RALPH MILIBAND was for many years senior lecturer in political science at the London School of Economics. He then became Professor of Politics at Leeds University. Since 1981 he has been a visiting Professor at Brandeis University. Ralph Miliband lives in London. Editor of *The Socialist Register*, his major publications include *Parliamentary Socialism* (1961), *The State in Capitalist Society* (1969), *Marxism and Politics* (1977) and *Capitalist Democracy in Britain* (1981).

Ralph Miliband

Verso

Class Power and State Power

For permission to use copyright material acknowledgement is made to the
following:
JAI Press for 'Political Action, Determinism and Contingency' from
Political Power and Social Theory, vol. 1 (1980) and Macmillan Press
Ltd. for 'The Politics of Peace and War' from *War, State and Society*
(1983).

First published 1983
© Ralph Miliband 1983

Verso Editions and NLB
15 Greek Street London W1V 5LF

Filmset in Times Roman by
Red Lion Setters, London

Printed in Great Britain by
The Thetford Press Ltd.
Thetford, Norfolk

ISBN 0 86091 073 3 (cloth)
      0 86091 773 8 (Paperback)

Contents

Preface   vii

I   The Capitalist State

1   Marx and the State   3
2   The Capitalist State: Two Exchanges with Nicos
    Poulantzas   26
3   Political Forms and Historical Materialism   50
4   State Power and Class Interests   63
5   The Coup in Chile   79
6   Constitutionalism and Revolution: Notes on
    Eurocommunism   108

II   Marxism and the Problem of Power

7   Political Action, Determinism and Contingency   131
8   Lenin's *The State and Revolution*   154
9   Stalin and After   167
10 Bettelheim and Soviet Experience   189
11 Rudolf Bahro's Alternative   203
12 Kolakowski's Anti-Marx   215
13 Military Intervention and Socialist Internationalism   230
14 The Politics of Peace and War   259

III   Britain

15 Class War Conservatism   279
16 Socialist Advance in Britain   286

Index   309

Preface

All but four of the essays collected in this volume have appeared in *The Socialist Register* and *New Left Review*; and only the first was written before 1970. The four essays which have appeared in other publications are: 'Political Action, Determinism and Contingency', in *Political Power and Social Theory*, vol. 1 (1980), edited by Maurice Zeitlin; 'Kolakowski's Anti-Marx', in *Political Studies*, vol. XXIX, no.1 (1981); 'The Politics of Peace and War', in Martin Shaw, ed., *War, State and Society* (1983); and 'Class War Conservatism', in *New Society*, 19 June 1980. I am grateful to the publishers for permission to reprint these essays.

Save for some minor corrections, I have made no changes in the texts themselves. The one exception is the essay entitled 'Military Intervention and Socialist Internationalism' where I have made more substantial changes, though these do not affect the main argument I seek to develop in the essay. In some cases, I have added a brief Introduction or Postscript. In one case, that of the article entitled 'Constitutionalism and Revolution: Notes on Eurocommunism', I thought that some substantial changes were required; but rather than make large modifications in the text, it seemed better to write a Postscript which may be taken as a critique of some parts of the essay.

Most of these essays are concerned with three main themes: first, with the ways in which state power is related to class forces; secondly, with the degree to which political action can affect the context in which it is inscribed; and thirdly, with the problems which the exercise of power presents for the socialist project. These themes are closely linked; and the reader will therefore find in the book a greater unity of subject and a more sustained argument than is often the case with an assemblage of texts written over a number of years.

I am very grateful to Perry Anderson for his probing comments on many of these texts; and to Neil Belton for his editorial help and encouragement.
August 1983   R.M.

I
The Capitalist State

1
Marx and the State

1965

As in the case of so many other aspects of Marx's work, what he thought about the state has more often than not come to be seen through the prism of later interpretations and adaptations. These have long congealed into *the* Marxist theory of the state, or into *the* Marxist-Leninist theory of the state, but they cannot be taken to constitute an adequate expression of Marx's own views. This is not because these theories bear *no* relation to Marx's views but rather that they emphasise some aspects of his thought to the detriment of others, and thus distort by over-simplification an extremely complex and by no means unambiguous body of ideas; and also that they altogether ignore certain strands in Marx's thought which are of considerable interest and importance. This does not, in itself, make later views better or worse than Marx's own: to decide this, what needs to be compared is not text with text, but text with historical or contemporary reality itself. This can hardly be done within the compass of an essay. But Marx is so inescapably bound up with contemporary politics, his thought is so deeply buried inside the shell of official Marxism and his name is so often invoked in ignorance by enemies and partisans alike, that it is worth asking again what he, rather than Engels, or Lenin or any other of his followers, disciples or critics, actually said and appeared to think about the state. This is the purpose of the present essay.

Marx himself never attempted to set out a comprehensive and systematic theory of the state. In the late 1850s he wrote that he intended, as part of a vast scheme of projected work, of which *Capital* was only to be the first part, to subject the state to systematic study.[1] But of this scheme, only one part of *Capital* was in fact

4

completed. His ideas on the state must therefore be taken from such historical *pièces de circonstance* as *The Class Struggle in France*, *The 18th Brumaire of Louis Bonaparte* and *The Civil War in France*, and from his incidental remarks on the subject in his other works. On the other hand, the crucial importance of the state in his scheme of analysis is well shown by his constantly recurring references to it in almost all of his writings; and the state was also a central preoccupation of the 'young Marx': his early work from the late 1830s to 1844 was largely concerned with the nature of the state and its relation to society. His most sustained piece of work until the 1844 *Economic and Philosophical Manuscripts*, apart from his doctoral dissertation, was his *Critique of Hegel's Philosophy of Law*.[2] It is in fact largely through his critique of Hegel's view of the state that Marx completed his emancipation from the Hegelian system. This early work of Marx on the state is of great interest; for, while he soon moved beyond the views and positions he had set out there, some of the questions he had encountered in his examination of Hegel's philosophy recur again and again in his later writings.

Marx's earliest views on the state bear a clear Hegelian imprint. In the articles which he wrote for the *Rheinische Zeitung* from May 1842 to March 1843, he repeatedly spoke of the state as the guardian of the general interest of society and of law as the embodiment of freedom. Modern philosophy, he writes in July 1842, 'looks on the state as the great organism, in which legal, moral and political freedom must be realised, and in which the individual citizen in obeying the laws of the state only obeys the natural laws of his own reason, of human reason'.[3]

On the other hand, he also shows himself well aware that this exalted view of the state is in contradiction with the real state's actual behaviour: 'a state that is not the realization of rational freedom is a bad state'[4], he writes, and in his article on the Rhineland Diet's repressive legislation against the pilfering of forest wood, he eloquently denounces the Diet's denial of the customary rights of the poor and condemns the assignation to the state of the role of servant of the rich against the poor. This, he holds, is a perversion of the state's true purpose and mission; private property may wish to degrade the state to its own level of concern, but any modern state, in so far as it remains true to its own meaning, must, confronted by such pretensions, cry out 'your ways are not my ways, your thoughts are not my thoughts!'[5]

More and more, however, Marx found himself driven to emphasize the external pressures upon the state's actions. Writing in January 1843 on the plight of the wine growers of the Moselle, he remarks that 'in investigating a situation *concerning the state* one is all too easily tempted to overlook the *objective nature of the circumstances* and to explain everything by the *will* of those empowered to act'[6].

It is this same insistence on the need to consider the 'objective nature of circumstances' which lies at the core of the *Critique of Hegel's Philosophy of Law*, which Marx wrote in the spring and summer of 1843, after the *Rheinische Zeitung* had been closed down. By then, his horizons had widened to the point where he spoke confidently of a 'break' in the existing society, to which 'the system of industry and trade, of ownership and exploitation of people lead even more rapidly than the increase in population'.[7] Hegel's 'absurdity', he also writes in the *Critique*, is that he views the affairs and activities of the state in an abstract fashion; he forgets that the activities of the state are human functions: '...that state functions, etc., are nothing but modes of being and modes of action of the social qualities of men'.[8]

The burden of Marx's critique of Hegel's concept of the state is that Hegel, while rightly acknowledging the separation of civil society from the state, asserts their reconciliation in the state itself. In his system, the 'contradiction' between the state and society is resolved in the supposed representation in the state of society's true meaning and reality; the alienation of the individual from the state, the contradiction between man as a private member of society, concerned with his own private interests, and as a citizen of the state finds resolution in the state as the expression of society's ultimate reality.

But, says Marx, this is not a resolution but a mystification. The contradiction between the state and society is real enough. Indeed, the political alienation which it entails is the central fact of modern, bourgeois society, since man's political significance is detached from his real private condition, while it is in fact this condition which determines him as a social being, all other determinations appearing to him as external and inessential: 'The *real human being* is the *private individual* of the present-day state constitution.'[9]

But the mediating elements which are supposed, in Hegel's system, to ensure the resolution of this contradiction—the sovereign, the bureaucracy, the middle classes, the legislature—are not in the least capable, says Marx, of doing so. Ultimately, Hegel's state, far from being above private interests and from representing the general interest, is in fact subordinate to private property. What, asks Marx, is the power of the state over private property? The state has only the illusion of being determinant, whereas it is in fact determined; it does, in time, subdue private and social wills, but only to give substance to the will of private property and to acknowledge its reality as the highest reality of the political state, as the highest moral reality.[10]

In the *Critique*, Marx's own resolution of political alienation and of the contradiction between the state and society is still envisaged in mainly political terms, i.e. in the framework of 'true democracy'. 'Democracy is the solved *riddle* of all constitutions'; in it 'the constitution appears as what it is, a free product of man'. 'All other *state forms* are definite, distinct, *particular forms of state*. In democracy the *formal* principle is at the same time the *material* principle.' It constitutes, therefore, the real unity of the universal and the particular.[11] Marx also writes: 'In all states other than democratic ones the *state*, the *law*, the *constitution* is what rules, without really ruling, i.e. without materially permeating the content of the remaining, non-political spheres. In democracy the constitution, the law, the state itself, insofar as it is a political constitution, is only the self-determination of the people, and a particular content of the people.'[12]

Democracy is here intended to mean more than a specific political form, but Marx does not yet define what else it entails. The struggle between monarchy and republic, he noted, is still a struggle within the framework of what he calls the 'abstract state', i.e. the state alienated from society; the abstract political form of democracy is the republic. 'Property, etc., in short, the entire content of the law and the state, is the same in North America as in Prussia, with few modifications. The *republic* there is thus a mere state *form*, as is the monarchy here.'[13] In a real democracy, however, the constitution ceases to be purely political; indeed, Marx quotes the opinion of 'some recent Frenchmen' to the effect that 'in true democracy the *political state is annihilated*'.[14] But the concrete contents of 'true democracy' remains here undefined.

The *Critique* already suggests the belief that political emancipation is not synonymous with human emancipation. The point, which is of course central to Marx's whole system, was made explicit in the two articles which he wrote for the *Franco-German Annals*, namely the *Jewish Question* and the '*Introduction*' to his *Contribution to the Critique of Hegel's Philosophy of Law*.

In the first essay, Marx criticizes Bruno Bauer for confusing political and human emancipation, and notes that 'the limits of political emancipation are evident at once from the fact that the *state* can free itself from a restriction without man being *really* free from this restriction, that the state can be a *free* state without man being a *free* man'.[15] Even so, political emancipation is a great advance; it is not the last form of human emancipation, but it is the last form of human emancipation within the framework of the existing social order.[16] Human emancipation, on the other hand, can only be realized by transcending bourgeois society, 'which has severed all the species-ties of man, put egoism and selfish need in the place of these species-ties, and dissolved the human world into a world of atomistic individuals who are inimically opposed to one another'.[17] The more specific meaning of that emancipation is defined in the *Jewish Question*, in Marx's strictures against 'Judaism', here deemed synonymous with trade, money and the commercial spirit which has come to affect all human relations. On this view, the political emancipation of the Jews, which Marx defends,[18] does not produce their social emancipation; this is only possible in a new society, in which practical need has been humanised and the commercial spirit abolished.[19]

In the *Introduction*, which he wrote in Paris at the end of 1843 and the beginning of 1844, Marx now spoke of 'the doctrine, that for man the root is man himself' and of the 'categorical imperative' which required the overthrow of all conditions in which 'man is a debased, enslaved, forsaken, despicable being.'[20] But he also added another element to the system he was constructing, namely the proletariat as the agent of the dissolution of the existing social order;[21]

as we shall see, this view of the proletariat is not only crucial for Marx's concept of revolution but also for his view of the state.

By this time, Marx had already made an assessment of the relative importance of the political realm from which he was never to depart and which also had some major consequence for his later thought. On the one hand, he does not wish to underestimate the importance of 'political emancipation', i.e. of political reforms tending to make politics and the state more liberal and democratic. Thus, in *The Holy Family*, which he wrote in 1844 in collaboration with Engels, Marx describes the 'democratic representative state' as 'the perfect modern state',[22] meaning the perfect modern *bourgeois* state, its perfection arising from the fact that 'the public system is *not* faced with any privileged exclusivity',[23] i.e. economic and political life are free from feudal encumbrances and constraints.

But there is also, on the other hand, a clear view that political emancipation is not enough, and that society can only be made truly human by the abolition of private property. 'It is natural necessity, *essential human properties*, however alienated they may seem to be, and *interest* that hold the members of civil society together; *civil*, not *political* life is their *real* tie. It is therefore not the state that holds the *atoms* of civil society together . . . only *political superstition* today imagines that social life must be held together by the state, whereas in reality, the state is held together by civil life.'[24] The modern democratic state 'is based on emancipated slavery, on bourgeois society . . . the society of industry, of universal competition, of private interest freely following its aims, of anarchy, of the self-alienated natural and spiritual individuality . . .';[25] the 'essence' of the modern state is that 'it is based on the unhampered development of bourgeois society, on the free movement of private interest.'[26]

A year later, in *The German Ideology*, Marx and Engels defined further the relation of the state to bourgeois society. 'By the mere fact that it is a *class* and no longer an *estate*, they wrote, 'the bourgeoisie is forced to organize itself no longer locally but nationally, and to give a general form to its mean average interest'; this 'general form' is the state, defined as 'nothing more than the form of organization which the bourgeois necessarily adopt both for internal and external purposes, for the mutual guarantee of their property and interest.'[27] This same view is confirmed in *The Poverty of Philosophy* of 1847, where Marx again states that 'political conditions are only the official expression of civil society' and goes on: 'It is the sovereigns who in all ages have been subject to economic conditions, but it is never they who have dictated laws to them. Legislation, whether political or civil, never does more than proclaim, express in words, the will of economic relations.'[28]

This whole trend of thought on the subject of the state finds its most explicit expression in the famous formulation of the *Communist Manifesto*: 'The executive of the modern state is but a committee for managing the common affairs of the whole bourgeoisie';[29] and political power is 'merely the organized power of one class for oppressing another.'[30] This is the classical Marxist view on the subject of the state, and it is the only one which is to be found in Marxism-Leninism. In regard to Marx himself, however, and this is true to a certain extent of Engels as well, it only constitutes what might be called a primary view of the state. For, as has occasionally been noted in discussions of Marx and the state,[31] there is to be found another view of the state in his work, which it is inaccurate to hold up as of similar status with the first,[32] but which is none the less of great interest, not least because it serves to illuminate, and indeed provides an essential context for, certain major elements in Marx's system, notably the concept of the dictatorship of the proletariat. This secondary view is that of the state as independent from and superior to all social classes, as being the dominant force in society rather than the instrument of a dominant class.

It may be useful, for a start, to note some qualifications which Marx made even to his primary view of the state. For in relation to the two most advanced capitalist countries of the day, England and France, he often makes the point that, at one time or another, it is not the ruling class as a whole, but a fraction of it, which controls the state;[33] and that those who actually run the state may well belong to a class which is not the economically dominant class.[34] Marx does not suggest that this *fundamentally* affects the state's class character and its rôle of guardian and defender of the interests of property; but it obviously does introduce an element of flexibility into his view of the operation of the state's bias, not least because the competition between different factions of the ruling class may well make easier the passage of measures favourable to labour, such as the Ten Hours Bill.[35]

The extreme manifestation of the state's independent rôle is, however, to be found in authoritarian personal rule, Bonapartism. Marx's most extensive discussion of this phenomenon occurs in *The 18th Brumaire of Louis Bonaparte*, which was written between December 1851 and March 1852. In this historical study, Marx sought very hard to pin down the precise nature of the rule which Louis Bonaparte's *coup d'état* had established.

The *coup d'état*, he wrote, was 'the victory of Bonaparte over parliament, of the executive power over the legislative power'; in parliament, 'the nation made its general will the law, that is, made the law of the ruling class its general will'; in contrast, 'before the executive power it renounces all will of its own and submits to the superior command of an alien will, to authority'; 'France, therefore, seems to have escaped the despotism of a class only to fall back beneath the despotism of an individual and, what is more, beneath the authority of an individual without authority. The struggle seems to be settled in such a way that all classes, equally impotent and equally mute, fall on their knees before the rifle butt.'[36]

Marx then goes on to speak of 'this executive power with its enormous bureaucratic and military organization, with its ingenious state machinery, embracing wide strata, with a host of officials numbering half a million, besides an army of another half million, this appalling parasitic body which enmeshes the body of French society like a net and chokes all its pores.'[37] This bureaucratic power, which sprang up in the days of the absolute monarchy, had, he wrote, first been 'the means of preparing the class rule of the bourgeoisie,' while 'under the Restoration, under Louis Philipre, under the parliamentary Republic, it was the instrument of the ruling class, however much it strove for power of its own.'[38] But the *coup d'état* had seemingly changed its rôle: 'only under the second Bonaparte does the state seem to have made itself completely independent'; 'as against civil society, the state machine has consolidated its position so thoroughly that the chief of the Society of December 10 [i.e. Louis Bonaparte] suffices for its head . . . .'[39]

This appears to commit Marx to the view of the Bonapartist state as independent of any specific class and as superior to society. But he then goes on to say, in an often quoted phrase: 'And yet the state power is not suspended in mid-air. Bonaparte represents a class, and the most numerous class of French society at that, *the small-holding peasants*.'[40] However, lack of cohesion makes these 'incapable of enforcing their class interests in their own name whether through a parliament or a convention';[41] they therefore require a representative who 'must at the same time appear as their master, as an authority over them, as an unlimited governmental power that protects them against the other classes and sends them rain and sunshine from above. The political influence of the small-holding peasants, therefore, finds its final expression in the executive power subordinating society to itself.'[42]

'Represent' is here a confusing word. In the context, the only meaning that may be attached to it is that the small-holding peasants *hoped* to have their interests represented by Louis Bonaparte. But this does not turn Louis Bonaparte or the state into the mere instrument of their will; at the most, it may limit the executive's freedom of action somewhat. Marx also writes that 'as the executive authority which has made itself an independent power, Bonaparte feels it his mission to safeguard 'bourgeois order.' But the strength of this bourgeois order lies in the middle class. He looks on himself, therefore, as the representative of the middle class and issues decrees in this sense. Nevertheless, he is somebody solely due to the fact that he has broken the political power of this middle class and daily breaks it anew'; and again, 'as against the bourgeoisie, Bonaparte looks on himself, at the same time, as the representative of the peasants and of the people in general, who wants to make the lower classes of the people happy within the frame of bourgeois society . . . But, above all, Bonaparte looks on himself as the chief of the Society of 10 December, as the representative of the *lumpen-proletariat* to which he himself, his *entourage*, his government and his army belong . . . .'[43]

On this basis, Louis Napoleon may 'represent' this or that class (and Marx stresses the 'contradictory task' of the man and the 'contradictions of his government, the confused groping about which seeks now to win, now to humiliate first one class and then another and arrays all of them uniformly against him . . . '[44]); but his power of initiative remains very largely unimpaired by the specific wishes and demands of any one class or fraction of a class.

On the other hand, this does *not* mean that Bonapartism, for Marx, is in any sense neutral as between contending classes. It may *claim* to represent all classes and to be the embodiment of the whole of society. But it does in fact exist, and has been called into being, for the purpose of maintaining and strengthening the existing social order and the domination of capital over labour. Bonapartism and the Empire, Marx wrote much later in *The Civil War in France*, had succeeded the bourgeois Republic precisely because 'it was the only form of government possible at a time when the bourgeoisie had already lost, and the working class had not yet acquired, the faculty of ruling the nation.'[45] It was precisely under its sway that 'bourgeois society, freed from political cares, attained a development unexpected even by itself.'[46] Finally, Marx then characterizes what he calls 'imperialism,' by which he means Napoleon's imperial régime, as 'at the same time, the most prostitute and the ultimate form of the State power which nascent middle-class society had commenced to elaborate as a means of its own emancipation from feudalism, and which full-grown bourgeois society had finally transformed into a means for the enslavement of labour by capital.'[47]

In *The Origin of the Family, Private Property and the State*, written a year after Marx's death, Engels also notes: 'By way of exception, however, periods occur in which the warring classes balance each other so nearly that the state power, as ostensible mediator, acquires, for the moment, a certain degree of independence of both.'[48] But the independence of which he speaks would seem to go much further than anything Marx had in mind; thus Engels refers to the Second Empire, 'which played off the proletariat against the bourgeoisie and the bourgeoisie against the proletariat' and to Bismarck's German Empire, where 'capitalists and workers are balanced against each other and equally cheated for the benefit of the impoverished Prussian cabbage junkers.'[49]

For Marx, the Bonapartist state, however independent it may have been *politically* from any given class, remains, and cannot in a class society but remain, the protector of an economically and socially dominant class.

In the *Critique of Hegel's Philosophy of Law*, Marx had devoted a long and involved passage to the bureaucratic element in the state,

and to its attempt 'to transform the purpose of the state into the purpose of the bureaucracy and the purpose of the bureaucracy into the
purpose of the state.'[50] But it was only in the early fifties that he
began to look closely at a type of society where the state appeared to
be genuinely 'above society,' namely societies based on the 'Asiatic
mode of production', whose place in Marx's thought has recently
attracted much attention.[51] What had, in the *Critique,* been a passing reference to Asiatic despotism, 'where the political realm is
nothing but the personal caprice of a single individual, where the
political realm, like the material, is a slave',[52] had, by 1859, become
one of Marx's four main stages of history: 'In broad outlines', he
wrote in the famous Preface to *A Contribution to the Critique of
Political Economy*, 'Asiatic, ancient, feudal and modern bourgeois
modes of production can be designated as progressive epochs in the
economic formation of society.'[53]

The countries Marx was mainly concerned with in this connection
were India and China, and also Russia as a 'semi-Asiatic' or 'semi-
Eastern' state. The Asiatic mode of production, for Marx and
Engels, has one outstanding characteristic, namely the absence of
private property in land: 'this,' Marx wrote to Engels in 1853, 'is the
real key, even to the Oriental heaven . . . '[54] 'In the Asiatic form (or
at least predominantly so),' he noted, 'there is no property, but
individual possession; the community is properly speaking the real
proprietor';[55] in Asiatic production, he also remarked, it is the state
which is the 'real landlord.'[56] In this system, he also wrote later, the
direct producers are not 'confronted by a private land-owner but
rather, as in Asia, [are] under direct subordination to a state which
stands over them as their landlord and simultaneously as sovereign';
'the state', he went on, 'is then the supreme lord. Sovereignty here
consists in the ownership of land concentrated on a national scale.
But, on the other hand, no private ownership of land exists,
although there is both private and common possession and use of
land.'[57]

A prime necessity of the Asiatic mode of production, imposed by
climate and territorial conditions, was artificial irrigation by canals
and waterworks; indeed, Marx wrote, this was 'the basis of Oriental
agriculture.' In countries like Flanders and Italy the need of an economical and common use of water drove private enterprise into

voluntary association; but it required 'in the Orient, where civilization was too low and the territorial extent too vast to call into life voluntary associations, the interference of the centralized power of Government. Hence an economical function devolved upon all Asiatic governments, the functions of providing public works.'[58]

Finally, in the *Grundrisse*, Marx speaks of 'the despotic government which is poised above the lesser communities,'[59] and describes that government as the *'all-embracing unity* which stands above all these small common bodies . . . since the *unity* is the real owner, and the real pre-condition of common ownership, it is perfectly possible for it to appear as something separate and superior to the numerous real, particular communities . . . the despot here appears as the father of all the numerous lesser communities, thus realizing the common unity of all.'[60]

It is therefore evident that Marx does view the state, in the conditions of Asiatic despotism, as the dominant force in society, independent of and superior to all its members, and that those who control its administration are society's authentic rulers. Karl Wittfogel has noted that Marx did not pursue this theme after the 1850s and that 'in the writings of the later period he emphasized the technical side of large scale waterworks, where previously he had emphasized their political setting.'[61] The reason for this, Professor Wittfogel suggests, is that 'obviously the concept of Oriental despotism contained elements that paralysed his search for truth';[62] hence his 'retrogressions' on the subject. But the explanation for Marx's lack of concern for the topic would seem much simpler and much less sinister; it is that he was, in the sixties and the early seventies, primarily concerned with Western capitalism. Furthermore, the notion of bureaucratic despotism can hardly have held any great terror for him since he had, in fact, worked through its nearest equivalent in capitalist society, namely Bonapartism, and had analysed it as an altogether different phenomenon from the despotism encountered in Asiatic society. Nor is it accurate to suggest, as does Mr Lichtheim, that 'Marx for some reason shirked the problem of the bureaucracy' in post-capitalist society.[63] On the contrary, this may be said to be a crucial element in Marx's thought in the late sixties and in the early seventies. His concern with the question, and with the state, finds expression in this period in his discussion of the nature of political power in post-capitalist societies, and particularly in his view of the dictatorship of the proletariat. This theme had last occupied Marx in 1851-52; after almost twenty years it was again brought to the fore by the Paris Commune, by his struggles with anarchism in the First International and by the programmatic pronouncements of German Social Democracy. It is to this, one of the most important and the most misunderstood aspects of Marx's work on the state, that we must now turn.

It is first of all necessary to go back to the democratic and representative republic, which must be clearly distinguished from the dictatorship of the proletariat: for Marx, the two concepts have nothing in common. An element of confusion arises from the fact that Marx bitterly denounced the class character of the democratic republic, yet supported its coming into being. The contradiction is only apparent; Marx saw the democratic republic as the most advanced type of political régime in *bourgeois society*, and wished to see it prevail over more backward and 'feudal' political systems. But it remained for him a system of class rule, indeed the system in which the bourgeoisie rules most directly.

The limitations of the democratic republic, from Marx's point of view, are made particularly clear in the *Address of the Central Committee of the Communist League* which he and Engels wrote in March 1850. 'Far from desiring to revolutionize all society for the revolutionary proletarians,' they wrote, 'the democratic petty bourgeois strive for a change in social conditions by means of which existing society will be made as tolerable and comfortable as possible for them.' They would therefore demand such measures as 'the diminution of state expenditure by a curtailment of the bureaucracy and shifting the chief taxes on to the big landowners and bourgeois ... the abolition of the pressure of big capital on small, through public credit institutions and laws against usury ... the establishment of bourgeois property relations in the countryside by the complete abolition of feudalism.' But in order to achieve their purpose they would need 'a democratic state structure, either constitutional or republican, that will give them and their allies, the peasants, a majority; also a democratic communal structure that will give them direct control over communal property and over a series of functions now performed by the bureaucrats.'[64] However, they added, 'as far as the workers are concerned, it remains certain that they are to remain wage workers as before; the democratic petty-bourgeois only desire better wages and a more secure existence for the workers ... they hope to bribe the workers by more or less concealed alms and to break their revolutionary potency by making their position tolerable for the moment.'[65]

But, Marx and Engels go on, 'these demands can in no wise suffice for the party of the proletariat'; while the petty-bourgeois democrats would seek to bring the revolution to a conclusion as quickly as possible, 'it is our interest and our task to make the revolution permanent, until all more or less possessing classes have been forced out of their position of dominance, until the proletariat has conquered state power, and the association of proletarians, not only in one country but in all the dominant countries of the world, has advanced so far that competition among the proletarians of these countries has ceased and that at least the decisive productive forces are concentrated in the hands of the proletarians. For us the issue cannot be the alteration of private property but only its annihilation, not the smoothing over of class antagonisms but the abolition of classes, not the improvement of existing society but the foundation of a new one.'[66]

At the same time, while the demands and aims of the proletarian party went far beyond anything which even the most advanced and radical petty-bourgeois democrats would accept, the revolutionaries must give them qualified support and seek to push the democratic movement into even more radical directions.[67] It was, incidentally, precisely the same strategy which dictated Marx's later attitude to all movements of radical reform, and which led him, as in the *Inaugural Address* of the First International in 1864, to acclaim the Ten Hours Act or the advances of the co-operative movement as the victories of 'the political economy of labour over the political economy of property.'[68]

In 1850, Marx and Engels had also suggested that one essential task of the proletarian revolutionaries would be to oppose the decentralizing tendencies of the petty-bourgeois revolutionaries. On the contrary, 'the workers must not only strive for a single and indivisible German republic, but also within this republic for the most determined centralization of power in the hands of the state authority . . . '[69]

This is not only the most extreme 'statist' prescription in Marx's (and Engels's) work—it is the only one of its kind, leaving aside Marx's first 'Hegelian' pronouncements on the subject. More important is the fact that the prescription is intended *not* for the proletarian but for the bourgeois democratic revolution.[70] In 1850, Marx and Engels believed, and said in the *Address*, that the German workers would not be able 'to attain power and achieve their own class interest without completely going through a lengthy revolutionary development.'[71] The proletarian revolution would see the coming into being of an altogether different form of rule than the democratic republic, namely the dictatorship of the proletariat.

In a famous letter to J. Weydemeyer in March 1852, Marx had revealed the cardinal importance he attached to this concept by saying that, while no credit was due to him for discovering the existence of classes in modern society or the struggles between them, 'what I did that was new was to prove (1) that the *existence of classes* is only bound up with *particular historical phases in the development of production*, (2) that the class struggle necessarily leads to the *dictatorship of the proletariat*, (3) that this dictatorship itself only constitutes the transition to *abolition of all classes* and to a *classless society*.'[72]

Unfortunately, Marx did not define in any specific way *what* the dictatorship of the proletariat actually entailed, and more particularly what was its relation to the state. It has been argued by Mr Hal Draper in an extremely well-documented article that it is a '*social description*, a statement of the class character of the political power. It is not a statement about the forms of the government machinery.'[73] My own view, on the contrary, is that, for Marx, the dictatorship of the proletariat is *both* a statement of the class character of the political power *and* a description of the political power itself; and that it is in fact the nature of the political power which it described which guarantees its class character.

In *The 18th Brumaire*, Marx had made a point which constitutes a main theme of his thought, namely that all previous revolutions had '(perfected this [state] machine instead of smashing it. The parties that contended in turn for domination regarded the possession of this huge state edifice as the principal spoils of the victors.'[74] Nearly twenty years later, in *The Civil War in France*, he again stressed how every previous revolution had consolidated 'the centralized State power, with its ubiquitous organs of standing army, police, bureaucracy, clergy and judicature'; and he also stressed how the political character of the state had changed 'simultaneously with the economic changes of society. At the same pace at which the progress of modern history developed, widened, intensified the class antagonism between capital and labour, the State power assumed more and more the character of the national power of capital over labour, of a public force organized for social enslavement, of an engine of class despotism. After every revolution marking a progressive phase in the class struggle, the purely repressive character of the State power stands out in bolder and bolder relief.'[75]

As Mr Draper notes, Marx had made no reference to the dictatorship of the proletariat in all the intervening years. Nor indeed did he so describe the Paris Commune. But what he acclaims above all in the Commune is that, in contrast to previous social convulsions, it sought not the further consolidation of the state power but its destruction. What it wanted, he said, was to have 'restored to the social body all the forces hitherto absorbed by the State parasite feeding upon, and clogging the free movement of, society.'[76] Marx also lays stress on the Commune's popular, democratic and egalitarian character, and on the manner in which 'not only municipal administration but the whole initiative hitherto exercised by the State was laid into the hands of the Commune.'[77] Moreover, while the communal form of government was to apply even to the 'smallest country hamlet,' 'the unity of the nation was not to be broken, but, on the contrary, to be organized by the Communal Constitution, and to become a reality by the destruction of the State power which claimed to be the embodiment of that unity independent of, and superior to, the nation itself, from which it was but a parasitic excrescence.'[78]

In notes which he wrote for *The Civil War in France*, Marx makes even clearer than in the published text the significance which he attached to the Commune's dismantling of the state power. As contributing evidence of his approach to the whole question, the following passage from the Notes is extremely revealing: 'This [i.e. the

Commune] was,' he wrote, 'a Revolution not against this or that, legitimate, constitutional, republican or Imperialist form of State power. It was a Revolution against the *State* itself, of this super-naturalist abortion of society, a resumption by the people for the people of its own social life. It was not a revolution to transfer it from one fraction of the ruling class to the other but a Revolution to break down this horrid machinery of Classdomination [*sic*] itself ...the Second Empire was the final form(?) [*sic*] of this State usurpation. The Commune was its definite negation, and, there-fore, the initiation of the social Revolution of the nineteenth cen-tury.'[79] It is in the light of such views that Marx's verdict on the Commune takes on its full meaning: this 'essentially working-class government,' he wrote, was 'the political form at last discovered under which to work out the economic emancipation of labour.'[80]

It is of course true that, while Engels, long after Marx's death, did describe the Paris Commune as the dictatorship of the proletarat,[81] Marx himself did not do so. The reason for this would seem fairly obvious, namely that, for Marx, the dictatorship of the proletariat would be the outcome of a socialist revolution on a national scale; the Commune, as he wrote in 1881, was 'merely the rising of a city under exceptional conditions,' while 'the majority of the Commune was in no wise socialist, nor could it be'.[82] Even so, it may justifiably be thought that the Commune, in its de-institutionalization of pol-itical power, did embody, for Marx, the essential elements of his concept of the dictatorship of the proletariat.

Precisely the opposite view has very generally come to be taken for granted; the following statement in Mr Lichtheim's *Marxism* is a typical example of a wide consensus: 'His (Marx's) hostility to the state was held in check by a decidedly authoritarian doctrine of pol-itical rule during the transition period: prior to being consigned to the dustbin of history, the state was to assume dictatorial powers. In different terms, authority would inaugurate freedom—a typically Hegelian paradox which did not worry Marx though it alarmed Proudhon and Bakunin ...'[83]

The trouble with the view that Marx had a 'decidedly authorit-arian doctrine' is that it is unsupported by any convincing evidence from Marx himself; and that there is so much evidence which runs directly counter to it.

Marx was undoubtedly the chief opponent of the anarchists in the International. But it is worth remembering that his central quarrel with them concerned above all the manner in which the struggle for a socialist revolution ought to be prosecuted, with Marx insisting on the need for political involvement within the existing political framework, against the anarchists' all-or-nothing rejection of mere politics; and the quarrel also concerned the question of the type of organization required by the international workers' movement, with Marx insisting on a *degree* of control by the General Council of the International over its affiliated organizations.

As for the rôle of the state in the period of transition, there is the well-known passage in the 'private circular' against the anarchists issued by the General Council in 1872, *Les Prétendues Scissions dans l'Internationale*, and most probably written by Marx: 'What all socialists understand by anarchism is this: as soon as the goal of the proletarian movement, the abolition of class, shall have been reached, the power of the state, whose function it is to keep the great majority of the producers beneath the yoke of a small minority of exploiters, will disappear, and governmental functions will be transformed into simple administrative functions. The Alliance [i.e. Bakunin's Alliance of Socialist Democracy] turns the thing upside down. It declares anarchism in the ranks of the workers to be an infallible means for disrupting the powerful concentration of social and political forms in the hands of the exploiters. Under this pretext, it asks the International, when the old world is endeavouring to crush our organization, to replace organization by anarchism. The international police could ask for nothing better . . .'[84]

This can hardly be construed as an authoritarian text; nor certainly is Marx's plaintive remark in January 1873 quoted by Lenin in *State and Revolution* that 'if the political struggle of the working class assumes violent forms, if the workers set up this revolutionary dictatorship in place of the dictatorship of the bourgeoisie, they commit the terrible crime of violating principles, for in order to satisfy their wretched, vulgar, everyday needs, in order to crush the resistance of the bourgeoisie, instead of laying down their arms and abolishing the state, they give the state a revolutionary and transitory form . . .'[85]

Nor is there much evidence of Marx's 'decidedly authoritarian doctrine' in his marginal notes of 1875 on the Gotha Programme of the German Social-Democratic Party. In these notes, Marx bitterly attacked the programme's reference to 'the free state' ('free state— what is this?') and this is well in line with his belief that the 'free state' is a contradiction in terms; and he then asked: 'What transformation will the state undergo in communist society? In other words, what social functions will remain in existence there that are analogous to present functions of the state?' Marx, however, did not answer the question but merely said that it could only be answered 'scientifically' and that 'one does not get a flea-hop nearer to the problem by a thousandfold combination of the word people with the word state.'[86] He then goes on: 'Between capitalist and communist society lies the period of the revolutionary transformation of the one into the other. There corresponds to this also a political transition period in which the state can be nothing but *the revolutionary dictatorship of the proletariat.*'[87]

This does not advance matters much, but neither does it suggest the slightest 'authoritarian' impulse. In the *Critique of the Gotha Programme* Marx (as always before) made a sharp distinction between the democratic republic and the dictatorship of the proletariat, and Engels was clearly mistaken when he wrote in 1891 that the democratic republic was 'even the specific form of the dictatorship of the proletariat.'[88] On the contrary, Marx's critical attitude towards the democratic republic in the *Critique of the Gotha Programme* shows that he continued to think of the dictatorship of the proletariat as an altogether different and immeasurably freer form of political power. 'Freedom,' he wrote in the *Critique of the Gotha Programme*, 'consists in converting the state from an organ superimposed upon society into one completely subordinated to it . . .'[89] This would seem a good description of Marx's view of the state in the period of the dictatorship of the proletariat. No doubt he would have endorsed Engels's view, expressed a few weeks after Marx's death, that 'the proletarian class will first have to possess itself of the organized political force of the state and with this aid stamp out the resistance of the capitalist class and reorganize society.'[90] But it is of some significance that, with the possible exception of his remark of January 1873, referred to earlier, Marx himself always chose to emphasize the liberating rather than the repressive aspects of post-capitalist political power; and it is also of some interest that, in the notes he made for *The Civil War in France*, which were not of course intended for publication, he should have warned the working class that the 'work of regeneration' would be 'again and again relented [*sic*] and impeded by the resistance of vested interests and class egotisms,' but that he should have failed to make any reference to the State as an agent of repression. What he did say was that 'great strides may be [made] at once through the communal form of political organization' and that 'the time has come to begin that movement for themselves and mankind.'[91]

The fact is that, far from bearing any authoritarian imprint, the whole of Marx's work on the state is pervaded by a powerful anti-authoritarian and anti-bureaucratic bias, not only in relation to a distant communist society but also to the period of transition which is to precede it. True, the state is necessary in this period. But the only thing which, for Marx, makes it tolerable is popular participation and popular rule. If Marx is to be faulted, it is not for any authoritarian bias, but for greatly understating the difficulties of the libertarian position. However, in the light of the experience of socialist movements since Marx wrote, this may perhaps be judged a rather less serious fault than its bureaucratic obverse.

1. K. Marx to F. Lassalle, 22 February 1858, and K. Marx to F. Engels, 2 April 1858, *Selected Correspondence*, Moscow n.d., pp.125, 126.
2. 1843. K. Marx and F. Engels, *Collected Works* (henceforth MECW), London 1975-, vol. 3, pp.3-130.
3. MECW, vol. 1, p.202.
4. *Ibid.*, p.100.
5. *Ibid.*, p.241.
6. *Ibid.*, p.337. Note also his contemptuous reference in an article of May 1842 on the freedom of the press to 'the empty, nebulous and blurry arguments of those German liberals who claim to honour freedom by placing it in the starry firmament of the imagination instead of on the solid ground of reality' (MECW, vol. 1, p.172; A. Cornu, *Karl Marx et Friedrich Engels. Leur Vie et Leur Oeuvre*, Paris 1958, vol. II, p.17).
7. Marx to A. Ruge, May 1843, MECW, vol. 3, p.141; see also Marx to Ruge, March 1843, pp.133-4.
8. *Ibid.*, pp.21-2.
9. *Ibid.*, p.81. See also J. Hyppolite, *Etudes sur Marx et Hegel*, Paris 1955, pp.123ff., and M. Rubel, *K. Marx. Essai de biographie intellectuelle*, Paris 1957, pp.58ff.
10. *Ibid.*, pp.98-9.

11. *Ibid.*, pp.29-30.
12. *Ibid.*, pp.30-31.
13. *Ibid.*, p.31.
14. *Ibid.*, p.30.
15. *Ibid.*, p.152.
16. *Ibid.*, pp.155-6.
17. *Ibid.*, p.173.
18. See S. Avineri, 'Marx and Jewish Emancipation', *Journal of the History of Ideas*, vol. XXV (July-September 1964), pp.445-50.
19. MECW, pp.168-74.
20. *Ibid.*, p.182.
21. *Ibid.*, pp.186-7.
22. K. Marx and F. Engels, *The Holy Family*, Moscow 1956, p.154.
23. *Ibid.*, p.157. Italics in original.
24. *Ibid.*, p.163. Italics in original.
25. *Ibid.*, p.164.
26. *Ibid.*, p.166.
27. K. Marx and F. Engels, *The German Ideology*, New York 1939, p.59. Italics in original.
28. K. Marx, *The Poverty of Philosophy*, London 1936, p.70.
29. K. Marx and F. Engels, *Selected Works*, hereafter noted as *S.W.*, Moscow 1950, I, p.35.
30. *Ibid.*, p.51.
31. See, e.g. J. Plamenatz, *German Marxism and Russian Communism*, London 1954, pp.144ff.; J. Sanderson, 'Marx and Engels on the State' in *Western Political Quarterley*, vol. XVI, no. 4 (December 1963), pp.946-55.
32. As is suggested by the two authors cited above.
33. See, e.g., *The Class Struggles in France*, passim, *The 18th Brumaire of Louis Bonaparte*, passim.
34. See, e.g., 'The Elections in Britain', in K. Marx and F. Engels, *On Britain*, Moscow 1953, pp.353ff. 'The Whigs are the *aristocratic representatives* of the bourgeoisie, of the industrial and commercial middle class. Under the condition that the bourgeoisie should abandon to them, to an oligarchy of aristocratic families, the monopoly of government and the exclusive possession of office, they make to the middle class, and assist it in conquering, all those concessions, which in the course of social and political developments have shown themselves to have become *unavoidable and undelayable*' (*Ibid.*, p.353. Italics as original.)
35. *Ibid.*, p.368.
36. *S.W.*, p.300.
37. *Ibid.*, p.301.
38. *Ibid.*, p.302.
39. *Ibid.*, p.302.
40. *Ibid.*, p.302. Italics in original.
41. Marx also notes that the identity of interest of the smallholding peasants 'begets no community, no national bond and no political organization among them', so that 'they do not form a class' (*'Ibid.*, p.302). For an interesting discussion of Marx's concept of class, see S. Ossowski, *Class Structure in the Social Consciousness*, London 1963, ch. V.
42. *S.W.*, I, p.303.
43. *Ibid.*, pp.308-9.

44. *Ibid.*, p.309.
45. K. Marx, *The Civil War in France, S.W.*, I, p.470.
46. *Ibid.*, p.470.
47. *Ibid.*, p.470.
48. F. Engels, *The Origin of the Family, Private Property and the State, S.W.*, II, p.290.
49. *Ibid.*, pp.290-291. For further comments on the subject from Engels, see also his letter to C. Schmidt, 27 October 1890, in *S.W.*, II, pp.446-47.
50. MECW, vol. 3, pp.40-54.
51. See, e.g. K. Wittfogel, *Oriental Despotism*, Yale 1957, ch. IX; G. Lichtheim, 'Marx and the "Asiatic Mode of Production"' in *St. Anthony's Papers*, no. 14, Far Eastern Affairs (London, 1963). Also K. Marx, *Pre-Capitalist Economic Formations*, with an introduction by E.J. Hobsbawm, London 1964. This is a translation of a section of Marx's *Grundrisse der Kritik der Politischen Ökonomie*, Berlin 1953.
52. MECW vol. 3, p.32.
53. *S.W.*, I, p.329.
54. K. Marx to F. Engels, 2 June 1853, *Sel. Cor.* p.99.
55. K. Marx, *Pre-Capitalist Economic Formations*, p.79.
56. *New York Daily Tribune*, 5 August 1853, in Lichtheim, p.94.
57. K. Marx, *Capital*, Moscow 1962, III, pp.771-72.
58. K. Marx and F. Engels, *The First Indian War of Independence* (1857-59), Moscow n.d., p.16. In *Capital* I, p.514, fn. 2, Marx also notes that 'one of the material bases of the power of the State over the small disconnected producing organisms in India, was the regulation of the water supply'; also, 'the necessity for predicting the rise and fall of the Nile created Egyptian astronomy, and with it the dominion of the priests, as directors of agriculture' (*Ibid.*, p.514, fn. 1); for some further elaboration on the same theme, see F. Engels, *Anti-Dühring*, Moscow 1962, p.248.
59. K. Marx, *Pre-Capitalist Economic Formations*, p.71.
60. *Ibid.*, p.69. Italics in original.
61. Wittfogel, p.381.
62. *Ibid.*, p.387.
63. Lichtheim, p.110.
64. K. Marx and F. Engels, *Address of the Central Committee to the Communist League, S.W.*, Ip.101.
65. *Ibid.*, p.101.
66. *Ibid.*, p.102.
67. *Ibid.*, p.101.
68. *Ibid.*, pp.307-9.
69. *Ibid.*, p.106.
70. It is, in this connection, of some interest that Engels should have thought it necessary to add a note to the 1885 edition of the Address, explaining that this passage was based on a 'misunderstanding' of French revolutionary experience and that 'local and provincial self-government' were not in contradiction with 'national centralization' (*Ibid.*, p.107).
71. *Ibid.*, p.108.
72. K. Marx to J. Weydemeyer, 5 March 1852, *Sel. Cor.*, p.86. Italics in original.
73. H. Draper, 'Marx and the Dictatorship of the Proletariat' in *New Politics*, vol. I, no. 4, p.102. Italics in original.
74. *S.W.*, I, p.301.

75. *Ibid.*, pp.468-69.
76. *Ibid.*, p.473.
77. *Ibid.*, p.471.
78. *Ibid.*, p.472.
79. *Marx-Engels Archives*, Moscow 1934, vol. III (VIII), p.324. Italics in original. I am grateful to Mr M. Johnstone for drawing my attention to these notes. Note also, e.g., the following: 'Only the proletarians, fired by a new social task to accomplish by them for all society, to do away with all classes and class rule, were the men to break the instrument of that class rule—the State, the centralized and organized governmental power usurping to be the master instead of the servant of society . . . It had sprung into life against them. By them it was broken, not as a peculiar form of governmental (centralized) power, but as its most powerful, elaborated into seeming independence from society expression and, therefore, also its most prostitute reality, covered by infamy from top to bottom, having centred in absolute corruption at home and absolute powerlessness abroad' (*Ibid.*, p.326). The peculiar English syntax of such passages is obviously due to the fact that they are only notes, not intended for publication.
80. *S.W.*, I, p.473.
81. 'Of late,' Engels wrote in an Introduction to the 1891 edition of *The Civil War in France*, 'the Social-Democratic philistine has once more been filled with wholesome terror at the words: Dictatorship of the Proletariat. Well and good, gentlemen, do you want to know what this dictatorship looks like? Look at the Paris Commune. That was the Dictatorship of the Proletariat' (*S.W.*, I. p.440.)
82. K. Marx to F. Domela-Niewenhuis, 22 February 1881, *Sel. Cor.*, p.410.
83. G. Lichtheim, *Marxism*, London 1961, p.374.
84. G.M. Stekloff, *History of the First International*, London 1928, pp.179-80; and J. Freymond, ed., *La Première Internationale*, Geneva 1962, II, p.295.
85. V.I. Lenin, *State and Revolution*, London 1933, p.54.
86. K. Marx, *Critique of the Gotha Programme, S.W.*, II, p.30.
87. *Ibid.*, p.30. Italics in original.
88. Quoted in Lenin, *The State and Revolution*, p.54. Lenin's own comment is also misleading: 'Engels,' he writes, 'repeats here in a particularly striking manner the fundamental idea which runs like a red thread through all of Marx's works, namely, that the democratic republic is the nearest approach to the dictatorship of the proletariat' (*Ibid.*, p.54). Engels's phrase does not bear this interpretation; and whatever may be said for the view that the democratic republic is the nearest approach to the dictatorship of the proletariat, it is not so in Marx.
89. *S.W.*, II, p.29.
90. F. Engels to P. Van Patten, 18 April 1883, *Sel. Cor.*, p.437.
91. *Marx-Engels Archives*, p.334.

2

The Capitalist State:

Two Exchanges with Nicos Poulantzas

Note: The first of these two texts was a 'reply' to a review of The
State in Capitalist Society *(1969), which Nicos Poulantzas
published in* New Left Review, *'The Problem of the Capital-
ist State' (no.58, Nov.-Dec. 1969). The second text, occa-
sioned by the publication of the English translation of his*
Political Power and Social Classes *(1973), appeared in* New
Left Review, *'Poulantzas and the Capitalist State' (no.82,
Nov.-Dec. 1973).*

*Poulantzas replied both to this review and to an article by
Ernesto Laclau, 'The Specificity of the Political: Around the
Poulantzas-Miliband Debate' (in* Economy and Society,
vol.5, no.1, Feb 1975, reprinted in E. Laclau, Politics and
Ideology in Marxist Theory, *London 1977) in* New Left
Review, *'The Capitalist State: A Reply to Miliband and Lac-
lau' (no.95, Jan.-Feb. 1976).*

As I note in the second text, Poulantzas's review of The
State in Capitalist Society *and my 'reply' to it attracted a
good deal of attention and was held to epitomize the division
between 'instrumentalists' (like myself) and 'structuralists'
such as Poulantzas. Whether this was or was not an over-
simplified view of our positions is a question that need not be
pursued here. But I do want to note one feature of this
'debate': namely, that it helped to clarify some important
issues and (I think) to advance the discussion. I certainly
learnt much from it; and it may be that it had some influence
on Poulantzas as well.*

The re-publication of these two texts also gives me an

opportunity to say something about Poulantzas's work, and I welcome that opportunity all the more because of the highly critical nature of my review of his Political Power and Social Classes: *this is that his work, taken as a whole, is without question the most creative and stimulating contribution to a Marxist political sociology to have been made in the sixties and seventies; and that his suicide at a tragically early age was a very great loss to its further advancement.*

I

1970

I very much welcome Nicos Poulantzas's critique of *The State in Capitalist Society* in the last issue of NLR: this is exactly the kind of discussion which is most likely to contribute to the elucidation of concepts and issues that are generally agreed on the Left to be of crucial importance for the socialist project, yet which have for a very long time received altogether inadequate attention, or even no attention at all. While some of Poulantzas's criticisms are, as I shall try to show, unwarranted, my purpose in the following comments is only incidentally to 'defend' the book; my main purpose is rather to take up some general points which arise from his review and which seem to me of particular interest in the investigation of the nature and role of the state in capitalist society. I hope that others may be similarly provoked into entering the discussion.

I. The Problem of Method

The first such point concerns the question of method. Poulantzas suggests that, notwithstanding the book's merits (about which he is more than generous), the analysis which it attempts is vitiated by the absence of a 'problematic' which would adequately situate the concrete data it presents. In effect, Poulantzas taxes me with what C. Wright Mills called 'abstracted empiricism', and with which I myself, as it happens, tax pluralist writers.[1] Poulantzas quite rightly states that 'a precondition of any scientific approach to the "concrete" is to make explicit the epistemological principles of its own treatment of it'; and he then goes on to say that 'Miliband nowhere deals with the Marxist theory of the state as such, although it is constantly implicit in his work' (p.69). In fact, I do quite explicitly give an outline of the Marxist theory of the state[2] but undoubtedly do so very briefly. One reason for this, quite apart from the fact that I have discussed Marx's theory of the state elsewhere,[3] is that, having outlined the Marxist theory of the state, I was concerned to set it against the dominant, democratic-pluralist view and to show the latter's deficiencies in the only way in which this seems to me to be possible, namely in empirical terms. It is perfectly proper for Poulantzas to stress the importance of an appropriate 'problematic' in such an undertaking, and it is probably true that mine is insufficiently elucidated; but since he notes that such a 'problematic' is 'constantly implicit in my work', I doubt that my exposition is quite as vitiated by empiricist deformations as he suggests; i.e. that the required 'problematic' is not absent from the work, and that I am not therefore led 'to attack bourgeois ideologies of the State whilst placing [myself] on their own terrain' (p.69).

Poulantzas gives as an example of this alleged failing the fact that, while I maintain against pluralist writers the view that a plurality of élites does not exclude the existence of a ruling class (and I do in fact entitle one chapter 'Economic Elites and Dominant Class'), I fail to provide a critique of the ideological notion of élite and do therefore place myself inside the 'problematic' which I seek to oppose. Here too, however, I doubt whether the comment is justified. I am aware of the degree to which the usage of certain words and concepts is ideologically and politically loaded, and indeed I provide a number of examples of their far from 'innocent' usage; and I did in fact, for this very reason, hesitate to speak of 'élites'. But I finally decided to do so, firstly because I thought, perhaps mistakenly, that it had by now acquired a sufficiently neutral connotation (incidentally, it may still have a much more ideological ring in its French usage than in its English one); and secondly because it seemed, in its neutral sense, the most convenient word at hand to suggest the basic point that, while there do exist such separate 'élites' inside the dominant class, which Poulantzas describes by the admittedly more neutral but rather weak word 'fractions', they are perfectly compatible with the existence of a dominant class, and are in fact parts of that class. He suggests that the 'concrete reality' concealed by the notion of 'plural élites' can only be grasped 'if the very notion of élite is rejected' (p.70). I would say myself that the concrete reality can only be grasped if the concept of élite is turned against those who use it for apologetic purposes and shown to require integration into the concept of a dominant or ruling class: i.e. there *are* concepts of bourgeois social science which can be used for critical as well as for apologetic purposes. The enterprise may often be risky, but is sometimes legitimate and necessary.[4]

However, the general point which Poulantzas raises goes far beyond the use of this or that concept. In fact, it concerns nothing less than the status of empirical enquiry and its relationship to theory. In this regard, I would readily grant that *The State in Capitalist Society* may be insufficiently 'theoretical' in the sense in which Poulantzas means it; but I also tend to think that his own approach, as suggested in his review and in his otherwise important book, *Pouvoir Politique et Classes Sociales*, a translation of which into English is urgently needed, errs in the opposite direction. To put the point plainly, I think it is possible, in this field at least, to be so profoundly concerned with the elaboration of an appropriate 'problematic' and with the avoidance of any contamination with opposed 'problematics', as to lose sight of the absolute necessity of empirical enquiry, and of the empirical demonstration of the falsity of these opposed and apologetic 'problematics'. Poulantzas declares himself not to be against the study of the 'concrete': I would go much farther and suggest that, of course on the basis of an appropriate 'problematic', such a study of the concrete is a *sine qua non* of the kind of 'demystifying' enterprise which, he kindly suggests, my book accomplishes. After all, it was none other than Marx who stressed the importance of empirical validation (or invalidation) and who spent many years of his life in precisely such an undertaking; and while I do not suggest for a moment that Poulantzas is unaware of this fact, I do think that he, and the point also goes for Louis Althusser and his collaborators, may tend to give it rather less attention than it deserves. This, I must stress, is not a crude (and false) contraposition of empiricist versus non- or anti-empiricist approaches: it is a matter of emphasis—but the emphasis is important.

2. The Objective Nature of the State

Poulantzas's critique of my approach also underlies other points of difference between us. But before dealing with these, I should like to take up very briefly what he calls 'the false problem of managerialism'. Managerialism *is* a false problem in one sense, not in another. It is a false problem in the sense that the 'motivations' of managers (of which more in a moment) are not such as to distinguish the latter in any fundamental way from other members of the capitalist class: i.e. he and I are agreed that the thesis of the 'soulful corporation' is a mystification. But he also suggests that I attribute to the managers 'an importance they do not possess' (p.72). This seems to me to underestimate the significance of the 'managerial' phenomenon in the internal organization of capitalist production (which, incidentally, Marx writing a hundred years ago, did not do).[5] Poulantzas for his own part chooses to stress 'the differences and relations between fractions of capital'. But while these *are* important and need to be comprehended in an economic and political analysis of contemporary capitalism, I would argue that the emphasis which he gives to these differences and relations may well obscure the underlying cohesion of these various elements—and may well play into the hands of those who focus on these differences in order to deny the fundamental cohesion of the capitalist class in the conditions of advanced capitalism.

More important, however, Poulantzas also suggests that I attach undue importance, indeed that I am altogether mistaken in attaching *any* importance to the 'motivations' of the managers. Thus, 'the characterization of the existing social system as capitalist in no way depends on the motivations of the conduct of the managers . . . to characterize the class position of managers, one need not refer to the motivations of their conduct, but only to their place in production and their relation to the ownership of the means of production' (p.71). I think myself that one must refer to both not because managerial 'motivations' are in themselves critical (and Poulantzas is mistaken in believing that I think they are)[6] but precisely in order to show why they are not. By ignoring them altogether, one leaves a dangerous gap in the argument which needs to be put forward against managerial apologetics. This is why, I take it, Baran and Sweezy, for instance, devote a good deal of attention to 'business behaviour' in their *Monopoly Capital*.

This issue of 'motivations' also arises, in a much more significant and far-reaching way, in connection with what I have called the state élite and its relation to the ruling class. Poulantzas notes that, in order to rebut the ideologies which affirm the neutrality of the state, I bring forward evidence to show that members of that class are themselves involved in government, and also show the degree to which those who man the command posts of the various parts of the state system are, by social origin, status, milieu (and, he might have added, ideological dispositions) connected with the ruling class. But, he also adds, this procedure, while having a 'capital *demystifying* importance',[7] is 'not the most significant one' (p.72). His reason for saying this is so basic that I must here quote him at some length: 'The relation between the bourgeois class and the State is an *objective relation*. This means that if the *function* of the State in a determinate social formation and the *interests* of the dominant class in this formation *coincide*, it is by reason of the system itself' (p.73).[8] Similarly, the members of the State apparatus 'function according to a specific internal unity. Their class origin—*class situation* — recedes into the background in relation to that which unifies them— their *class position*: that is to say, the fact that they belong precisely to the State apparatus and that they have as their *objective function* the actualization of the role of the State. The totality of this role coincides with the interests of the ruling class' (pp.73-4).[9]

I should like to make two comments about this. The first and less important is that Poulantzas greatly under-estimates the extent to which I myself do take account of the 'objective relations' which affect and shape the role of the state. In fact, I repeatedly note how government and bureaucracy, irrespective of social origin, class situation and even ideological dispositions, are subject to the structural constraints of the system. Even so, I should perhaps have stressed this aspect of the matter more.

But however that may be, I believe—and this is my second point—
that Poulantzas himself is here rather one-sided and that he goes
much too far in dismissing the nature of the state élite as of altogether no account. For what his *exclusive* stress on 'objective relations' suggests is that what the state does is in every particular and at
all times *wholly* determined by these 'objective relations': in other
words, that the structural constraints of the system are so absolutely
compelling as to turn those who run the state into the merest functionaries and executants of policies imposed upon them by 'the system'. At the same time, however, he also rejects the 'long Marxist
tradition (which) has considered that the State is only a simple tool
or instrument manipulated at will by the ruling class' (p.74).
Instead, he stresses the 'relative autonomy of the state'. But all that
this seems to me to do is to substitute the notion of 'objective structures' and 'objective relations' for the notion of 'ruling' class. But
since the ruling class is a dominant element of the system, we are in
effect back at the point of total subordination of the state élite to
that class; i.e. the state is not 'manipulated' by the ruling class into
doing its bidding: it does so autonomously but totally because of the
'objective relations' imposed upon it by the system. Poulantzas condemns the 'economism' of the Second and Third Internationals and
attributes to it their neglect of the state (p.68). But his own analysis
seems to me to lead straight towards a kind of structural determinism, or rather a structural super-determinism, which makes impossible a truly realistic consideration of the dialectical relationship between the state and 'the system'.

For my own part, I do believe that 'the state in these class societies
is primarily and inevitably the guardian and protector of the economic interests which are dominant in them. Its 'real' purpose and
mission is to ensure their continued predominance, not to prevent
it'.[10] But I also believe that within this 'problematic', the state élite is
involved in a far more complex relationship with the 'system' and
with society as a whole than Poulantzas's scheme allows; and that at
least to a certain but definite and important extent that relationship
is shaped by the kind of factors which I bring into the analysis and
which Poulantzas dismisses as of no account.

The political danger of structural super-determinism would seem
to me to be obvious. For if the state élite is as totally imprisoned in

objective structures as is suggested, it follows that there is *really* no difference between a state ruled, say, by bourgeois constitutionalists, whether conservative or social-democrat, and one ruled by, say, Fascists. It was the same approach which led the Comintern in its 'class against class' period fatally to under-estimate what the victory of the Nazis would mean for the German working-class movement. This is an ultra-left deviation which is also not uncommon today; and it is the obverse of a right deviation which assumes that changes in government, for instance the election of a social-democratic government, accompanied by some changes in the personnel of the state system, are sufficient to impart an entirely new character to the nature and role of the state. Both are deviations, and both are dangerous.

It is the same sort of obliteration of differences in the forms of government and state which appears in Poulantzas's references to the 'relative autonomy' of the state. He suggests that Marx designated Bonapartism as the 'religion of the bourgeoisie', and takes Marx to mean that Bonapartism was 'characteristic of *all* forms of the capitalist state' (p.74).[11] I stand to be corrected but I know of no work of Marx which admits of such an interpretation; and if he had said anything which did admit of such an interpretation, he would have been utterly mistaken. For in any meaningful sense of the concept, Bonapartism has *not* been characteristic of all forms of the capitalist state—rather the reverse. What Marx did say was that Bonapartism in France 'was the only form of government possible at the time when the bourgeoisie had already lost, and the working class had not yet acquired, the faculty of ruling the nation'.[12] It is perfectly true that all states are in some degree 'autonomous', and Poulantzas misreads me when he suggests that I 'finally admit this autonomy only in the extreme case of Fascism' (p.74).[13] What I do say is that Fascism is the extreme case of the state's autonomy in the context of capitalist society, which is not at all the same thing—and that between the kind of autonomy which is achieved by the state under Fascism, and that which is achieved by it under the conditions of bourgeois democracy, there is a large gulf, which it is dangerous to underestimate. This scarcely leads me to an apotheosis of bourgeois democracy. It leads me rather to say that 'the point of the socialist critique of 'bourgeois freedoms' is not (or should not be) that they are of no consequence, but that they are profoundly inadequate, and need to be extended by the radical transformation of the context, economic, social and political, which condemns them to inadequacy and erosion'.[14]

3. The Ideological Institutions

Poulantzas's references to the sections of my book devoted to ideology also raise points of great substance. He suggests that both he and I 'have ended by considering that ideology only exists in ideas, customs and morals without seeing that ideology can be embodied, in the strong sense, in *institutions*' (p.76).[15] I myself must plead not guilty to the charge. What he, again most generously, calls my 'long and excellent analyses' of the subject largely focus precisely on the institutions which are the purveyors of ideology, and on the degree to which they are part and parcel, as institutions, of the general system of domination—and I do this in relation to parties, churches, pressure groups, the mass media, education, and so on. What value my analyses may have lies, I think, in my attempted demonstration of the fact that 'political socialization' *is* a process performed by institutions, many of which never cease to insist on their 'un-ideological', 'un-political' and 'neutral' character.

The much more important point is that Poulantzas suggests that these institutions 'belong to the system of the State' and he proposes the thesis that this system of the State 'is composed of *several apparatuses or institutions* of which certain have a principally repressive role, and others a principally ideological role', and among these he lists the Church, political parties, unions, the schools, the mass media and, from a certain point of view, the family (p.77).[16]

I am extremely dubious about this. I suggest in *The State in Capitalist Society* that the state is increasingly involved in the process of 'political socialization' and that it plays, in certain respects, an extremely important role in it.[17] But I also think that, just as it is necessary to show that the institutions mentioned earlier *are* part of a system of power, and that they are, as Poulantzas says, increasingly linked to and buttressed by the state, so it is important not to blur the fact that they are not, in bourgeois democracies, part of the state but of the political system. These institutions *are* increasingly subject to a process of 'statization'; and as I also note in the book, that process is likely to be enhanced by the fact that the state must, in the conditions of permanent crisis of advanced capitalism, assume ever greater responsibility for political indoctrination and mystification. But to suggest that the relevant institutions are actually part of the state system does not seem to me to accord with reality, and tends to obscure the difference in this respect between these political systems and systems where ideological institutions are indeed part of a state monopolistic system of power. In the former systems, ideological institutions do retain a very high degree of autonomy; and are therefore the better able to conceal the degree to which they do belong to the system of power of capitalist society. The way to show that they do, is not to claim that they are part of the state system, but to show how they do perform their ideological functions outside it; and this is what I have tried to do.

Finally, Poulantzas notes that my book says very little by way of 'political conclusions'. If by 'political conclusions' is meant 'where do we go from here?' and 'how?', the point is well taken. I have no difficulties in suggesting that the aim of socialists is to create an 'authentically democratic social order, a truly free society of self-governing men and women, in which, in Marx's phrase, the state will be converted "from an organ superimposed upon society into one completely subordinate to it"'.[18] But this obviously raises very large and complex questions which I did not believe it possible to tackle, let alone answer with any kind of rigour, at the tail-end of this particular book.

II

1973

One or two preliminary remarks about this review-article may be in order. In *New Left Review 58* (November-December 1969), Nicos

Poulantzas wrote a very stimulating and generous review of my book *The State in Capitalist Society*; and in the following issue of NLR, I took up some of his comments and tried to meet some of his criticisms. This exchange attracted a good deal of attention, both in this country and elsewhere: obviously, and whether adequately or not, we had touched on questions concerning the state which Marxists and others felt to be important. I thought that the publication in English of Poulantzas's own book on the state[19] (it first appeared in French in 1968) would provide an opportunity to continue with the discussion that was then started, and to probe further some of the questions which were then raised. Unfortunately, the attempt to do this must, so far as I am concerned, be made in a much more critical vein than I had expected. The reason for this is that on re-reading the book in English five years after reading it in the original, I am very much more struck by its weaknesses than by its strengths. This is not a matter of poor translation: a random check suggests that the team of translators which was required for the task struggled valiantly and not unsuccessfully with an exceedingly difficult French text. It is a pity that the book is so obscurely written for any reader who has not become familiar through painful initiation with the particular linguistic code and mode of exposition of the Althusserian school to which Poulantzas relates. But too much ought not to be made of this: serious Marxist work on the state and on political theory in general is still sufficiently uncommon to make poor exposition a secondary defect—though the sooner it is remedied, the more likely it is that a Marxist tradition of political analysis will now be encouraged to take root.

Nor need a second and different objection that might be made against the book be taken as decisive, or even as particularly significant. This is its abstractness. The sub-title of the book in French (which the English edition does not reproduce) is: *de l'Etat Capitaliste*. But the fact is that the book hardly contains any reference at all to an actual capitalist state anywhere. Poulantzas says at the beginning of the work 'I shall also take into consideration not simply in research but also in exposition, concrete capitalist social formations' (p.24). But he doesn't, not at least as I understand the meaning of the sentence. He seems to me to have an absurdly exaggerated fear of empiricist contamination ('Out, out, damned fact'); but all the same, accusations of abstractness are rather facile and in many ways off the point—the question is what kind of abstractness and to what purpose. In any case, and notwithstanding the attention to concrete social formations promised in the above quotation, Poulantzas makes it quite clear that his main concern is to provide a 'reading' of texts from Marx and Engels, and also from Lenin, on the state and politics. Such a 'reading', in the Althusserian sense, is, of course, not a presentation or a collation of texts; nor is it a commentary on them or even an attempt at interpretation, though it is partly the latter. It is primarily a particular theorization of the texts. Poulantzas makes no bones about the nature of the exercise: 'In order to use the texts of the Marxist classics as a source of information, particularly on the capitalist state,' he writes, 'it has been necessary to complete them and to subject them to a particular critical treatment.'[20] Similarly, he notes that 'these texts are not always explicit . . . Marx and Engels often analyse historical realities by explicitly referring to notions insufficient for their explanation. These texts contain valuable guide lines, so long as the necessary scientific concepts contained in them are deciphered, concepts which are either absent, or, as is more commonly the case, are present in the practical state.'[21] One may feel a bit uneasy about this 'complementation' of texts and at their subjection to 'particular critical treatment'. But at least, the author appears to be playing fair in declaring what he is doing, and the enterprise is not in itself illegitimate—indeed, there is no other way of effecting a theorization. The question here too is how well the enterprise has been conducted, and whether the 'deciphering' has produced an accurate message. I will argue below that it has not and that much of Poulantzas's 'reading' constitutes a serious misrepresentation of Marx and Engels and also of the actual reality he is seeking to portray.

I. Structures and Levels

I want to start by noting that the basic theme of the book, its central 'problematic', is absolutely right; and that Poulantzas, whatever else may be said about his work, directs attention to questions whose core importance not only *for* but *in* the Marxist analysis of politics cannot be sufficiently emphasized. What he is concerned to re-affirm is that the political realm is not, in classical Marxism, the mere reflection of the economic realm, and that in relation to the state, the notion of the latter's 'relative autonomy' is central, not only in regard to 'exceptional circumstances', but in *all* circumstances. In fact, this notion may be taken as the starting-point of Marxist political theory. As with Althusser, 'economism' is for Poulantzas one of the three cardinal sins (the other two being 'historicism' and 'humanism'); and even though his anti-'economism' is so obsessive as to produce its own 'deviations', there is no doubt that 'economistic' misinterpretations of the politics of classical Marxism have been so common among enemies and adherents alike that even some stridency in the assertion of the central importance of the concept of the relative autonomy of the political in Marxist theory may not come amiss.[22]

Still, to insist on this *is* only a starting-point, however important. Once it has been established, the questions follow thick and fast: how relative is relative? In what circumstances is it more so, or less? What form does the autonomy assume? And so on. These are the key questions of a Marxist political sociology, and indeed of political sociology *tout court*. It would be absurd to blame Poulantzas for not having, in this book, provided an answer to all these questions. The real trouble, as I see it, is that his *approach* to these questions prevents him from providing a satisfactory answer to them. In my *Reply* to Poulantzas in NLR 59, I said that his mode of analysis struck me as leading towards what I then called 'structural super-determinism'. I think that was right but that a more accurate description of his approach and of its results would be *structuralist abstractionism*. By this I mean that the world of 'structures' and 'levels' which he inhabits has so few points of contact with historical or contemporary reality that it cuts him off from any possibility of achieving what he describes as 'the political analysis of a concrete conjuncture'.[23] 'Everything happens,' he writes, 'as if social classes were the result of an ensemble of structures and of their relations, firstly at the economic level, secondly at the political level and thirdly at the ideological level.'[24] But even if we assume that classes are the product of such an 'ensemble', we want to know the nature of the dynamic which produces this 'ensemble', and which welds the different 'levels' into the 'ensemble'. Poulantzas has no way that I can discern of doing this: the 'class struggle' makes a dutiful appearance; but in an exceedingly formalized ballet of evanescent shadows. What is lacking here is both any sense of history or for that matter of social analysis. One example is Poulantzas's treatment of the notion of 'class-in-itself' and 'class-for-itself'. These are described as '1847 formulae' of Marx, which 'are merely Hegelian reminiscences. Not only do they fail to explain anything, but they have for years misled Marxist theorists of social classes'.[25] But what, it may then be asked, is to take the place of these 'Hegelian reminiscences', since we clearly do need some means of tracing the dynamic whereby a class (or a social aggregate) becomes an 'ensemble' in which the economic, the political and the ideological 'levels' achieve the necessary degree of congruence?

Poulantzas sees the problem: 'A class', he says, 'can be considered as a distinct and autonomous class, as a social force, inside a social formation, only when its connection with the relations of production, its economic existence, is reflected on the other levels by a specific presence'.[26] Leaving aside this oddly 'economistic' reflectionism, after so much denunication of it, one must ask what is a 'specific presence'? The answer is that 'this presence exists when the relation to the relations of production, the place in the process of production, is reflected on the other levels by *pertinent effects*.'[27] What then are 'pertinent effects'? The answer is that 'we shall designate by "pertinent effects" the fact that the reflection of the place in the process of production on the other levels constitutes a *new element* which cannot be inserted in the typical framework which these levels would present without these elements'.[28] This might be interpreted to mean that a class assumes major significance when it makes a major impact upon affairs—which can hardly be said to get us very far. But Poulantzas does not even mean that. For he also tells us, 'the dominance of the economic struggle' (i.e. 'economism' as a form of working-class struggle—R.M.) does *not* mean 'an absence of "pertinent effects" at the level of political struggle'—it only means 'a certain form of political struggle, which Lenin criticizes by considering it as ineffectual'.[29] So, at one moment a class can only be considered as distinctive and autonomous if it exercises 'pertinent effects', i.e. a decisive impact, next moment, these 'pertinent effects' may be 'ineffectual'. Poulantzas never ceases to insist on the need for 'rigorous' and 'scientific' analysis. But what kind of 'rigorous' and 'scientific' analysis is this? Indeed, what kind of analysis at all?

2. Class Power and State Power

I now want to return to the issue of the relative autonomy of the state and show how far Poulantzas's *structuralist abstractionism* affects his treatment of the question. Not only does his approach seem to me to stultify his attempt to explain the nature of the state's relationship to the dominant class: it also tends to subvert the very concept of relative autonomy itself. Driven out through the front door, 'economism' re-appears in a new guise through the back. Thus, Poulantzas tells us that 'power is not located in the levels of structures, but is an effect of the ensemble of these levels, while at the same time characterizing each of the levels of the class struggle'.[30] From this proposition, (which strikes me as extremely dubious, but let it pass), Poulantzas moves on to the idea that 'the concept of power cannot thus be applied to one level of the structure. When we speak for example of *state power*, we cannot mean by it the mode of the state's articulation at the other levels of the structure; *we can only mean the power of a determinate class* to whose interests (rather than to those of other social classes) the state corresponds'.[31] Now this, I should have thought, is manifestly incorrect: it is simply not true that by 'state power', we can only mean 'the power of a determinate class'. For this, *inter alia*, is to deprive the state of any kind of autonomy at all and to turn it *precisely* into the merest instrument of a determinate class—indeed all but to conceptualize it out of existence. Lest it be thought that I exaggerate, consider this: 'The various social institutions, in particular the institutions of the state, do not, strictly speaking, have any power. Institutions considered from the point of view of power, can be related only to *social classes which hold power*.'[32]

As if uneasily aware of the implications of what he is saying, Poulantzas assures us that 'this does not mean that power centres, the various institutions of an economic, political, military, cultural, etc, character are mere instruments, organs or appendices of the power of social classes. They possess their autonomy and *structural* specificity which is not as such immediately reducible to an analysis in terms of power.'[33] This half-hearted concession does not dissipate the confusion: it only compounds it. The reason for that confusion, or at least one reason for it, is Poulantzas's failure to make the necessary distinction between *class power* and *state power*. State power is the main and ultimate—but not the only—means whereby class power is assured and maintained. But one of the main reasons for stressing the importance of the notion of the relative autonomy of the state is that there is a basic distinction to be made between class power and state power, and that the analysis of the meaning and implications of that notion of relative autonomy must indeed focus on the forces which cause it to be greater or less, the circumstances in which it is exercised, and so on. The blurring of the distinction between class power and state power by Poulantzas[34] makes any such analysis impossible: for all the denunciations of 'economism', politics does here assume an 'epiphenomenal' form.

This is particularly evident in Poulantzas's scattered and cursory references to the bourgeois-democratic form of the capitalist state. Two instances may be given to illustrate the point. The first concerns the relationship between different elements of the state system. For Poulantzas, 'the actual relation of the state's institutional powers, which is conceived as a "separation" of these powers, is in fact fixed in the capitalist state as a mere *distribution* of power, out of the undivided unity of state sovereignty'.[35] This formulation slurs over some important questions concerning the nature of the bourgeois-democratic form of state. No doubt, in the strong sense in which it has commonly been used, the notion of the separation of powers is a mystification which serves apologetic purposes. But to dismiss the actual separation of power which occurs in this form of state as a 'mere distribution of power' out of 'the undivided unity of state sovereignty' is to ignore processes which it is the task of a Marxist political theory to situate in a proper perspective. Thus, to take a topical example, the constitutional struggles around Watergate may or may not produce large results. But there is something badly wrong with a mode of analysis which suggests that 'the actual relation of the state's institutional powers' (in this case the American state) is 'a mere distribution of power, out of the undivided unity of state sovereignty'. It begs too many questions and leaves too much unanswered.

Similarly, and more important, Poulantzas appears to me systematically to underestimate the significance of the role performed by bourgeois political parties in organizing and articulating the interests and demands of various classes, notably the dominant class. 'The political parties of the bourgeois class and of its fractions are unable', he tells us, 'to play an autonomous organizational role, let alone one analogous to the role of the working-class's parties'.[36] This too is surely an untenable claim. The idea that the Conservative Party in Great Britain or Christian Democracy in Germany or Italy have not played this role is absurd—indeed, they have played it much *more* effectively than working-class parties have played it for the working class. 'In fact', Poulantzas goes on, 'the bourgeois parties, in general, utterly fail to fill that autonomous role as organiser of these classes which is precisely necessary for the maintenance of existing social relations: this role falls to the state'.[37] But this is not right. The state may in various ways *help* these parties to fulfil their role, and also in competing on terms of advantage with their working-class rivals. But the main task to which Poulantzas refers is, in the bourgeois-democratic form of the capitalist state, performed by the parties themselves. It is only in periods of acute and prolonged crisis, when these parties show themselves incapable of performing their political task, that their role may be taken over by the state.[38]

Towards the end of the book, Poulantzas notes the existence of a current of thought, which he sees as originating with Max Weber, and which seeks to present the state 'either as the exclusive foundations of political power, independent of the economic, or as the foundation of political power, independent from, but parallel to, economic power';[39] and he suggests that 'the major defect of these theories consists in the fact that they do not provide any *explanation* of the foundation of political power'.[40] Unfortunately, the same has to be said of his own text, in so far as what I called in my NLR 59 article his 'structural super-determinism' makes him *assume* what has to be *explained* about the relationship of the state to classes in the capitalist mode of production. There is in this schema a 'derealization' of classes, whose 'objective interests' are so loosely defined as to make possible almost anything and everything;[41] and the same is true of the state itself, whose relative autonomy, as I have suggested earlier, turns into complete instrumentalization.[42]

3. Bonapartism

Poulantzas does not really seem interested in the bourgeois-democratic form of state at all. His primary interest is in the form which the capitalist state assumes in crisis circumstances, or rather in one of these forms, namely the Bonapartist state.[43] There is nothing wrong with this: but there is a lot which is wrong, as I suggested earlier, with his treatment of it, particularly in his 'reading' of the work of Marx and Engels on the subject.

Some quotations are required here. 'Constantly throughout their concrete political analyses,' Poulantzas writes, 'Marx and Engels relate Bonapartism (the religion of the bourgeoisie), as characteristic of the capitalist type of state, to its intrinsic unity and to the relative autonomy which it derives from its function *vis-à-vis* the power bloc and the hegemonic class or fraction.'[44] Even more categorically, we are told that 'Marx and Engels *systematically conceive* Bonapartism not simply as a concrete form of the capitalist state, *but as a constitutive theoretical characteristic of the very type of capitalist state.*'[45] Categorical and italicized though these assertions may be, it has to be said that they are untrue. For one thing, the notion that Marx and Engels 'systematically' conceived this or that form of state is inaccurate, as Poulantzas himself, as may be recalled from my previous quotations, suggests at the beginning of his book. But in any case and much more important, there is absolutely nothing in their writings to warrant the assertion that they conceived (systematically or otherwise) Bonapartism 'as a constitutive theoretical characteristic of the very type of capitalist state'. It may be that they should have done: but they did not. Nor is Poulantzas able to adduce the textual evidence needed for so definite a 'reading'.

The evidence upon which he does rely is a letter which Engels addressed to Marx on 13 April 1866, commenting on Bismarck's proposals for constitutional reform in Prussia on the basis of universal suffrage. The relevant passage, of which Poulantzas only provides an abbreviated version, goes as follows: 'It would seem that, after a little resistance, the German citizens will agree, for Bonapartism is after all the real religion of the modern bourgeoisie. I see ever more clearly that the bourgeoisie is not capable of ruling directly, and that where there is no oligarchy, as there is in England, to take on the task of leading the state and society in the interests of the bourgeoisie for a proper remuneration, a Bonapartist semi-dictatorship is the normal form; it takes in hand the big material interests of the bourgeoisie even against the bourgeoisie, but leaves it with no part in the process of governing. On the other hand, this dictatorship is itself compelled to adopt against its will the material interests of the bourgeoisie.'[46]

This is an interesting and a very suggestive text, but no more than that. Poulantzas also claims that 'Engels returns to this point in the famous foreward to the third edition of *The Eighteenth Brumaire*'. But even the most careful study of this text fails to substantiate the claim. On the contrary, it could well be argued that it makes the *opposite* point, since Engels says there that 'France demolished feudalism in the Great Revolution and established *the unalloyed rule of the bourgeoisie* in a classical purity unequalled by any other European land'.[47] Thirdly, and finally as far as texts are concerned, Poulantzas argues that Marx, in his own 1869 Preface to *The Eighteenth Brumaire*, 'opposes Bonapartism *as the political form of the modern class struggle in general* to the political forms of formations dominated by modes of production other than the capitalist mode'.[48] This is without foundation. There is nothing in the quotation which Poulantzas gives from this Preface, or in the rest of the text, which bears the interpretation he gives to it, on any kind of 'reading'.

Poulantzas lays great emphasis on Engels's reference to Bonapartism as 'the religion of the bourgeoisie'. Even if one agreed to treat a single passing reference in a letter from Engels to Marx as a main pillar in the construction of a Marxist theory of the state, one would be bound to say that Engels was wrong in describing Bonapartism as the *religion* of the bourgeoisie, if this is taken to mean that the bourgeoisie has an irrepressible hankering for such a type of regime. As the extreme inflation of executive power and the forcible demobilization of all political forces in civil society, Bonapartism is not the religion of the bourgeoisie at all—it is its last *resort* in conditions of political instability so great as to present a threat to the maintenance of the existing social order, including of course the system of domination which is the central part of that order.

In this instance, care and scruple in textual quotation are not simply matters of scholarship: they also involve large political issues. The insistence that Marx and Engels did believe that Bonapartism *was* the 'constitutive theoretical characteristic of the very type of capitalist state' is not 'innocent': it is intended to invoke their authority for the view that there is *really* no difference, or at least no *real* difference between such a form of state and the bourgeois-democratic form. Thus Poulantzas writes that 'in the framework of the capitalist class state, parliamentary legitimacy is no "closer to the people" than that legitimacy which corresponds to the predominance of the executive. In fact, these are always *ideological* processes in both cases'.[49] But this is to pose the issues in a perilously confusing manner: the issue is not one of 'legitimacy' or 'closeness to the people': it is whether there is a real difference in the manner of operation between different forms of the capitalist state, and if so, what are the implications of these differences. But suppose we do pose the question in the terms chosen by Poulantzas. Both the Weimar Republic and the Nazi state were capitalist class states. But is it the case that 'parliamentary legitimacy' was no 'closer to the people' than 'that legitimacy which corresponds to the predominance of the executive'? Let us not be melodramatic about this, but after all fifty million people died partly at least in consequence of the fact that German Comintern-Marxism, at a crucial moment of time, saw no *real* difference between the two forms of state. Poulantzas also writes, in the same vein, that 'the popular sovereignty of political democracy finds its expression equally well in a classical parliamentarism and in a Bonapartist semi-dictatorship'.[50] But neither is the issue here one of 'popular sovereignty'. This too is to confuse matters and to lend credence to confusions that in the past have proved catastrophic in their consequences.

The point is not, of course, to claim for bourgeois-democratic forms of the capitalist state virtues which they do not possess; or to suggest that such regimes are not given to repression and to Bonapartist-type modes of behaviour; or to imply that the dominant classes in *any* of them are immune from Bonapartist temptations and promptings, given the right circumstances and opportunities. Chile is only the latest example of this. But to say all this is not the same as obliterating differences between forms of the capitalist state which are of crucial importance, not least to working class movements.

To conclude, I have no wish to suggest that the reader will not find useful, suggestive and important ideas in *Political Power and Social Classes*. But I am also bound to say, with genuine regret, that it does not seem to me to be very helpful in the development of that Marxist political sociology which Poulantzas quite rightly wants to see advanced.

1. *The State in Capitalist Society*, p.172.

2. *Ibid*., pp.5, 93.

3. 'Marx and the State' in *The Socialist Register*, 1965, reprinted above as essay 1.

4. Here is one example. 'Governments may be solely concerned with the better running of "the economy". But the descriptions of systems as "the economy" is part of the idiom of ideology, and obscures the real process. For what is being improved is a *capitalist* economy; and this ensures that whoever may or may not gain, capitalist interests are least likely to lose' (*op. cit.*, p.79, italics in original).

5. In fact, *his* formulations may go rather further than is warranted: 'A large part of the social capital is employed by people who do not own it and who consequently tackle things quite differently from the owner' (*Capital*, Moscow 1962, III, p.431). 'This is the abolition of the capitalist mode of production within the capitalist mode of production itself, and hence a self-dissolving contradiction, which *prima facie* represents a mere phase of transition to a new form of production' (*Ibid*., p.429).

6. 'Like the vulgar owner-entrepreneur of the bad old days, the modern manager, however bright and shiny, must also submit to the imperative demands inherent in the sytem of which he is both master and servant; and the most important such demand is that he should make the "highest possible" profits. Whatever his motives and aims may be, they can only be fulfilled on the basis of his success in this regard.' (*The State in Capitalist Society*, p.34.)

7. Italics in text.

8. *Ibid*.

9. *Ibid*.

10. *Op. Cit.*, p.265.

11. Italics in text.

12. *The Civil War in France*, in *Selected Works*, Moscow 1950, I, p.469.

13. It is, incidentally, this recognition on my part of the 'relative autonomy' of the state which leads me, *inter alia*, to suggest that Poulantzas also misreads me when he states that my analysis 'converges with the orthodox communist thesis of *State monopoly capitalism*, according to which the present form of the State is specified by increasingly close inter-personal relations between the monopolies and the members

of the State apparatus, by the "fusion of the State and monopolies into a single mechanism"' (p.71). In fact, I think this scheme to be *simpliste* and explicitly question its usefulness. (*The State in Capitalist Society*, p.11, ft.2.).

14. *Ibid.*, p.267.
15. Italics in text.
16. *Ibid.*
17. *Op. cit.*, pp.183ff.
18. *Op. cit.*, p.277.

II

19. Nicos Poulantzas, *Political Power and Social Classes*, London 1973 (henceforth *PPSC*).
20. *PPSC*.
21. *PPSC*, pp.257-8.
22. A simple illustration of the point is the common interpretation of the most familiar of all the Marxist formulations on the state, that which is to be found in the *Communist Manifesto*, where Marx and Engels assert that 'the modern State is but a committee for managing the common affairs of the whole bourgeoisie'. This has regularly been taken to mean not only that the state acts *on behalf* of the dominant or 'ruling' class, which is one thing, but that it acts *at the behest* of that class, which is an altogether different assertion and, as I would argue, a vulgar deformation of the thought of Marx and Engels. For what they are saying is that 'the modern state is but a committee for managing the *common* affairs of the *whole* bourgeoisie': the notion of common affairs assumes the existence of particular ones; and the notion of the whole bourgeoisie implies the existence of separate elements which make up that whole. This being the case, there is an obvious need for an institution of the kind they refer to, namely the state; and the state *cannot* meet this need without enjoying a certain degree of autonomy. In other words, the notion of autonomy is embedded in the definition itself, is an intrinsic part of it.
23. PPSC, p.91.
24. PPSC, p.63.
25. PPSC, p.76. See, in the same vein, his rejection of the notion of true and false consciousness as a 'mythology', pp.60-1.
26. PPSC, p.78.
27. PPSC, p.79 (italics in original).
28. PPSC, p.79 (italics in original).
29. PPSC, p.83.
30. PPSC, p.99.
31. PPSC, p.100 (italics in original).
32. PPSC, p.115 (italics in original).
33. PPSC, p.115 (italics in original).
34. This is perhaps best exemplified by reference to an article of Poulantzas, '*On Social Classes*', NLR 78, March-April 1973, in which he writes: 'The state is composed of *several apparatuses*: broadly, the *repressive* apparatus and the *ideological apparatus*, the principal role of the former being repression, that of the latter being the elaboration and incubation of ideology. The ideological apparatuses include the churches, the educational system, the bourgeois and petty-bourgeois political parties, the press, radio, television, publishing, etc. These apparatuses belong to the state system because of their objective function of elaborating and inculcating ideology, irrespective of their formal juridical status as nationalized (public) or private' (p.47).

48

This carries to caricatural forms the confusion between different forms of class domination and, to repeat, makes impossible a serious analysis of the relation of the state to society, and of state power to class power.

35. PPSC, p.279 (italics in original).
36. PPSC, p.299.
37. PPSC, p.299.
38. Here too, confusion is compounded by the contradictory statements which abound in the text. Thus on page 320, Poulantzas notes that 'the predominance of the executive implies an increased state autonomy vis-à-vis these classes and fractions only when it is combined with a characteristic of the parties' organizational role *reflected right in the political scene*' (italics in text). So parties which on page 299 fail to play an organizatorial role do play such a role twenty-one pages later.
39. PPSC, p.327.
40. PPSC, p.330.
41. PPSC, p.112.
42. This may account for, though it hardly excuses, such major errors of interpretation as the attribution to C. Wright Mills of the view that 'the heads of economic corporations', the 'political leaders' (including the heights of the bureaucracy) and the 'military leaders', that is to say all the elites, belong to what he (i.e. Mills—R.M.) calls the "corporate rich"' (p.329). This is a complete misunderstanding of Mills's basic characterization of the 'power elite' and of the interrelationship of its component parts.
43. At least in this book. For a wider and much more solid discussion of the 'crisis state' see his *Fascisme et Dictature* (English Edition, *Fascism and Dictatorship*, Verso 1979).
44. PPSC, p.302.
45. PPSC, p.258.
46. K. Marx-F. Engels *Werke*, Berlin 1965, Vol. 31, p.208. Poulantzas's quotation goes as follows: 'Bonapartism is after all *the real religion of the modern bourgeoisie*. It is becoming ever clearer to me that the bourgeoisie has not the stuff in it for ruling directly itself, and that therefore . . . a Bonapartist semi-dictatorship is the normal form; it upholds the big material interests of the bourgeoisie (even against the will of the bourgeoisie) but allows the bourgeoisie no part in the power of government', PPSC, p.259. The italics are not in the original text of Engels.
47. K. Marx and F. Engels, *Selected Works*, Moscow 1950, vol. 1, p.223. There is another text of Engels, from a pamphlet written in 1865, *Die preussische Militärfrage und die deutsche Arbeiterpartei*, where Engels anticipates, in a modified form, a famous formulation of Marx, in stating that 'Bonapartism is the necessary form of state in a country where the working class, though having achieved a high level of development in the towns, remains numerically inferior to the small peasants in the countryside, and has been defeated in a great revolutionary struggle by the capitalist class, the petty bourgeoisie and the army' (*Werke*, Vol. 16, p.71). Compare Marx's formulation (which Poulantzas quotes in a different context) in *The Civil War in France* that the Bonapartist regime 'was the only form of government at the time when the bourgeoisie had already lost, and the working class had not yet acquired, the faculty of ruling the nation' (*Selected Works*, I, p.470). Neither Engels's not Marx's formulation serves to buttress Poulantzas's claims, although, like their other writings of the subject, they are of great interest. For a comprehensive review of these writings, scholarly but weak in interpretation, see M. Rubel, *Karl Marx devant le Bonapartisme*, Paris/The Hague 1960.

48. PPSC, p.259.
49. PPSC, p.312.
50. PPSC, p.312.

3
Political Forms
and Historical Materialism
1975

In *Passages from Antiquity to Feudalism* and *Lineages of the Absolutist State*, the enterprise on which Perry Anderson is engaged is the production of a comparative history of the forms which political power has assumed in different parts of Europe (though not only of Europe); and of the purposes which that political power has served. In effect, he is aiming to produce nothing less than a history of political power and of the state in different social formations and modes of production, notably in slave-labour societies, under feudalism, and under capitalism, but not forgetting the 'Asiatic mode of production', to which a 100-page 'Note' is devoted in the second of the present volumes, *and* taking due account of many different geographical and national specifications. The two books now published carry the analysis from Antiquity to the eve of the overthrow of the Absolutist state in England in the 17th century, in France at the end of the 18th, and in Russia at the beginning of the 20th, a matter of some two and a half thousand years, with no part of Europe left out, and with chapters on the Ottoman Empire and Japanese feudalism.

This is an extraordinary undertaking, whose vastness has induced in the author a certain diffidence about the status of his work. Anderson describes these volumes as 'essays', whose analyses, 'for reasons of both competence and space, are rudimentary diagrams: no more. Brief sketches for another history, they are intended to propose elements for discussion, rather than to expound closed or comprehensive theses' (1,8-9).* This modesty may be commendable

* The volumes are not numbered I and II but I will, as a matter of convenience, so number the references to them. All italics are in the original texts, unless otherwise stated.

but it is quite unnecessary: if the undertaking is extraordinary, the achievement is scarcely less so; and the analyses here put forward are anything but rudimentary diagrams or brief sketches. Anderson has a solid grip on scholarly sources in eight or nine languages. He advances swiftly and surely over terrain after terrain each of which has usually been explored only by specialist historians. He writes with limpid precision, often with controlled eloquence, and with a rare gift for the illuminating aphorism. His books are historical writing in the great tradition. But what gives them quite exceptional significance is that they are historical writing of a particular kind, in so far as they have been shaped by the perspectives and methods of historical materialism. There are by now many Marxist historians. But there are, so far as I know, not many such historians anywhere who have written Marxist history at this pitch of conceptual intensity and with such a specific and sustained consciousness of what they were *theoretically* doing. This is of course not to say that Anderson's work is beyond questioning, not least by other Marxists; and I will presently suggest one or two central questions which these volumes seem to me to raise. I am sure that many different questions will be raised about and around these books, which is as it should be. But I am also sure that, whatever reservation or criticism there may be regarding this or that thesis of Anderson's, what he has now produced constitutes an outstanding contribution to historical writing in the historical materialist mode; as Marxist historiography these volumes stand in a class apart.

The Method of Historical Materialism

In the Foreword to his second volume, Anderson notes that 'Marxist historians, the authors of a now impressive corpus of research, have not always been directly concerned with the theoretical questions or implications raised by their work'; and that, for their part, 'Marxist philosophers, who have sought to clarify or solve the basic theoretical problems of historical materialism, have often done so at a considerable remove from the specific empirical issues posed by historians' (II, 7). This is a very delicate way of describing a situation in which Marxist historians have tended to be hazily impressionistic

about the historiographical method to which they formally sub-
scribed; and where Marxist philosophers have tried to deal with (and
have even claimed to resolve) large historical questions by conceptual acrobatics as a substitute for hard historical work. Anderson
has attempted, he says, 'to explore a mediate ground between the
two', and thus 'to try to hold together in tension two orders of
reflection which have often been unwarrantably divorced in Marxist
writing, weakening its capacity for rational and controllable theory
in the domain of history.' (II, 8) I have already indicated my belief
that he has done this remarkably well. But it is necessary to define
wherein he has succeeded theoretically, that is to say in terms of his
use of historical materialism as a method.

In one sense, the answer is quite simple, although what goes into
the making of it is infinitely complex. That answer lies in *beginning*
with the mode of production of a given society but in not ending
there; in other words, in the attribution of a primacy to the 'economic base' which does not lead to a view of the 'superstructure' as a
mere reflection of that 'base'. Anderson has taken seriously some of
the guidelines provided by Marx and Engels, starting with what has
perhaps been the most influential of any text of Marx in this field,
the Preface to *A Contribution to the Critique of Political Economy*
of 1859, in which Marx asserts that 'the mode of production of
material life conditions the social, political and intellectual life process in general.'[1] This can be, and often has been, easily turned into
a more or less primitive economic determinism. But it was not so
envisaged by Marx or Engels. Marx emphatically warned that one
should beware of using 'as one's master key a general historico-
philosophical theory', 'the supreme virtue of which,' he noted
ironically 'consists in being super-historical,'[2] and his own historical
work, including that which is to be found in *Capital*, shows well
enough how alien to him was the notion of turning historical
materialism into a 'super-historical master key.' So was it alien to
Engels, who was even more explicit and specific about it than Marx,
as for instance in his famous letters to J. Bloch and C. Schmidt in
1890.[3]

Obviously, these are no more than guidelines, but Anderson has
used them well, as may be seen from some direct quotations. In his
first volume, he notes that it was the slave mode of production in the

Graeco-Roman world 'which provided the ultimate basis both for its accomplishments and its eclipse.' 'The Ancient World as a whole was never continuously or ubiquitously marked by the predominance of slave labour. But its great *classical* epochs, when the civilisations of Antiquity flowered – Greece in the 5th and 4th centuries B.C. and Rome from the 2nd century B.C. to the 2nd century A.D. —were those in which slavery was massive and general, amidst other labour systems.' (I, 21-2) But with this as a starting-point, he also has a very strong sense of the related but distinct and powerful other influences which went into the shaping of the societies in question. Thus, 'the structural constraint of slavery on technology . . . lay not so much in a direct intra-economic causality, although this was important in its own right, as in the mediate social ideology which enveloped the totality of manual work in the classical world, contaminating hired and even independent labour with the stigma of debasement.' (I, 27). Similarly, 'the classical *polis* was based on the new conceptual discovery of liberty, entrained by the systematic institution of slavery: the free citizen now stood out in full relief, against the background of slave labourers' (I, 36). Again, but this time for France in the 16th century, he has a passage which shows well the 'blending' of a variety of elements to explain the 'far-reaching limitations of the central State' namely 'the insurmountable organizational problems of imposing an effective apparatus of royal rule over the whole country, amidst an economy without a unified market or modernized transport system, in which the dissociation of primary feudal relations in the village was by no means complete. The social ground for vertical political centralization was not yet ready, despite the notable gains registered by the monarchy' (II, 89). Anderson aptly sums up the approach when he says, at the end of his second volume, that 'the modes of production of any pre-capitalist social formation are always specified by the politico-juridicial apparatus of class rule which enforces the extra-economic coercion peculiar to it' (II, 543). Nor does he find any difficulty, quite rightly, in accepting the fact that there are elements of the 'superstructure' which historical materialism has not so far been able (or for that matter been much concerned) to integrate into its general perspectives. Thus, in a passage of compelling grace, he writes that 'one single institution . . . spanned the whole transition from Antiquity to the Middle Ages in essential continuity: the Christian Church. It was, indeed, the main, frail aqueduct across which the cultural reservoirs of the Classical World now passed to the new universe of feudal Europe, where literacy had become clerical. Strange historical object *par excellence*, whose peculiar temporality has never coincided with that of a simple sequence from one economy or policy to another, but has overlapped and outlived several in a rhythm of its own, the Church has never received theorization within historical materialism' (I, 131).

What Anderson is doing is not simply to take due account of 'factors' other than the 'economic factor'. Such an eclectic accumulation of 'factors' as a way of escaping 'economic determinism' is not historical materialism. That method does include, at its very core, a notion of the primacy of the mode of production. As Marx also put it in the *Grundrisse*, in a passage which Anderson quotes, 'in all forms of society it is a determinate production and its relations which assign every other production and its relations their rank and influence. It is a general illumination in which all other colours are plunged and which modifies their specific tonalities. It is a special ether which defines the specific gravity of everything found in it.' (I, 27) These formulations suggest well enough the broadness of the concept—and who says 'broad' does not necessarily say 'loose'. Certainly in Anderson's handling of it, it yields a controlled and illuminating set of results. Specialists will no doubt tell us in due course what particular weaknesses they find in his account. But no such weakness can invalidate the general method itself: to invalidate it, there would be required a demonstrably superior, analytically richer and more fruitful method.

How great is the freedom of analytical manoeuvre *inside* the realm of historical materialism is also demonstrated by one of Anderson's most telling generalisations: '...contrary to widely received beliefs among Marxists', he writes, 'the characteristic "figure" of a crisis in a mode of production is not one in which vigorous (economic) forces of production burst triumphantly through retrograde (social) relations of production, and promptly establish a higher productivity and society on their ruins. On the contrary, the forces of production typically tend to *stall* and *recede* within the existent relations of production; these then must themselves be radically changed and recorded *before* new forces of production can be created and combined for a globally new mode of production. In other words, the relations of production generally change *prior* to the forces of production in an epoch of transition, and not vice versa' (I, 204). Whether the process thus described is 'typical' or not, the point is one of extreme importance, for it firmly helps to shift the focus of attention onto human agencies since 'relations of production' are of course the relations between producers and owners/controllers, in this instance in the context of slave-labour and feudal modes of production. What is involved in this process is the *expression* of manifold 'contradictions' in and through the consciousness of individuals envisioned as different and antagonistic socio-economic aggregates-classes: in other words, in and through class struggle. Thus, Anderson notes that between the 9th and the 13th century in Western Europe, 'both prosperous and pauper peasants were structurally opposed to the lords who battened on them, and constant, silent rent struggles between the two were waged throughout the feudal epoch (occasionally erupting into open warfare, of course . . .)' (I, 186-7).

It is class struggle which both results from, and which ultimately resolves the 'contradictions' of a given mode of production. But here too, Anderson is very careful not to over-simplify, and therefore to distort, a complex process. He rejects any interpretation which 'tends to inflect Marx's theory of complex objective contradictions into a simple subjective contest of class wills'; and he notes that while 'the *resolution* of structural crises in a mode of production always depends on the direct intervention of the class struggle', 'the *germination* of such crises may well take all social classes by surprise in a given historical totality, by deriving from other structural levels of it than their own immediate confrontation' (I, 198, footnote 3). Indeed, he writes in a different connection, 'no class in history immediately comprehends the logic of its own historical situation, in epochs of transition: a long period of disorientation and confusion may be necessary for it to learn the necessary rules of its own sovereignty' (II, 55). This is well said, and gives the right emphasis to the exceedingly entangled nature of the 'class consciousness' which is produced by the relations of production and the 'contradictions' of a given mode of production.

At this point, however, it may be apposite to enter a doubt as to whether the socio-economic aggregates dealt with in Anderson's account are sufficiently delineated and differentiated; and whether the encounter between antagonistic classes is identified in adequately specific terms. The classes which make their appearance in his analyses suffer somewhat from over-abstract treatment. Classes are rather more complicated entities than is often allowed for here; and while it would be wrong to require a detailed analysis of class structures and class struggles in an account such as this, it may be that a greater concern with questions of social stratification would have enabled Anderson to provide more differentiated analyses of conflicts *within* classes as well as *between* them. As it is, the socio-economic aggregates to which he refers often have a bloc-like quality which obviously belies actual reality: that reality is *also* shaped—and not least shaped—by the separate and conflicting interests of different strata within given classes. The point has a considerable bearing on the question of the role of the Absolutist State (and of the state in general, for that matter), and it is to this that I now turn.

The Absolutist State and its 'Relative Autonomy'

In the Foreword to his second volume, Anderson refers to the fact that it is the state which forms his 'central theme for reflection'; and he recalls 'one of the basic axioms of historical materialism', namely that 'secular struggle between classes is ultimately resolved at the *political*—not at the economic or cultural—level of society . . . it is the construction and destruction of States which seal the basic shifts in the relations of production, so long as classes subsist' (II, 11). This is true; and the question which this volume sets itself concerns the character of the Absolutist State and the role it played in the class configuration of Europe, East and West, in the periods, different for different countries, in which it held sway.

Anderson begins with a straightforward rejection of the view held by Marx and Engels that the Absolutist State represented some sort of 'equilibrium' between the landowning aristocracy and the bourgeoisie. (II, 15-16). His own thesis, which echoes what he describes as 'the consensus of a generation of Marxist historians, from England and Russia', is that 'Absolutism was essentially . . . a *redeployed and recharged apparatus of feudal domination*, designed to clamp the peasant masses back into their traditional social position—despite and against the gains they had won by the widespread commutation of dues' (II, 18). Anderson clearly attaches great importance to the idea of a 'redeployed and recharged' state apparatus. I believe that he is right to do so. For the Absolute monarchies, which introduced, as he notes, standing armies, a permanent bureaucracy, national taxation and a codified system of law, constituted very different state forms from the political systems which had preceded them; and changes of political form, here as anywhere else, also had many different and important implications for state action and non-action. On the other hand, his reference in the previous quotation to the state and the 'peasant masses' is too summary in so far as it leaves out the Absolutist State's relation to the new bourgeoisie; and Anderson himself corrects the formulation a few pages later when he writes that 'the threat of peasant unrest, unspokenly constitutive of the Absolutist State, was . . . always conjoined with the pressure of mercantile or manufacturing capital within the Western economies as a whole, in moulding the contours of aristocratic class power in the new age'. Indeed, he adds, 'the peculiar form of the Absolutist State in the West derives from this double determination' (II, 23-24).

What is at issue here is the very large question of the relationship of the Absolutist State to the West European bourgeoisie, and therefore the very nature and role of that form of state. What Anderson is saying is that the Absolutist State served the interests of a particular class—the class in question being the feudal nobility. This is one thing. But he is in fact saying a great deal more than that—not only that the Absolutist State was an instrument wielded *for* the feudal nobility; but that it was also for the most part wielded *by* the feudal nobility, and for the latter's own purposes. This is a very different thing; and taken as a *general* statement about the Absolutist State, a much more questionable one, which is in fact contradicted by many of Anderson's own formulations. The problem this raises has in recent years been much discussed in regard to the capitalist state, namely the 'relative autonomy of the state'; but it is also of major importance in regard to the Absolutist State. I think that Anderson is right to argue that Marx and Engels greatly *over-stated* the autonomy of the Absolutist State, and that the notion of 'equilibrium' is indeed a misleading one. But it also seems to me that in many of his formulations he himself greatly *under-states* the 'relative autonomy' of the Absolutist State—and the fact that he tends to use inconsistent formulations on this issue suggests a weakness of conceptualisation which is, for him, most unusual, and which has fairly far-reaching consequences.

At the outset, Anderson states that 'the lords who remained the proprietors of the fundamental means of production in any pre-industrial society were, of course, the noble landowners. Throughout the early modern epoch, the dominant class—economically *and politically*—was thus the *same* as in the mediaeval epoch itself: the feudal aristocracy. This nobility underwent profound metamorphoses in the centuries after the close of the Middle Ages: *but from the beginning to the end of the history of Absolutism, it was never dislodged from its command of political power*' (II, 17-18. Italics mine except for the word 'same'). This is a very rash and simple way to describe a very complex situation and Anderson is compelled almost immediately to qualify the statement. 'This new State machine, however,' he also writes, 'was also by its nature vested with a coercive force capable of breaking or disciplining individuals or groups *within* the nobility itself. The arrival of Absolutism was thus . . . never a smooth evolutionary process for the dominant class itself: it was marked by extremely sharp ruptures and conflicts within the feudal aristocracy to whose collective interests it ultimately ministered' (II, 19-20). At the very least, this means that the Absolutist State had a great deal more 'play' vis-à-vis the feudal nobility than the first statement allows, and that its motivations were therefore much more complex than that statement suggests. Indeed, he notes somewhat later in relation to 'nascent absolutism' that for the whole of Western Europe except Spain 'the primary pattern was the suppression of aristocratic rather than burgher revolts, even where the two were closely mingled' (II, 68). Similarly, he writes of France in the 17th century that 'the very depth of the plebeian unrest revealed by the Fronde shortened the last emotional breakaway of the dissident aristocracy from the monarchy', (II,

100) a formulation which obviously and rightly implies a considerable tension between that aristocracy and the monarchy.

The problem in Anderson's exposition to which I am pointing is perhaps best illustrated in the following quotation:

> The kings who presided over the new monarchies could never transgress the unseen limits of their power: those of the material conditions of reproduction of the class to which they themselves belonged. Commonly, these sovereigns were aware of their membership of the aristocracy which surrounded them; their individual pride of station was founded on a collective solidarity of sentiment. Thus while capital was slowly accumulated beneath the glittering superstructures of Absolutism, exerting an ever greater gravitational pull on them, the noble landowners of early modern Europe retained their historical predominance, *in and through the monarchies which now commanded them*. Economically guarded, socially privileged and culturally matured, *the aristocracy still ruled*: the Absolutist State adjusted its paramountcy to the steady burgeoning of capital within the composite social formations of Western Europe (II, 430. My italics).

This very fine piece of writing, which is typical of both these volumes, seems to me to be seriously flawed by the blurred conceptualisation that is present in the formulations which I have italicized. It is perfectly reasonable to maintain that the aristocracy under the Absolutist State remained a 'dominant class'. It is equally reasonable to stress the affinities that linked the absolute monarchs to the aristocracy, affinities epitomised by the remark of Catherine II which Anderson quotes: '*Je suis une aristocrate, c'est mon métier*' (II, 231). It is even permissible to say, in a loose sense, that the aristocracy remained a 'ruling class'. But to say, as Anderson does, that it 'still ruled', in the sense that it was in charge of the state power, is not an acceptable generalisation at all. For, as suggested earlier, it deprives the Absolutist State of the relative autonomy which it enjoyed, and which it required, *in order* to fulfil the very task which Anderson assigns to it, namely the protection of the aristocracy; and the point is as valid for Eastern as for Western Europe. Anderson writes, in this connection that 'the Absolutist State in the West was the redeployed political apparatus of a feudal class which had accepted the commutation of dues. It was a *compensation for the disappearance of serfdom*, in the context of an increasingly urban economy which it did not completely control and to which it had to adapt. The Absolutist State in the East, by contrast, was the repressive machine of a feudal class that had just erased the traditional communal freedoms of the poor. It was a *device for the consolidation of serfdom*, in a landscape scoured of autonomous urban life or resistance' (II, 195). But in *both* cases, the state power was always distinct and to a greater or lesser extent politically independent from the class power of the aristocracy.

This relative autonomy is institutionally emphasised in the case of the Absolutist State by the fact that state power was lodged in the absolute monarch and such advisers as he (or she) might choose to have around him (or her), and these were of course often drawn from outside the ranks of the feudal aristocracy. There is in this form of state an exceptionally strong element of individual, monarchical and monarchically-derived, intervention and policy-making, which further enhances the notion of relative autonomy. Anderson writes of the direct and manifold impact of French Absolutism that 'Henry IV fixed royal presence and power centrally in Paris for the first time, rebuilding the city and making it into the permanent capital of the kingdom. Civic pacification was accompanied by official care for agricultural recovery and promotion of export trades. The popular prestige of the monarchy was restored by the personal magnetism of the founder of the new Bourbon monarchy himself. The Edict of Nantes and its supplementary articles contained the problem of Protestantism, by conceding it limited regional autonomy. No Estates-General was summoned, despite promises to do so made during the civil war. External peace was maintained, and with it administrative economy. Sully, the Huguenot Chancellor, doubled the net revenues of the State, mainly by shifting to indirect taxes, rationalizing tax-farms and cutting expenses' (II, 94); and there is more of the same in the French as well as in most other cases. The picture is clearly not at all one of a state closely confined within the narrow walls created for it by aristocratic class forces. Even so, it is perfectly reasonable to argue that the Absolutist State *was* the state of the feudal aristocracy—but a state, to use a necessary distinction, which acted *on behalf* of that class rather than at *its behest*.

The blurring, in Anderson's account, of the conceptual (and actual) significance of this element of independence enjoyed by the Absolutist State makes more difficult the proper perception and analysis of some major aspects of its nature and role. One such aspect is the intensity of the opposition which it had to overcome on the part of landowning aristocracies, torn between the fear of a centralized and powerful authority on the one hand, and their awareness of the need for such authority on the other. The parallel with the bourgeoisie's attitude to the state is obvious.

Another aspect that needs stressing is the crucial role which the Absolutist State played in the development of Western capitalism. The notion of 'equilibrium' between aristocracy and bourgeoisie is not required to account for the reasons why and the ways in which it played that role. But the notions of 'mediation' and of 'relative autonomy' *are* required for the purpose. An Absolutist State as thoroughly subordinated to aristocratic class power as is suggested by many (but by no means all) of Anderson's formulations would not, it may be surmised, have been able or willing to be as beneficial as it was to the new bourgeoisie.

Anderson argues that even though Absolutism in Western Europe 'represented an apparatus for the protection of aristocratic property and privileges,' 'yet at the same time the means whereby this protection was promoted could *simultaneously* ensure the basic interests of the nascent mercantile and manufacturing classes.' (II, 40) But this too understates the policy *choices* which the Absolutist State often had to make, and the *conflicting claims* which these choices had to resolve: the notion of 'simultaneity' devalues this element of policy choices as between competing interests within and between classes. The absolute monarchs did makes choices and could only make them because the state which they and their advisers commanded was not the mere 'instrument' of aristocratic class power. Here too, Anderson hints at the point when he says, in the passage from which I have already quoted, that the Absolutist State 'adjusted' the paramountcy of the aristocracy 'to the steady burgeoning of capital within the composite social formations of Western Europe' (II, 430). Such 'adjustments', as made by the Absolutist State, could not have been made had it not enjoyed a certain freedom of manoeuvre—nor in any case does the notion of 'adjustment' seem adequate for the description and analysis of the processes and policies in question. In the end, and as a result of their combined if uneven economic, social, political and cultural development, the various strata which made up the bourgeois class found it necessary to seek the radical transformation of the Absolutist State; and this will no doubt occupy a very large place in Anderson's next volume. But it is as well to stress how much that bourgeois development had at least in part been fostered by the Absolutist State, notwithstanding its aristocratic class basis; and also that matters would have proceeded very differently had it not been able to play a 'mediating' role, born of the degree of autonomy which it had, and which was further extended, of course in different measure in each case, by the absolute monarchs.

This last point too may be worth somewhat greater emphasis than it is accorded in Anderson's account. He rightly notes that 'the sway of Absolutism ultimately operated within the necessary bounds of the class whose interest it secured' (II, 51). But these 'necessary bounds' were not very firmly fixed, and the absolute monarchs had something to do with this fact. Clearly, what they could achieve, as individual rulers, was also circumscribed by forces and circumstances beyond their control. But even though these monarchs were only 'absolute' in name, they did introduce a certain element of contingency in the historical process of which they were a part. Here as elsewhere, there is in historical materialism a permanent danger of over-determinism.

To conclude, I want to say that the reservations which have been voiced here do not in the least affect the view expressed at the beginning, namely that these volumes constitute a quite outstanding contribution to Marxist historical work in particular and to Marxist intellectual work in general. The present notice has only concentrated on a very few aspects of the work, and cannot do justice to the richness of the material presented here and to the scholarship and intellectual power with which it is handled. These books offer a double challenge: to historians and others who reject the method of historical materialism; but also to those who subscribe to it, or whose work is influenced by it. The impact of that challenge will be strongly felt for a long time to come.

1. K. Marx, Preface to *A Contribution to the Critique of Political Economy*, in K. Marx and F. Engels, *Selected Works*, Moscow 1950, I, p.329.

2. K. Marx to the Editorial Board of *Otechestvenniye Zapiski*, November 1877, in K. Marx and F. Engels, *Selected Correspondence*, Moscow n.d., p.329.

3. *Ibid.*, pp.495 ff.

4

State Power and Class Interests

1983

Work done in the last fifteen years or so by people writing within a broad Marxist perspective on the subject of the state in capitalist society now fills a great many bookshelves; and however critical one may be of one or other article, book or trend, it is undoubtedly very useful that this work should be available. There is, however, a very large gap in the literature, in so far as very little of it is specifically concerned with the question of the autonomy of the state.[1] How ~~self governing~~ great a degree of autonomy does the state have in capitalist society? What purpose is its autonomy intended to serve? And what purpose does it actually serve? These and many other such questions are clearly of the greatest theoretical and practical importance, given the scope and actual or potential impact of state action upon the society over which the state presides, and often beyond. Yet, the issue has remained poorly explored and 'theorized' in the Marxist perspective.[2] The present article is intended as a modest contribution to the work that needs to be done on it.[3]

In the first volume of *Karl Marx's Theory of Revolution*, Hal Draper very usefully sets out what Marx and Engels said on the subject of the autonomy of the state, and shows how large a place it occupied in their political thinking and writings.[4] It was also this that I was trying to suggest in an article on 'Marx and the State' published in 1965, where I noted, in a formulation which I do not find very satisfactory, that there was a 'secondary' view of the state in Marx (the first one being of the state as the 'instrument' of a ruling class so designated by virtue of its ownership or control—or both—of the main means of economic activity). This 'secondary' view was of the state 'as independent from and superior to all social classes',

64

as being the dominant force in society rather than the instrument of a 'dominant class', with Bonapartism as 'the extreme manifestation of the state's independent role' in Marx's own lifetime.[5] On the other hand, I also noted then that, for Marx, the Bonapartist state, 'however independent it may have been politically from any given class, remains, and cannot in a class society but remain, the protector of an economically and socially dominant class'.[6] Some years later, in the course of a review of *Political Power and Social Classes* by the late and greatly-missed Nicos Poulantzas, I reformulated the point by suggesting that a distinction had to be made between the state autonomously acting *on behalf* of the ruling class, and its acting *at the behest* of that class, the latter notion being, I said, 'a vulgar deformation of the thought of Marx and Engels'.[7] What I was rejecting there was the crude view of the state as a mere 'instrument' of the ruling class obediently acting at its dictation.

The Debate over State 'Autonomy'

[handwritten: Using marx perspective its ignore that the state is autonomous it h own interest that may diff from ruling class]

However, it is undoubtedly to Poulantzas that belongs the credit for the most thorough exploration of the concept of the autonomy of the state; and it was he who coined the formulation which has remained the basis for most subsequent discussion of the subject, namely the 'relative autonomy of the state'. In essence, the view that this formulation encapsulated was that the state might indeed have a substantial degree of autonomy, but that, nevertheless, it remained for all practical purposes the state of the ruling class.

There has been considerable discussion among Marxists and others about the nature of the constraints and pressures which cause the state to serve the needs of capital—notably whether these constraints and pressures were 'structural' and impersonal, or produced by a ruling class armed with an arsenal of formidable weapons and resources. But beyond the differences that were expressed in these discussions, there was also a fundamental measure of agreement that the state *was* decisively constrained by forces *external to it*, and that the constraints originated in the national and international capitalist context in which it operated. The state might be constrained by the imperative requirement of capital for its reproduction and accumulation; or by the pressure from lobbies and organizations and agencies at the service of capital or one or other of its 'fractions'; or by the combined impact of these and international forces such as other capitalist states or the World Bank or the International Monetary Fund. But *these* at any rate were the kind of factors which had to be taken into account to explain the actions of the state. As has occasionally been noted in this connection, this Marxist view of the state as impelled by forces external to it shares its 'problematic' with the liberal or 'democratic pluralist' view of the state, notwithstanding the other profound differences between them: whereas the Marxist view attributes the main constraints upon the state to capital or capitalists or both, the 'democratic pluralist' one attributes them to the various pressures exercised upon a basically democratic state by a plurality of competing groups, interests and parties in society. In both perspectives, the state does not originate action but responds to external forces: it may *appear* to be the 'historical subject', but is in fact the object of processes and forces at work in society.

It is this whole perspective which has come under challenge in recent years, not only from the right, which has long insisted on the primacy of the state, but from people strongly influenced by Marxism. Two notable examples of this challenge are Ellen Kay Trimberger's *Revolution from Above: Military Bureaucrats and Development in Japan, Turkey, Egypt and Peru*,[8] and more explicitly Theda Skocpol's much-acclaimed *States and Social Revolution*,[9] which is, however, not concerned with the contemporary state but with the state in relation to the French, Russian and Chinese Revolutions.[10]

In the Marxist tradition, Skocpol writes, 'whatever the variations of its historical forms, the state as such is seen as a feature of all class-divided modes of production; and, invariably, the one necessary and inescapable function of the state—by definition—is to contain class conflict and to undertake other policies in support of the dominance of the surplus-appropriating and property-owning class.' This, she argues, fails to treat the state 'as an autonomous structure —a structure with a logic and interests of its own not necessarily equivalent to, or fused with, the interests of the dominant class in society or the full set of member groups in the polity'.[11]

This seems to me to be a valid criticism: the Marxist tradition does tend to under-emphasize or simply to ignore the fact that the state does have interests of its own or, to put it rather more appropriately, that the people who run it believe it has and do themselves have interests of their own. The failure to make due allowance for this naturally inhibits or prevents the exploration of the ways in which class interests and state interests are related and reconciled.

For her part, Skocpol goes much further than merely stating that the state has interests of its own or that those who run it do have such interests. For she goes on to argue that the Marxist perspective makes it 'virtually impossible even to raise the possibility that fundamental conflicts of interest might arise between the existing dominant class or set of groups, on the one hand, and the state rulers on the other'.[12] But contrary to what she appears to believe, this second argument does not follow from the first, and in fact raises an entirely different question, of great interest, but which should not be confused with the first one. That first proposition refers to the interests which the state may have of its own, and leaves open the question of how these may be reconciled with other interests in society. The second proposition, on the other hand, assumes that the state may have interests 'fundamentally' opposed to those of all forces and interests in society. This is a much stronger version of the autonomy of the state, and needs to be discussed separately from the other, and much weaker, one.

The Scope of State Action

Perhaps the first thing to note in this discussion is how very large is the sphere of action which the state in capitalist societies does have in all areas of life. It is deeply and pervasively involved in every aspect of economic life. It is a permanent and active presence in class conflict and in every other kind of conflict. It plays a great and growing role in the manipulation of opinion and in the 'engineering of consent'. It has, in Max Weber's famous phrase, a 'monopoly of the legitimate use of physical force'. It is alone responsible for international affairs and for deciding what the level and character of the country's armaments should be.

To speak of 'the state' in this manner is of course to use a shorthand which can be misleading. The reference is to certain people who are in charge of the executive power of the state—presidents, prime ministers, their cabinets and their top civilian and military advisers. But this assumes a unity of views and interests which may not exist: great divisions between the people concerned are in fact very common, with ministers at odds with their colleagues, and civilian and military advisers at odds with their political superiors. If these divisions are so deep as to make a workable compromise impossible and as to paralyse the executive power, some kind of reconstruction of the decision-making apparatus has to occur. In the end, decisions do have to be made; and it is the executive power which makes them, 'on its own'.

No doubt, there are many powerful influences and constraints, from outside the state, international as well as indigenous, which affect the nature of the decisions taken; and these may well be very strong and compelling. But it is ultimately a very small group of people in the state—often a single person—who decide what is to be done or not done; and it is only in very exceptional cases that those who make the decisions are left with no range of choice at all. Much more often, there is some degree of choice: even where governments are subjected to the imperative will of other governments, they are usually left with some freedom of decision in relation to matters which directly and greatly affect the lives of those whom they govern. Perhaps the best way to highlight the meaning of the autonomy of the state is to note that if nuclear war should occur, either between the 'superpowers' or between lesser powers armed with the capacity to wage such a war, it will occur because governments will have so decided, without reference to anybody else. There is no democratic procedure for starting a nuclear war.

The degree of autonomy which the state enjoys for most purposes in relation to social forces in capitalist society depends above all on the extent to which class struggle and pressure from below challenge the hegemony of the class which is dominant in such a society. Where a dominant class is truly hegemonic in economic, social, political and cultural terms, and therefore free from any major and effective challenge from below, the chances are that the state itself will also be subject to its hegemony, and that it will be greatly constrained by the various forms of class power which the dominant class has at its disposal. Where, on the other hand, the hegemony of a dominant class is persistently and strongly challenged, the autonomy of the state is likely to be substantial, to the point where, in conditions of intense class struggle and political instability, it may assume 'Bonapartist' and authoritarian forms, and emancipate itself from constraining constitutional checks and controls.

It is worth noting that the capitalist class has very seldom enjoyed anything like full hegemony in economic, social, political and cultural terms. One major capitalist country where it has come nearest to such hegemony is the United States—the prime example in the capitalist world of a society where business has not had to share power with an entrenched aristocracy, and where it has also been able to avoid the emergence of a serious political challenge by organized labour. Everywhere else, business has had to reach an accommodation with previously established social forces, and meet the challenge of labour. Moreover, it has also had to deal with state structures of ancient provenance and encrusted power that were strongly resistant to change. Capitalist hegemony has therefore been much more contested and partial in the rest of the 'late' capitalist world than in the United States; and even in the United States, economic and social contradictions and pressure from below, particularly since the Great Depression, have strengthened the state and given it greater autonomy than it enjoyed between, say, the Civil War and the early thirties.

The idea that class struggle is of decisive importance in determining the nature and form of the state is a familiar part of classical Marxism;[13] and so too is the view that the purpose of the state's autonomy is the better to protect and serve the existing social order and the dominant class which is the main beneficiary of that social order. As I noted earlier, it is this latter proposition which is under challenge; and rightly so. For the question: 'What is the state's autonomy *for*?' cannot simply be answered in these familiar terms: the point is *not* that these terms are wrong; but rather that they are inadequate to explain the dynamic of state action and cannot provide a satisfactory 'model' of the state in relation to society in a capitalist context. The dynamic of state action is explained by Marxism in terms of the imperative requirements of capital or the inexorable pressure of capitalists; and these are indeed of very great importance

But to focus exclusively on them is to leave out of account other very powerful impulses to state action generated from within the state by the people who are in charge of the decision-making power. These impulses undoubtedly exist; and they cannot be taken to be synonymous with the purposes of dominant classes.

The Impulses of Executive Power

The two main impulses which are generated by the executive power of the state are self-interest on the one hand, and a conception of the 'national interest' on the other.

People in power wish for the most part to retain it. It is a spurious kind of wordly wisdom which affirms that all 'politicians' and people in power are moved by nothing but self-interest and are only concerned to serve themselves by acquiring and clinging to office. But it is naive to think that, whatever else moves such people, they are not also moved by self-interest, meaning above all the wish to obtain and retain power. Of one man of power, the late Lyndon Johnson, president of the United States, it has been said that he exhibited from early days 'the desire to dominate, the *need* to dominate, to bend others to his will . . . the overbearingness with subordinates that was as striking as the obsequiousness with superiors . . . the viciousness and cruelty, the joy in breaking backs and keeping them broken, the urge not just to defeat but to destroy . . . above all, the ambition, the all-encompassing personal ambition that made issues impediments and scruples superfluous. And present also was the fear—the loneliness, the terrors, the insecurities—that underlay, and made savage, the aggressiveness, the energy and the ambition.'[14]

No doubt, Lyndon Johnson was a very repulsive politician. But the sentiments and motives ascribed to him are hardly unique; and the different terms that may be used to describe the drives of other men and women in power do not affect the point: this is that there are many people for whom the exercise of great power is an exceedingly satisfying experience, for whose sake acts of extraordinary cruelty have been committed throughout history. The point would hardly be worth making if it was not so imperfectly integrated into the Marxist view of the state.

The reason for this, or at least one reason for it, has already been touched on, and lies in Marxism's emphasis on economic and social processes as determinants of political action. The emphasis is perfectly legitimate but is easily deformed into an under-estimation of the weight which political processes themselves do have. The tendency to one form or another of 'economic reductionism' has had a marked influence on the Marxist discussion of politics and the state, even when the deformation has been acknowledged and pledges made to correct it.

The state is not the only institution which makes the exercise of great power possible; but it is by far the most important one. Nor does it only make possible the exercise of power as such, crucial though that is: it is also the source of high salaries, status, privilege and access to well-paid and otherwise desirable positions outside the state.[15] Nor is this only relevant for those people who are at the very centre of the decision-making process. Thousands of people in the upper reaches of the state are involved, whom the state provides with high salaries and all that goes with state service at this level, not only in government departments, but also in innumerable boards, commissions, councils and other public bodies. Such people constitute a 'state bourgeoisie', linked to but separate from those who are in charge of corporate capitalist enterprise. Their first concern is naturally with their jobs and careers. Capitalist interests are in no danger of being overlooked; but they are not the sole or primary concern of these office holders.

Those who seek state power find it easy to persuade themselves that their achievement of it, and their continued hold on it, are synonymous with the 'national interest', whose service, they proclaim, is their paramount and overriding consideration. Here too, it would be short-sighted to treat these proclamations as mere sham, and as elicited purely by the wish to obtain and retain state power. It is much more reasonable to think that people in power *are* moved by what they conceive to be the 'national interest', in addition to being deeply concerned with their own jobs. This is all the more likely to be the case in that the 'national interest' is woven into a larger and very powerful sentiment, namely nationalism. There was in classical Marxism the hope and belief that a different sentiment, namely proletarian or revolutionary internationalism, would move not only the working class but its leaders, in opposition but also in power. The collapse of internationalism in 1914 dealt a shattering blow to this hope; and so, in different ways, did the fact that the Soviet regime alone survived the revolutionary convulsions which followed the First World War. Even if manifestations of revolutionary internationalism may occasionally be read into the actions of people in power (Cuba in Africa?), it is nationalism and what is taken to be the 'national interest' which everywhere form the main and even the exclusive frame of reference for state action today; and this is easily compatible with the pursuit of the self-interest of those who control state power.

If it is agreed that self-interest and a conception of the 'national interest' have been and are powerful influences in shaping the policies and actions of the people in control of state power, the question which immediately arises is how this relates to the interests of the dominant class—in other words, what is the relationship of state power to class interests?

The answer is that, throughout the history of capitalism, that relationship has on the whole been very good. The people in charge of the state have generally been strongly imbued with the belief that the 'national interest' was bound up with the well-being of capitalist enterprise, or at least that no conceivable alternative arrangement, least of all socialism, could possibly be more advantageous to the 'national interest'; and they have therefore been particularly attentive to the interests of capitalist enterprise, whatever view they might take of capitalists. However, being attentive to these interests might well mean refusing to pay heed to capitalist wishes: very often, it was precisely because they wanted to ensure the best conditions for capitalism that they did things which ran counter to the wishes of capitalists.

A certain tension between state power and class interests is in fact inevitable, however good their relationship may fundamentally be. The dynamic of capitalism is the reproduction and accumulation of capital, and the maximization of long-term profit for each individual firm. This is the paramount aim, the all but exclusive concern of those who are in charge of the private sector of economic life: all else passes through this and must be subordinate to it. But this cannot be the dynamic of state power. For those who control that power,

72

the 'national interest' in essence requires the defence of the existing social order against any internal challenge to it, and also the best defence they believe they can mount against commercial, military and ideological competition from other states. Of course, this may also include, and often has included, offensive action abroad. These twin concerns encompass, or at least seek to encompass, capitalist class interests: but this is not at all the same as saying that state action and these class interests precisely coincide. In fact, there is always likely to be some unhingement between what the state does, however much those who control it may be devoted to capitalist interests, and these interests. The state, for instance, needs revenue; and it cannot obtain all the revenue it needs from the subordinate classes. It must levy taxes upon capital and capitalists, and thereby drain off some of the surplus which accrues to them: hence the constant lamentations of businessmen, large and small, about the state's taxation policies, and their complaints that the state, in its blind bureaucratic and greedy bungling, is forever undermining private enterprise. Similarly with reform and regulation: the containment of pressure from below, and indeed the maintenance of a viable and efficient labour force, demand that the state should undertake some measures of reform and regulation, which capital finds disagreeable and constraining, and which it certainly would not undertake on its own.

State and Class: a Partnership?

In short, an accurate and realistic 'model' of the relationship between the dominant class in advanced capitalist societies and the state is one of *partnership between two different, separate forces*, linked to each other by many threads, yet each having its own separate sphere of concerns. The terms of that partnership are not fixed but constantly shifting, and affected by many different circumstances, and notably by the state of class struggle. It is not at any rate a partnership in which the state may be taken necessarily to be the junior partner. On the contrary, the contradictions and shortcomings of capitalism, and the class pressures and social tensions this produces, require the state to assume an ever more pronounced role in the defence of the social order. The end of that process is one form or another of 'Bonapartism'. Meanwhile, it makes for a steady inflation of state power within the framework of a capitalist-democratic order whose democratic features are under permanent threat from the partnership of state and capital.

This 'model' of partnership seeks to give due importance to the independent and 'self-regarding' role of the state, and to make full allowance for what might be called the Machiavellian dimension of state action, which Marxism's 'class-reductionist' tendencies have obscured.[16] This is not a question of the 'primacy of politics': that formulation goes rather too far the other way, and suffers from a 'state-reductionist' bias.

By speaking of partnership between the state and the dominant class, I seek to avoid both forms of 'reductionism': the notion makes allowance for all the space which political and state action obviously has in practice; but it also acknowledges a capitalist context which profoundly affects everything the state does, particularly in economic matters where capitalist interests are directly involved. The idea of the 'primacy of politics' tends to abstract from the hard reality of this capitalist context: but no government can be indifferent to it. So long as a government works within it, so long does the partnership hold. If it seeks to pose a fundamental threat to capitalist interests, or a threat which capitalist interests judge to be fundamental, the partnership is dissolved and replaced by the determination of these interests to see the government destroyed. Nor in such a case is that determination likely to be confined to capitalist interests: it would be shared to the full by many other forces in society, and by people located in the state itself—military people, top civil servants, and many others.

The notion of partnership is scarcely contradicted by the experience of the governments of the left which have come to power (or to office) in capitalist countries in this century. For all practical purposes, the partnership has endured between such governments and capital, perhaps with more tensions and disagreements than when governments of the right have been in office, but not so as to bring about a complete break in relations. Great antagonism to the government might be expressed by members of the dominant class, business interests and their many agencies; but there was always a clear understanding on the part of these class forces that, even though the government might be doing some reprehensible things, it was also seeking to maintain the existing social order, to help business, to discipline and subdue labour, and to defend, in international and defence matters (and in colonial ones in an earlier day), what dominant class interests and the government both agreed to be the 'national interest'. In any case, capital also knew that it was only a small part of the state that was now in alien hands: the top reaches of the civil service, the police, the military, the judiciary remained more or less intact, and vigilantly concerned to limit the damage which the government might do. Moreover, the hegemony exercised by the dominant class in civil society was never much affected by the arrival in office of a government of the left. All the 'earthworks' which that dominant class occupied remained under its control. For their part, governments of the left have always sought to contain the activism of their own supporters and to bid them wait patiently and obediently for socialist ministers to get on with their tasks. The one case where the partnership between a government of the left and dominant class interests *was* broken was that of Salvador Allende's government in Chile. Given that break, the government's only hope of obviating the dangers which it faced was to forge a new partnership between itself and the subordinate classes. It was unable to achieve this, or did not sufficiently strive to achieve it. Its autonomy was also its death warrant.

This proposed model of partnership stands in opposition to Theda Skocpol's model of the 'state for itself' referred to earlier. According to that model, it will be recalled, 'fundamental conflicts of interest might arise between the existing dominant class or set of groups, on the one hand, and the state rulers on the other'. In this view, the state would be no one's partner or ally: it would be 'for itself' and against all classes and groups in society. In relation to countries with a solid class structure and a well-entrenched dominant class, such a model does not seem appropriate. For it is surely very difficult to see, in such countries, what the interests of 'state rulers' would be which would also place these rulers in *fundamental* conflict with *all* classes or groups in society. I have already noted that there are things which the state wants and does, and which are very irksome to the dominant class: but this is a very different matter from there being a fundamental conflict between them. Moreover, if such a conflict between them did occur, the state would in all likelihood be acting in ways that would favour some other class or classes. In other words, a new partnership would have been created; or the state would be acting, for whatever reason, in favour of a class or classes without any such partnership having been established. In neither case would the state be 'neutral', or acting solely 'for itself'.

Of course, state rulers, in pursuing what they conceive to be their interest, and the 'national interest', may use the autonomy they have to adopt policies and take actions which turn out to be disadvantageous or disastrous for everybody (quite possibly including those who took the decisions). History is full of such failures of statecraft; and recent examples abound. Thus, it may be argued that the American decision to wage war in Vietnam was very disadvantageous to all classes in the United States, not to speak of the disaster it represented for the people of Vietnam. But it can hardly be claimed that the decision to wage war in Vietnam was taken in the interests of state rulers in fundamental opposition to the interests of the capitalist class in the United States. On the contrary, there was a perfectly good 'fit' between the two, as witness the support which most capitalist interests there gave to the war until its very end. Another instance is that of Hitler's expansionist ventures, including his decision to take Germany into war. This turned out badly for everybody concerned: but there was no fundamental opposition between business interests in Germany and the Nazi leaders; and here again, there was ample support from business for Nazi policies. In this case, however, it is possible to argue that the Nazi regime provides an example of the interests of those in charge of the state being fundamentally opposed to the interests of everybody else: the war was clearly lost by 1943, and the only people whose interest it was *not* to bring it to an end were the Nazi leaders. Other instances of this sort could no doubt be adduced. But they do not provide a firm basis for a 'model' of the state as being 'for itself' and against everybody else.

State Power under Socialism

It seems to me that the 'model' of partnership advanced here can be useful in defining the relationship of the state to the working class in a socialist society. In the classical Marxist perspective, this relationship is defined in terms of the dictatorship of the proletariat. As may be deduced from Marx's *Civil War in France*, and as it is presented in Lenin's *The State and Revolution*, this means in effect the virtual dissolution of state power into class power. The state is not abolished but its functions and powers become largely residual and subordinate. Göran Therborn is well within this tradition in saying that 'a strategy for socialism or for a transitional stage of "advanced democracy" must dismantle the government, administration, judicial and repressive apparatus of the existing bourgeois state', and in urging 'a political programme of changes in the organization of the state that will bring about a popular democracy'.[17]

For their part, both social democratic and Communist parties have adopted perspectives and strategies of a very different kind, according to which class power is strictly subordinated to state power. For social democracy, class power has always tended to mean the deployment of electoral strength by the working class and the election of a social democratic or labour government. Once this is achieved, the task of the 'voters' is done, save for the routine activities of the party or parties which support the government. Indeed, any manifestation of class power (for instance strike action) is frowned upon, disowned and opposed.

Communist parties place a great emphasis in their pronouncements and programmes on grassroots activism, but the focus tends to be on the achievement of legislative and ministerial power in what is in effect the old state with a partially renewed personnel. Whatever might happen to the hegemony of the dominant class, it is not on this basis likely to be inherited by the hitherto subordinate classes. Partnership between state power and class power in a socialist context means something rather different. It requires the achievement of real power by organs of popular representation in all spheres of life, from the workplace to local government; and it also involves the thorough democratization of the state system and the strengthening of democratic control upon every aspect of it. But it nevertheless also means that state power endures and that the state does not, in any strong sense, 'wither away'. It must, in fact, long continue to remain in being and carry out many functions which it alone can fulfil. Indeed, it requires some degree of autonomy to carry them out. For the working class is not a homogeneous bloc, with one clear interest and one voice; and the state alone is capable of acting as a mediator between the 'fractions' which constitute the newly hegemonic majority. Furthermore, it is also upon the state that falls a large part of the responsibility for safeguarding the personal, civic and political freedoms which are intrinsic to the notion of socialist citizenship. In this sense, and with proper controls, state power in a post-capitalist society is not in conflict with class power, but its essential complement.

1. For an interesting survey of the bulk of this literature, see Bob Jessop, *The Capitalist State: Marxist Theories and Methods*, London 1982. The autonomy of the state, however, is not accorded any particular attention in this book and does not appear in the index.

2. For a recent discussion of the subject by a 'mainstream' political scientist, which shows well how limited is an approach that takes no serious account of the state's capitalist context, see E. Nordlinger, *On the Autonomy of the Democratic State*, New York 1981. Actual case studies are discussed in S.D. Krasner, *Defending the National Interest: Raw Materials Investments and US Foreign Policy*, New York 1978.

3. This article is exclusively concerned with 'late' capitalist societies. The question presents itself rather differently in countries in the capitalist world which are poorly developed, and very differently indeed in Soviet-type regimes. Here again serious theoretical work has only commenced.

4. Volume One: *State and Bureaucracy*, New York 1977, Chs. 14-23.

5. See my 'Marx and the State', in *The Socialist Register 1965*, London 1965, p.283. Reprinted above as essay 1.

6. *Ibid.*, p.285.

7. See my 'Poulantzas and the Capitalist State', NLR 82 November-December 1973, p.85, footnote 4. Reprinted above as essay 2.II.

8. New York 1977.

9. Cambridge 1979.

10. See also Fred Block, 'The Ruling Class Does Not Rule', *Socialist Revolution* 33, May-June 1977; and 'Beyond Relative Autonomy', in *The Socialist Register 1980*, where he speaks of the 'relative autonomy thesis' as a 'cosmetic modification of Marxism's tendency to reduce state power to class power' (p.229).

11. Skocpol, p.27.

12. *Ibid.*

13. See Marx's famous description of the Second Empire as 'the only form of government possible at a time when the bourgeoisie had already lost, and the working class had not yet acquired, the faculty of ruling the nation' (*The Civil War in France*, in *Selected Works*, I, p.470). Also Engels's equally well-known remark: 'By way of exception, however, periods occur in which the warring classes balance each other so nearly that the state power, as ostensible mediator, acquires, for the moment, a certain degree of independence of both' (*The Origin of the Family, Property and the*

State, in *Ibid.*, II, p.290). For many other such examples, see Draper, *Karl Marx's Theory of Revolution*.

14. The quotation appears in Murray Kempton, 'The Great Lobbyist', *New York Review of Books*, 17 February 1983 and is drawn from R.A. Caro, *The Years of Lyndon Johnson: The Path to Power*, New York 1982.

15. A recent example is provided by Sir David McNee, who retired in 1982 as Metropolitan Police Commissioner, and who was appointed non-executive chairman of the Scottish *Express* Newspapers: 'Sir David, who left last September on an index-linked pension of £22,000, will be paid between £5,000 and £10,000 for the job. He recently sold his memoirs to the *Sunday Mirror* for £120,000, joined Clydesdale Bank for £5,000 a year as non-executive director, and in November the British Airways Board for £10,000 a year. In December he was nominated president of the National Bible Society for Scotland' (*The Guardian*, 27 January 1983).

16. Thus Göran Therborn dissolves state power into class power when he asserts that 'state power is a relation between social class forces expressed in the content of state policies' (*What Does the Ruling Class Do When it Rules?*, NLB, London 1978, p.34). Note also Jessop's characterization of Poulantzas's view of the state: 'The state reflects and condenses all the contradictions in a class-divided social formation . . . political practices are always class practices . . . state power is always the power of a definite class to whose interests the state corresponds' (*The Capitalist State* p.159).

17. Therborn, p.25.

5
The Coup in Chile

1973

Note: This article was written immediately after the coup, and the literature produced since then on the coup and on the three preceding years of Salvador Allende's presidency is very extensive. What I have read of it does not seem to me to contradict any of the main points I made in the article. In particular, there has been ample confirmation since the coup, not least from official American sources, of the involvement of the American government and the CIA in the 'destabilization' and overthrow of Allende. On this, see e.g. J. Petras and M. Morley, The United States and Chile *(1975) and Seymour M. Hersh,* The Price of Power: Kissinger in Nixon's White House *(1983).*

What happened in Chile on 11 September 1973 did not suddenly reveal anything new about the ways in which men of power and privilege seek to protect *their* social order: the history of the last 150 years is spattered with such episodes. Even so, Chile has at least forced upon many people on the Left some uncomfortable reflections and questions about the 'strategy' which is appropriate in Western-type regimes for what is loosely called the 'transition to socialism'.

Of course, the Wise Men of the Left, and others too, have hastened to proclaim that Chile is not France, or Italy, or Britain. This is quite true. No country is like any other: circumstances are always different, not only between one country and another, but between one period and another in the same country. Such wisdom makes it possible and plausible to argue that the experience of a country or period cannot provide conclusive 'lessons'. This is also true; and as a matter of general principle, one should be suspicious of people who have instant 'lessons' for every occasion. The chances are that they had them well before the occasion arose, and that they are merely trying to fit the experience to their prior views. So let us indeed be cautious about taking or giving 'lessons'.

All the same, and however cautiously, there are things to be learnt from experience, or unlearnt, which comes to the same thing. Everybody said, quite rightly, that Chile, alone in Latin America, *was* a constitutional, parliamentary, liberal, pluralist society, a country which had politics; not exactly like the French, or the American, or the British, but well within the 'democratic', or, as Marxists would call it, the 'bourgeois-democratic' fold. This being the case, and however cautious one wishes to be, what happened in Chile does pose certain questions, requires certain answers, may even provide certain reminders and warnings. It may for instance suggest that stadiums which can be used for purposes other than sport—such as herding left-wing political prisoners—exist not only in Santiago, but in Rome and Paris or for that matter London; or that there *must* be something wrong with a situation in which *Marxism Today*, the monthly 'Theoretical and Discussion Journal of the (British) Communist Party' has as its major article for its September 1973 issue a speech delivered in July by the General Secretary of the Chilean Communist Party, Luis Corvalan (now in jail awaiting trial, and possible execution),[1] which is entitled '*We Say No to Civil War! But Stand Ready to Crush Sedition*'. In the light of what happened, this worthy slogan seems rather pathetic and suggests that there is something badly amiss here, that one must take stock, and try to see things more clearly. In so far as Chile was a bourgeois democracy, what happened there is about bourgeois democracy, and about what may also happen in other bourgeois democracies. After all, *The Times*, on the morrow of the coup, was writing (and the words ought to be carefully memorized by people on the Left): ' . . . Whether or not the armed forces were right to do what they have done, the circumstances were such that a reasonable military man could in good faith have thought it his *constitutional* duty to intervene'.[2] Should a similar episode occur in Britain, it is a fair bet that, whoever else is inside Wembley Stadium, it won't be the Editor of *The Times*: he will be busy writing editorials regretting this and that, but agreeing, however reluctantly, that, taking all circumstances into account, and not-withstanding the agonizing character of the choice, there was no alternative but for reasonable military men ... and so on and so forth.

When Salvador Allende was elected to the presidency of Chile in September 1970, the regime that was then inaugurated was said to constitute a test case for the peaceful or parliamentary transition to socialism. As it turned out over the following three years, this was something of an exaggeration. It achieved a great deal by way of economic and social reform, under incredibly difficult conditions— but it remained a deliberately 'moderate' regime: indeed, it does not seem far-fetched to say that the cause of its death, or at least one main cause of it, was its stubborn 'moderation'. But no, we are now told by such experts as Professor Hugh Thomas, from the Graduate School of Contemporary European Studies at Reading University:* the trouble was that Allende was *much* too influenced by such people as Marx and Lenin, 'rather than Mill, or Tawney, or Aneurin Bevan, or any other European democratic socialist'. This being the case, Professor Thomas cheerfully goes on, 'the Chilean coup d'état cannot by any means be regarded as a defeat for democratic social-ism but for Marxist socialism'. All's well then, at least for democatic socialism. Mind you, 'no doubt Dr Allende had his heart in the right place' (we must be *fair* about this), but then 'there are many reasons for thinking that his prescription was the wrong one for Chile's mal-adies, and of course the result of trying to apply it may have led an "iron surgeon" to get to the bedside. The right prescription, of course, was Keynesian socialism, not Marxist'.[3] *That*'s it: the trouble with Allende is that he was not Harold Wilson, surrounded by advisers steeped in 'Keynesian socialism' as Professor Thomas obviously is.

We must not linger over the Thomases and their ready under-standing of why Allende's policies brought an 'iron surgeon' to the beside of an ailing Chile. But even though the Chilean experience may not have been a test case for the 'peaceful transition to social-ism', it still offers a very suggestive example of what may happen

* Now Lord Thomas, Director of Research at the (Conservative) Centre for Policy Studies.

when a government does give the impression, in a bourgeois democracy, that it genuinely intends to bring about really serious changes in the social order and to move in socialist directions, in however constitutional and gradual a manner; and whatever else may be said about Allende and his colleagues, and about their strategies and policies, there is no question that this is what they wanted to do. They were not, and their enemies knew them not to be, mere bourgeois politicians mouthing 'socialist' slogans. They were not 'Keynesian socialists'. They were serious and dedicated people, as many have shown by dying for what they believed in. It is this which makes the conservative response to them a matter of great interest and importance, and which makes it necessary for us to try to decode the message, the warning, the 'lessons'. For the experience may have crucial significance for other bourgeois democracies: indeed, there is surely no need to insist that *some* of it is bound to be directly relevant to any 'model' of radical social change in this kind of political system.

Perhaps the most important such message or warning or 'lesson' is also the most obvious, and therefore the most easily overlooked. It concerns the notion of class struggle. Assuming one may ignore the view that class struggle is the result of 'extremist' propaganda and agitation, there remains the fact that the Left is rather prone to a perspective according to which the class struggle is something waged by the workers and the subordinate classes against the dominant ones. It is of course that. But class struggle also means, and often means *first of all*, the struggle waged by the dominant class, and the state acting on its behalf, against the workers and the subordinate classes. By definition, struggle is not a one way process; but it is just as well to emphasize that it is actively waged by the dominant class or classes, and in many ways much more effectively waged by them than the struggle waged by the subordinate classes.

Secondly, but in the same context, there is a vast difference to be made—sufficiently vast as to require a difference of name—between on the one hand 'ordinary' class struggle, of the kind which goes on day in and day out in capitalist societies, at economic, political, ideological, micro- and macro-, levels, and which is *known* to constitute no threat to the capitalist framework within which it occurs; and, on the other hand, class struggle which either does, or which is thought likely to, affect the social order in really fundamental ways. The first form of class struggle constitutes the stuff, or much of the stuff, of the politics of capitalist society. It is not unimportant, or a mere sham; but neither does it stretch the political system unduly. The latter form of struggle requires to be described not simply as *class struggle*, but as *class war*. Where men of power and privilege (and it is not necessarily those with most power and privilege who are the most uncompromising) do believe that they confront a real threat from below, that the world they know and like and want to preserve seems undermined or in the grip of evil and subversive forces, *then* an altogether different form of struggle comes into operation, whose acuity, dimensions and universality warrants the label 'class war'.

Chile had known class struggle within a bourgeois democratic framework for many decades: that was its tradition. With the coming to the Presidency of Allende, the conservative forces progressively turned class struggle into class war—and here too, it is worth stressing that it was the *conservative forces* which turned the one into the other.

Before looking at this a little more closely, I want to deal with one issue that has often been raised in connection with the Chilean experience, namely the matter of electoral percentages. It has often been said that Allende, as the presidential candidate of a six-party coalition, only obtained 36 per cent of the votes in September 1970, the implication being that if only he had obtained say, 51 per cent of the votes, the attitude of the conservative forces towards him and his administration would have been very different. There is one sense in which this may be true; and another sense in which it seems to me to be dangerous nonsense.

To take the latter point first: one of the most knowledgeable French writers on Latin America, Marcel Niedergang, has published one piece of documentation which is relevant to the issue. This is the testimony of Juan Garces, one of Allende's personal political advisers over three years who, on the direct orders of the president, escaped from the Moneda Palace after it had come under siege on September 11. In Garces' view, it was precisely after the governmental coalition had increased its electoral percentage to 44% in the legislative elections of March 1973 that the conservative forces began to think seriously about a coup. 'After the elections of March', Garces said, 'a legal coup d'état was no longer possible, since the two thirds majority required to achieve the constitutional impeachment of the President could not be reached. The Right then understood that the electoral way was exhausted and that the way which remained was that of force.'[4] This has been confirmed by one of the main promoters of the coup, the Air Force general Gustavo Leigh, who told the correspondent in Chile of the *Corriere della Sera* that 'we began preparations for the overthrow of Allende in March 1973, immediately after the legislative elections'.[5]

Such evidence is not finally conclusive. But it makes good sense. Writing before it was available, Maurice Duverger noted that while Allende was supported by a little more than a third of Chileans at the beginning of his presidency, he had almost half of them supporting him when the coup occurred; and that half was the one that was most hard hit by material difficulties. 'Here', he writes, 'is probably the major reason for the military putsch. So long as the Chilean Right believed that the experience of Popular Unity would come to an end by the will of the electors, it maintained a democratic attitude. It was worth respecting the Constitution while waiting for the storm to pass. When the Right came to fear that it would not pass and that the play of liberal institutions would result in the maintenance of Salvador Allende in power and in the development of socialism, it preferred violence to the law.'[6] Duverger probably exaggerates the 'democratic attitude' of the Right and its respect for the Constitution before the elections of March 1973, but his main point does, as I suggested earlier, seem very reasonable.

Its implications are very large: namely, that as far as the conservative forces are concerned, electoral percentages, however high they may be, do not confer legitimacy upon a government which appears to them to be bent on policies they deem to be actually or potentially disastrous. Nor is this in the least remarkable: for here, in the eyes of the Right, are vicious demagogues, class traitors, fools, gangsters and crooks supported by an ignorant rabble, engaged in bringing about ruin and chaos upon an hitherto peaceful and agreeable country, etc. The script is familiar. The idea that, from such a perspective, percentages of support are of any consequence is naïve and absurd: what matters, for the Right, is not the percentage of votes by which a left-wing government is supported, but the purposes by which it is moved. If the purposes are wrong, deeply and fundamentally wrong, electoral percentages are an irrelevance.

There is, however, a sense in which percentages *do* matter in the kind of political situation which confronts the Right in Chilean-type conditions. This is that the higher the percentage of votes cast in any election for the Left, the more likely it is that the conservative forces will be intimidated, demoralized, divided, and uncertain as to their course. These forces are not homogeneous; and it is obvious that electoral demonstrations of popular support are very useful to the Left, in its confrontation with the Right, so long as the Left does not take them to be decisive. In other words, percentages may help to *intimidate* the Right—but not to *disarm* it. It may well be that the Right would not have dared strike *when it did* if Allende had obtained higher electoral percentages. But if, having obtained these percentages, Allende had continued to pursue the course on which he was bent, the Right would have struck whenever opportunity had offered. The problem was to deny it the opportunity; or, failing this, to make sure that the confrontation would occur on the most favourable possible terms.

I now propose to return to the question of class struggle and class war and to the conservative forces which wage it, with particular reference to Chile, though the considerations I am offering here do not only apply to Chile, least of all in terms of the nature of the conservative forces which have to be taken into account, and which I shall examine in turn, relating this to the forms of struggle in which these different forces engage:
(a) *Society as Battlefield*. To speak of 'the conservative forces', as I have done so far, is not to imply the existence of a homogeneous economic, social or political bloc, either in Chile or anywhere else. In Chile, it was among other things the divisions between different elements among these conservative forces which made it possible for Allende to come to the presidency in the first place. Even so, when these divisions have duly been taken into account, it is worth stressing that a crucial aspect of class struggle is waged by these forces as a whole, in the sense that the struggle occurs all over 'civil society',

has no front, no specific focus, no particular strategy, no elaborate leadership or organization: it is the daily battle fought by every member of the dissaffected upper and middle classes, each in his own way, and by a large part of the lower middle class as well. It is fought out of a sentiment which Evelyn Waugh, recalling the horrors of the Attlee regime in Britain after 1945, expressed admirably when he wrote in 1959 that, in those years of Labour government, 'the kingdom seemed to be under enemy occupation'. Enemy occupation invites various forms of resistance, and everybody has to do his little bit. It includes middle class 'housewives' demonstrating by banging pots and pans in front of the Presidential Palace; factory owners sabotaging production; merchants hoarding stocks; newspaper proprietors and their subordinates engaging in ceaseless campaigns against the government; landlords impeding land reform; the spreading of what was, in wartime Britain, called 'alarm and despondency' (and incidentally punishable by law): in short, *anything* that influential, well-off, educated (or not so well-educated) people can do to impede a hated government. Taken as a 'detotalized totality', the harm that can thus be done is very considerable—and I have not mentioned the upper professionals, the doctors, the lawyers, the state officials, whose capacity to slow down the running of a society, of any society, must be reckoned as being high. Nothing very dramatic is required: just an individual rejection in one's daily life and activity of the regime's legitimacy, which turns by itself into a vast collective enterprise in the production of disruption.

It may be assumed that the vast majority of members of the upper and middle classes (not all by any means) will remain irrevocably opposed to the new regime. The question of the lower middle class is rather more complex. The first requirement in this connection is to make a radical distinction between lower professional and white collar workers, technicians, lower managerial staffs, etc., on the one hand, and small capitalists and micro-traders on the other. The former are an integral part of that 'collective worker', of which Marx spoke more than a hundred years ago; and they are involved, like the industrial working class, in the production of surplus value. This is not to say that this class or stratum will necessarily see itself as part of the working class, or that it will 'automatically' support left-wing policies (nor will the working class proper); but it does mean that there is here at least a solid basis for alliance.

This is much more doubtful, in fact most probably untrue, for the other part of the lower middle class, the small entrepreneur and the micro-trader. In the article quoted earlier. Maurice Duverger suggests that 'the first condition for the democratic transition to socialism in a Western country of the French type is that a left-wing government should reassure the *classes moyennes* about their fate under the future regime, so as to dissociate them from the kernel of big capitalists who are for their part condemned to disappear or to submit to a strict control'.[7] The trouble with this is that, in so far as the *'classes moyennes'* are taken to mean small capitalists and small traders (and Duverger makes it clear that he does mean them), the attempt is doomed from the start. In order to accommodate them, he wants 'the evolution towards socialism to be very gradual and very slow, so as to rally at each stage a substantial part of those who feared it at the start'. Moreover, small enterprises must be assured that their fate will be better than under monopoly or oligopolistic capitalism.[8] It is interesting, and would be amusing if the matter was not very serious, that the realism which Professor Duverger is able to display in regard to Chile deserts him as soon as he comes closer to home. His scenario is ridiculous; and even if it were not, there is no way in which small enterprises *can* be given the appropriate assurances. I should not like to give the impression that I am advocating the liquidation of middle and small urban French *kulaks*: what I *am* saying is that to adapt the pace of the transition to socialism to the hopes and fears of this class is to advocate paralysis or to prepare for defeat. Better not to start at all. *How* to deal with the problem is a different matter. But it is important to start with the fact that as a class or social stratum, this element must be reckoned as part of the conservative forces.

This certainly appears to have been the case in Chile, notably with regard to the now notorious 40,000 lorry owners, whose repeated strikes helped to increase the Government's difficulties. These strikes, excellently coordinated, and quite possibly subsidized from outside sources, highlight the problem which a left-wing government must expect to face, to a greater or lesser degree depending on the country, in a sector of considerable economic importance in terms of distribution. The problem is further and ironically highlighted by the fact that, according to United Nations statistical sources, it was this *'classe moyenne'* which had done best under Allende's regime in regard to the distribution of the national income. Thus, it would appear that the poorest 50% of the population saw its share of the total increase from 16·1% to 17·6%; that of the 'middle class' (45% of the population) increased from 53·9% to 57·7%; while the richest 5% dropped from 30% to 24·7%.[9] This is hardly the picture of a middle class squeezed to death—hence the significance of its hostility.

(b) *External conservative intervention.* It is not possible to discuss class war anywhere, least of all in Latin America, without bringing into account external intervention, more specifically and obviously the intervention of United States imperialism, as represented both by private concerns and by the American state itself. The activities of I.T.T. have received considerable publicity, as well as its plans for plunging the country into chaos so as to get 'friendly military men' to make a coup. Nor of course was I.T.T. the only major American firm working in Chile: there was in fact no important sector of the Chilean economy that was not penetrated and in some cases dominated by American enterprises: their hostility to the Allende regime must have greatly increased the latter's economic, social and political difficulties. Everybody knows that Chile's balance of payments very largely depends on its copper exports: but the world price of copper, which had almost been halved in 1970, remained at that low level until the end of 1972; and American pressure was exercised throughout the world to place an embargo on Chilean copper. In addition, there was strong and successful pressure by the United States on the World Bank to refuse loans and credits to Chile, not that much pressure was needed, either on the World Bank or on other banking institutions. A few days after the coup, the *Guardian* noted that 'the net new advances which were frozen as a result of the U.S. pressure, included sums totalling £30 millions: all for projects which the World Bank had already cleared as worth backing'.[10] The president of the World Bank is of course Mr Robert McNamara. It was at one time being said that Mr McNamara had undergone some kind of spiritual conversion out of remorse for his part, when U.S. Secretary of State for Defence, in inflicting so much suffering on the Vietnamese people: under his direction, the World Bank was actually going to *help* the poor countries. What those who were peddling this stuff omitted to add was that there was a condition—that the poor countries should show the utmost regard, as Chile did not, for the claims of private enterprise, notably American private enterprise.

Allende's regime was, from the start, faced with a relentless American attempt at economic strangulation. In comparison with this fact, which must be taken in conjunction with the economic sabotage in which the internal conservative economic interests engaged, the mistakes which were committed by the regime are of relatively minor importance—even though so much is made of them not only by critics but by friends of the Allende government. The really remarkable thing, against such odds, is not the mistakes, but that the regime held out economically as long as it did; the more so since it was systematically impeded from taking necessary action by the opposition parties in Parliament.

In this perspective, the question whether the United States government was or was not directly involved in the preparation of the military coup is not particularly important. It certainly had foreknowledge of the coup. The Chilean military had close associations with the United States military. And it would obviously be stupid to think that the kind of people who run the government of the United States would shrink from active involvement in a coup, or in its initiation. The important point here, however, is that the U.S. government had done its considerable best over the previous three years to lay the ground for the overthrow of the Allende regime by waging economic warfare against it.

(c) *The conservative political parties.* The kind of class struggle conducted by conservative forces in civil society to which reference was made earlier does ultimately require direction and political articulation, both in Parliament and in the country at large, if it is to be turned into a really effective political force. This direction is provided by conservative parties, and was mainly provided in Chile by Christian Democracy. Like the Christian Democratic Union in Germany and the Christian Democratic Party in Italy, Christian Democracy in Chile included many different tendencies, from various forms of radicalism (though most radicals went off to form their own groupings after Allende came to power) to extreme conservatism. But it represented in essence the conservative constitutional right, the party of government, one of whose main figures, Eduardo Frei, had been President before Allende.

With steadily growing determination, this conservative constitutional right sought by every means in its power this side of legality to block the government's actions and to prevent it from functioning properly. Supporters of parliamentarism always say that its operation depends upon the achievement of a certain degree of cooperation between government and opposition; and they are no doubt right. But Allende's government was denied this cooperation from the very people who never cease to proclaim their dedication to parliamentary democracy and constitutionalism. Here too, on the legislative front, class struggle easily turned into class war. Legislative assemblies are, with some qualifications that are not relevant here, part of the state system; and in Chile, the legislative assembly was solidly under opposition control. So were other important parts of the state system, to which I shall turn in a moment.

The opposition's resistance to the government, in Parliament and out, did not assume its full dimensions until the victory which the Popular Unity coalition scored in the elections of March 1973. By the late spring, the erstwhile constitutionalists and parliamentarists were launched on the course towards military intervention. After the abortive *putsch* of June 29, which marks the effective beginning of the final crisis, Allende tried to reach a compromise with the leaders of Christian Democracy, Alwyn and Frei. They refused, and increased their pressure on the government. On August 22, the National Assembly which their party dominated actually passed a motion which effectively *called* on the Army 'to put an end to situations which constituted a violation of the Constitution'. In the Chilean case at least, there can be no question of the direct responsibility which these politicians bear for the overthrow of the Allende regime.

No doubt, the Christian Democratic leaders would have preferred it if they could have brought down Allende without resort to force, and within the framework of the Constitution. Bourgeois politicians do not like military coups, not least because such coups deprive them of their role. But like it or not, and however steeped in constitutionalism they may be, most such politicians will turn to the military where they feel circumstances demand it.

The calculations which go into the making of the decision that circumstances do demand resort to illegality are many and complex. These calculations include pressures and promptings of different kinds and weight. One such pressure is the general, diffuse pressure of the class or classes to which these politicians belong. *'Il faut en finir'*, they are told from all quarters, or rather from quarters to which they pay heed; and this matters in the drift towards *putschism*. But another pressure which becomes increasingly important as the crisis grows is that of groups on the right of the constitutional conservatives, who in such circumstances become an element to be reckoned with.

(d) *Fascist-type groupings*. The Allende regime had to contend with much organized violence from fascist-type groupings. This extreme right-wing guerilla or commando activity grew to fever pitch in the last months before the coup, involved the blowing up of electric pylons, attacks on left-wing militants, and other such actions which contributed greatly to the general sense that the crisis must somehow be brought to an end. Here again, action of this type, in 'normal' circumstances of class conflict, are of no great political significance, certainly not of such significance as to threaten a regime or even to indent it very much. So long as the bulk of the conservative forces remain in the constitutionalist camp, fascist-type groupings remain isolated, even shunned by the traditional right. But in exceptional circumstances, one speaks to people one would not otherwise be seen dead with in the same room; one gives a nod and a wink where a frown and a rebuke would earlier have been an almost automatic response. 'Youngsters will be youngsters', now indulgently say their conservative elders. 'Of course, they are wild and do dreadful things. But then look whom they are doing it to, and what do you expect when you are ruled by demagogues, criminals and crooks.' So it came about that groups like *Fatherland and Freedom* operated more and more boldly in Chile, helped to increase the sense of crisis, and encouraged the politicians to think in terms of drastic solutions to it.

(e) *Administrative and judicial opposition*. Conservative forces anywhere can always count on the more or less explicit support or acquiescence or sympathy of the members of the upper echelons of the state system; and for that matter, of many if not most members of the lower echelons as well. By social origin, education, social status, kinship and friendship connections, the upper echelons, to focus on them, are an intrinsic part of the conservative camp; and if none of these factors were operative, ideological dispositions would certainly place them there. Top civil servants and members of the judiciary may, in ideological terms, range all the way from mild liberalism to extreme conservatism, but mild liberalism, at the progressive end, is where the spectrum has to stop. In 'normal' conditions of class conflict, this may not find much expression except in terms of the kind of implicit or explicit bias which such people must be expected to have. In crisis conditions, on the other hand, in times when class struggle assumes the character of class war, these members of the state personnel become active participants in the battle and are most likely to want to do their bit in the patriotic effort to save their beloved country, not to speak of their beloved positions, from the dangers that threaten.

The Allende regime inherited a state personnel which had long been involved in the rule of the conservative parties and which cannot have included many people who viewed the new regime with any kind of smypathy, to put it no higher. Much in this respect was changed with Allende's election, in so far as new personnel, which supported the Popular Unity coalition, came to occupy top positions in the state system. Even so, and in the prevailing circumstances perhaps inevitably, the middle and lower ranks of that system continued to be staffed by established and traditional bureaucrats. The power of such people can be very great. The writ may be issued from on high: but they are in a good position to see to it that it does not run, or that it does not run as it should. To vary the metaphor, the machine does not respond properly because the mechanics in actual charge of it have no particular desire that it should respond properly. The greater the sense of crisis, the less willing the mechanics are likely to be; and the less willing they are, the greater the crisis.

Yet, despite everything, the Allende regime did not 'collapse'. Despite the legislative obstruction, administrative sabotage, political warfare, foreign intervention, economic shortages, internal divisions, etc.—despite all this, the regime held. That, for the politicians and the classes they represented, was the trouble. In an article which

I shall presently want to criticize, Eric Hobsbawm notes quite rightly that 'to those commentators on the right, who ask what other choice remained open to Allende's opponents but a coup, the simple answer is: not to make a coup'.[11] This, however, meant incurring the risk that Allende might yet pull out of the difficulties he faced. Indeed, it would appear that, on the day before the coup, he and his ministers had decided on a last constitutional throw, namely a plebiscite, which was to be announced on September 11. He hoped that, if he won it, he might give pause to the *putschists*, and give himself new room for action. Had he lost, he would have resigned, in the hope that the forces of the Left would one day be in a better position to exercise power.[12] Whatever may be thought of this strategy, of which the conservative politicians must have had knowledge, it risked prolonging the crisis which they were frantic to bring to an end; and this meant acceptance of, indeed active support for, the coup which the military men had been preparing. In the end, and in the face of the danger presented by popular support for Allende, there was nothing for it: the murderers had to be called in.

(f) *The military*. We had of course been told again and again that the military in Chile, unlike the military in every other Latin American country, was non-political, politically neutral, constitutionally-minded, etc.; and though the point was somewhat overdone, it was broadly speaking true that the military in Chile did not 'mix in politics'. Nor is there any reason to doubt that, at the time when Allende came to power and for some time after, the military did not wish to intervene and mount a coup. It was after 'chaos' had been created, and extreme political instability brought about, *and the weakness of the regime's response in the face of crisis had been revealed* (of which more later) that the *conservative dispositions* of the military came to the fore, and then decisively tilted the balance. For it would be nonsense to think that 'neutrality' and 'non-political attitudes' on the part of the armed forces meant that they did not have definite ideological dispositions, and that these dispositions were not definitely conservative. As Marcel Niedergang also notes, 'whatever may have been said, there never were high ranking officers who were socialists, let alone communists. There were two camps: the partisans of legality and the enemies of the left-wing government. The second, *more and more* numerous, finally won out.'[13]

The italics in this quotation are intended to convey the crucial dynamic which occurred in Chile and which affected the military as well as all other protagonists. This notion of dynamic process is essential to the analysis of any such kind of situation: people who are thus and thus at one time, and who are or are not willing to do this or that, *change* under the impact of rapidly moving events. Of course, they mostly change *within* a certain range of choices: but in such situations, the shift may nevertheless be very great. Thus conservative but constitutionally-minded army men, in certain situations, become just this much more conservative-minded; and this means that they cease to be constitutionally-minded. The obvious question is what it is that brings about the shift. In part, no doubt, it lies in the worsening 'objective' situation; in part also, in the pressure generated by conservative forces. But to a very large extent, it lies in the position adopted, and seen to be adopted, by the government of the day. As I understand it, the Allende administration's weak response to the attempted coup of June 29, its steady retreat before the conservative forces (and the military) in the ensuing weeks, and its loss by resignation of General Prats, the one general who had appeared firmly prepared to stand by the regime—all this must have had a lot to do with the fact that the enemies of the regime in the armed forces (meaning the military men who were prepared to make a coup) grew 'more and more numerous'. In these matters, there is one law which holds: the weaker the government, the bolder its enemies, *and* the more numerous they become day by day.

Thus it was that these 'constitutional' generals struck on September 11, and put into effect what had—significantly in the light of the massacre of left wingers in Indonesia—been labelled *Operation Djakarta*. Before we turn to the next part of this story, the part which concerns the actions of the Allende regime, its strategy and conduct, it is as well to stress the savagery of the repression unleashed by the coup, and to underline the responsibility which the conservative politicians bear for it. Writing in the immediate aftermath of the Paris Commune, and while the Communards were still being killed, Marx bitterly noted that 'the civilization and justice of bourgeois order comes out in its lurid light whenever the slaves and drudges of that order rise against their masters. Then this civilization and order stand forth as undisguised savagery and lawless revenge'.[14] The words apply well to Chile after the coup. Thus, that not very left-wing magazine *Newsweek* had a report from its correspondent in Santiago shortly after the coup, headed 'Slaughterhouse in Santiago', which went as follows:

> Last week, I slipped through a side door into the Santiago city morgue, flashing my junta press pass with all the impatient authority of a high official. One hundred and fifty dead bodies were laid out on the ground floor, awaiting identification by family members. Upstairs, I passed through a swing door and there in a dimly lit corridor lay at least fifty more bodies, squeezed one against another, their heads propped up against the wall. They were all naked.
>
> Most had been shot at close range under the chin. Some had been machine-gunned in the body. Their chests had been slit open and sewn together grotesquely in what presumably had been a pro forma autopsy. They were all young and, judging from the roughness of their hands, all from the working class. A couple of them were girls, distinguishable among the massed bodies only by the curves of their breasts. Most of their heads had been crushed. I remained for perhaps two minutes at most, then left.
>
> Workers at the morgue have been warned that they will be court-martialled and shot if they reveal what is going on there. But the women who go in to look at the bodies say there are between 100 and 150 on the ground floor every day. And I was able to obtain an official morgue body-count from the daughter of a member of its staff: by the fourteenth day following the coup, she said, the morgue had received and processed 2796 corpses.[15]

On the same day as it carried this report, the London *Times* commented in an editorial that 'the existence of a war or something very like it clearly explains the drastic severity of the new regime which has taken so many observers by surprise'. The 'war' was of course *The Times*' own invention. Having invented it, it then went on to observe that 'a military government confronted by widespread armed opposition(?) is unlikely to be over-punctilious either about constitutional niceties or even about basic human rights'. Still, lest it be thought that it *approved* the 'drastic severity' of the new regime, the paper told its readers that 'it must remain the hope of Chile's friends abroad, as no doubt of the great majority of Chileans, that human rights will soon be fully respected and that constitutional government will before long be restored'.[16] Amen.

No one knows how many people have been killed in the terror that followed the coup, and how many people will yet die as a result of it. Had a left-wing government shown one tenth of the junta's ruthlessness, screaming headlines across the whole 'civilized' world would have denounced it day in day out. As it is, the matter was quickly passed over and hardly a pip squeaked when a British Government rushed in, eleven days after the coup, to recognize the junta. But then so did most other freedom-loving Western governments.

We may take it that the well-to-do in Chile shared and more than shared the sentiments of the Editor of the London *Times* that, given the circumstances, the military could not be expected to be 'overpunctilious'. Here too, Hobsbawm puts it very well when he says that 'the left has generally underestimated the fear and hatred of the right, the ease with which well-dressed men and women acquire a taste for blood'.[17] This is an old story. In his *Flaubert*, Sartre quotes Edmond de Goncourt's Diary entry for 31 May 1871, immediately after the Paris Commune had been crushed: 'It's good. There has been no conciliation or compromise. The solution has been brutal. It has been pure force . . . a bloodletting such as this, by killing the militant part of the population (*la partie bataillante de la population*) puts off by a generation the new revolution. It is twenty years of rest which the old society has in front of it if the rulers dare all that needs to be dared at this moment'.[18] Goncourt, as we know, had no need to worry. Nor has the Chilean middle class, if the military not only dare, but are able, i.e. are allowed, to give Chile 'twenty years of rest'. A woman journalist with a long experience of Chile reports, three weeks after the coup, the 'jubilation' of her upper class friends who had long prayed for it.[19] These ladies would not be likely to be unduly disturbed by the massacre of left-wing militants. Nor would their husbands.

What did apparently disturb the conservative politicians was the thoroughness with which the military went about restoring 'law and order'. Hunting down and shooting militants is one thing, as is book-burning and the regimentation of the universities. But dissolving the National Assembly, denouncing 'politics' and toying with the idea of a Fascist-type 'corporatist' state, as some of the generals are doing, is something else, and rather more serious. Soon after the coup, the leaders of Christian Democracy, who had played such a major role in bringing it about, and who continued to express support for the junta, were nevertheless beginning to express their 'disquiet' about some of its inclinations. Indeed, ex-President Frei went so far, stout fellow, as to confide to a French journalist his belief that 'Christian Democracy will have to go into opposition two or three months from now'[20]—presumably after the military had butchered enough left-wing militants. In studying the conduct and declarations of men such as these, one understands better the savage contempt which Marx expressed for the bourgeois politicians he excoriated in his historical writings. The breed has not changed.

The configuration of conservative forces which has been presented in the previous section must be expected to exist in any bourgeois democracy, not of course in the same proportions or with exact parallels in any particular country—but the pattern of Chile is not unique. This being the case, it becomes the more important to get as close as one can to an accurate analysis of the response of the Allende regime to the challenge that was posed to it by these forces.

As it happens, and while there is and will continue to be endless controversy on the Left as to who bears the responsibility for what went wrong (if anybody does), and whether there was anything else that could have been done, there can be very little controversy as to what the Allende regime's strategy actually was. Nor in fact is there, on the Left. Both the Wise Men and the Wild Men of the Left are at least agreed that Allende's strategy *was* to effect a constitutional and peaceful transition in the direction of socialism. The Wise Men of the Left opine that this was the only possible and desirable path to take. The Wild Men of the Left assert that it was the path to disaster. The latter turned out to be right: but whether for the right reasons remains to be seen. In any case, there are various questions which arise and which are much too important and much too complex to be resolved by slogans. It is with some of these questions that I should like to deal here.

To begin at the beginning: namely with the manner in which the Left's coming to power—or to office—must be envisaged in bourgeois democracies. The overwhelming chances are that this will occur via the electoral success of a Left coalition of Communists, Socialists and other groupings of more or less radical tendencies. The reason for saying this is not that a crisis might not occur, which would open possibilities of a different kind—it may be for instance that May 1968 in France was a crisis of such a kind. But whether for good reasons or bad, the parties which might be able to take power in this type of situation, namely the major formations of the Left, including in particular the Communist Parties of France and Italy, have absolutely no intention of embarking on any such course, and do in fact strongly believe that to do so would invite certain disaster and set back the working class movement for generations to come. Their attitude *might* change if circumstances of a kind that cannot be anticipated arose—for instance the clear imminence or actual beginning of a right-wing coup. But this is speculation. What is not speculation is that these vast formations, which command the support of the bulk of the organized working class, and which will go on commanding it for a very long time to come, are utterly committed to the achievement of power—or of office—by electoral and constitutional means. This was also the position of the coalition led by Allende in Chile.

There was a time when many people on the Left said that, if a Left clearly committed to massive economic and social changes looked like winning an election, the Right would not 'allow' it to do so—i.e. it would launch a pre-emptive strike by way of a coup. This has ceased to be a fashionable view: it is rightly or wrongly felt that, in 'normal' circumstances, the Right would be in no position to decide whether it could or could not 'allow' elections to take place. Whatever else it and the government might do to influence the results, they could not actually take the risk of preventing the elections from being held.

The present view on the 'extreme' left tends to be that, even if this is so, and admitting that it is likely to be so, any such electoral victory is, by *definition*, bound to be barren. The argument, or one of the main arguments on which this is based, is that the achievement of an electoral victory can only be bought at the cost of so much manoeuvre and compromise, so much 'electioneering' as to mean very little. There seems to me to be rather more in this than the Wise Men of the Left are willing to grant; but not *necessarily* quite as much as their opponents insist *must* be the case. Few things in these matters are capable of being settled by definition. Nor have opponents of the 'electoral road' much to offer by way of an alternative, *in relation to bourgeois democracies in advanced capitalist societies*; and such alternatives as they do offer have so far proved entirely unattractive to the bulk of the people on whose support the realization of these alternatives precisely depends; and there is no very good reason to believe that this will change dramatically in any future that must be taken into account.

In other words, it must be assumed that, in countries with this kind of political system, it is by way of electoral victory that the forces of the Left will find themselves in office. *The really important question is what happens then.* For as Marx also noted at the time of the Paris Commune, electoral victory only gives one the *right* to rule, not the *power* to rule. Unless one takes it for granted that this right to rule cannot, in these circumstances, ever be transmitted into the power to rule, it is at this point that the Left confronts complex questions which it has so far probed only very imperfectly: it is here that slogans, rhetoric and incantation have most readily been used as substitutes for the hard grind of realistic political cogitation. From this point of view, Chile offers some extremely important pointers and 'lessons' as to what is, or perhaps what is not, to be done.

The strategy adopted by the forces of the Chilean Left had one characteristic not often associated with the coalition, namely a high degree of inflexibility. In saying this, I mean that Allende and his allies had decided upon certain lines of action, and of inaction, well before they came to office. They had decided to proceed with careful regard to constitutionalism, legalism and gradualism; and also, relatedly, that they would do everything to avoid civil war. Having decided upon this before they came to office, they stuck to it right through, up to the very end, notwithstanding changing circumstances. Yet, it may well be that what was right and proper and inevitable at the beginning had become suicidal as the struggle developed. What is at issue here is not 'reform versus revolution': it is that Allende and his colleagues were wedded to a particular version of the 'reformist' model, which eventually made it impossible for them to respond to the challenge they faced. This needs some further elaboration.

To achieve office by electoral means involves moving into a house long occupied by people of very different dispositions—indeed it involves moving into a house many rooms of which continue to be occupied by such people. In other words, Allende's victory at the polls—such as it was—meant the occupation by the Left of one element of the state system, the presidential-executive one—an extremely important element, perhaps the most important, but not obviously the only one. Having achieved this partial occupation, the President and his administration began the task of carrying out their policies by 'working' the system of which they had become a part.

In so doing, they were undoubtedly contravening an essential tenet of the Marxist canon. As Marx wrote in a famous letter to Kugelmann at the time of the Paris Commune ' . . . the next attempt of the French Revolution will be no longer, as before, to transfer the bureaucratic-military machine from one hand to another, but to *smash* it, and this is the preliminary condition for every real people's revolution on the continent'.[21] Similarly in *The Civil War in France*, Marx notes that 'the working class cannot simply lay hold of the ready-made state machinery, and wield it for its own purposes';[22] and he then proceeded to outline the nature of the alternative as foreshadowed by the Paris Commune.[23] So important did Marx and Engels think the matter to be that in the Preface to the 1872 German edition of the *Communist Manifesto*, they noted that 'one thing especially was proved by the Commune', that thing being Marx's observation in *The Civil War in France* that I have just quoted.[24] It is from these observations that Lenin derived the view that 'smashing the bourgeois state' was the essential task of the revolutionary movement.

I have argued elsewhere[25] that in one sense in which it appears to be used in *The State and Revolution* (and for that matter in *The Civil War in France*) i.e. in the sense of the establishment of an extreme form of council (or 'soviet') democracy on the very morrow of the revolution as a substitute for the smashed bourgeois state, the notion constitutes an impossible projection which can be of no immediate relevance to any revolutionary regime, and which certainly was of no immediate relevance to Leninist practice on the morrow of the Bolshevik revolution; and it is rather hard to blame Allende and his colleagues for not doing something which they never intended in the first place, and to blame them in the name of Lenin, who certainly did not keep the promise, and could not have kept the promise, spelt out in *The State and Revolution*.

However, disgracefully 'revisionist' though it is even to suggest it, there may be other possibilities which are relevant to the discussion of revolutionary practice, and to the Chilean experience, and which also differ from the particular version of 'reformism' adopted by the leaders of the Popular Unity coalition.

Thus, a government intent upon major economic, social and political changes does, in some crucial respects, have certain possibilities, even if it does not contemplate 'smashing the bourgeois state'. It may, for instance, be able to effect very considerable changes in the personnel of the various parts of the state system; and in the same vein, it may, by a variety of institutional and political devices, begin to attack and outflank the existing state apparatus. In fact, it must do so if it is to survive; and it must eventually do so with respect to the hardest element of all, namely the military and police apparatus.

The Allende regime did some of these things. Whether it could have done more of them, in the circumstances, must be a matter of argument; but it seems to have been least able or willing to tackle the most difficult problem, that presented by the military. Instead, it appears to have sought to buy the latter's support and good will by conciliation and concessions, right up to the time of the coup, notwithstanding the ever-growing evidence of the military's hostility. In the speech he made on July 8 of this year, and to which I referred at the beginning of this article, Luis Corvalan observed that 'some reactionaries have begun to seek new ways to drive a wedge between the people and the armed forces, maintaining little less than we are intending to replace the professional army. No, sirs! We continue to support the absolutely professional character of the armed institutions. Their enemies are not amongst the rank of the people but in the reactionary camp.'[26] It is a pity that the military did not share this view: one of their first acts after their seizure of power was to release the fascists from the *Fatherland and Freedom* group who had belatedly been put in jail by the Allende government. Similar statements, expressing trust in the constitutional-mindedness of the military were often made by other leaders of the coalition, and by Allende himself. Of course, neither they nor Corvalan were under much illusion about the *support* they could expect from the military: but it would seem nevertheless that most of them thought that they could buy off the military; and that it was not so much a coup on the classical 'Latin American' pattern that Allende feared as 'civil war'.

Régis Debray has written from personal knowledge that Allende had a 'visceral refusal' of civil war; and the first thing to be said about this is that it is only people morally and politically crippled in their sensitivities who would scoff at this 'refusal' or consider it ignoble. This however does not exhaust the subject. There are different ways of trying to avoid civil war; and there may be occasions where one cannot do it *and* survive. Debray also writes (and his language is itself interesting) that 'he (i.e. Allende) was not duped by the phraseology of "popular power" and he did not want to bear the responsibility of thousands of useless deaths: the blood of others horrified him. That is why he refused to listen to his Socialist Party which accused him of useless manoeuvring and which was pressing him to take the offensive.'[27]

It would be useful to know if Debray himself believes that 'popular power' is necessarily a 'phraseology' by which one should not be 'duped'; and what was meant by 'taking the offensive'. But at any rate, Allende's 'visceral refusal' of civil war, as Debray does make clear, was only one part of the argument for conciliation and compromise; the other was a deep scepticism as to any possible alternative. Debray's account, describing the argument that went on in the last weeks before the coup, has a revealing paragraph on this: '"Disarm the plotters?" "With what?" Allende would reply. "Give me first the forces to do it". "Mobilize them," he was told from all sides. For it is true (this is Debray speaking—R.M.) that he was gliding up there, in the superstructures, leaving the masses without ideological orientations or political direction. "Only the direct action of the masses will stop the coup d'etat." "And how many masses does one need to stop a tank?" Allende would reply.'[28]

Whether one agrees that Allende was 'gliding up there in the superstructures' or not, this kind of dialogue has the ring of truth; and it may help to explain a good deal about the events in Chile.

Considering the manner of Salvador Allende's death, a certain reticence is very much in order. Yet, it is impossible not to attribute to him at least some of the responsibility for what ultimately occurred. In the article from which I have just quoted, Debray also tells us that one of Allende's collaborators, Carlos Altamirano, the general secretary of the Socialist Party, had said to him, Debray, with anger at Allende's manoeuvrings, that 'the best way of precipitating a confrontation and to make it even more bloody is to turn one's back upon it'.[29] There were others close to Allende who had long held the same view. But, as Marcel Niedergang has also noted, all of them 'respected Allende, the centre of gravity and the real "patron" of the Popular Unity coalition';[30] and Allende, as we know, was absolutely set on the course of conciliation—encouraged upon that course by his fear of civil war and defeat; by the divisions in the coalition he led and by the weaknesses in the organization of the Chilean working class; by an exceedingly 'moderate' Communist Party; and so on.

The trouble with that course is that it had all the elements of self-fulfilling catastrophe. Allende believed in conciliation because he feared the result of a confrontation. But because he believed that the Left was bound to be defeated in any such confrontation, he had to pursue with ever-greater desperation his policy of conciliation; but the more he pursued that policy, the greater grew the assurance and boldness of his opponents. Moreover, and crucially, a policy of conciliation of the regime's opponents held the grave risk of discouraging and demobilizing its supporters. 'Conciliation' signifies a tendency, an impulse, a direction, and it finds practical expression on many terrains, whether intended or not. Thus, in October 1972, the Government had got the National Assembly to enact a 'law on the control of arms' which gave to the military wide powers to make searches for arms caches. In practice, and given the army's bias and inclinations, this soon turned into an excuse for military raids on factories known as left-wing strongholds, for the clear purpose of intimidating and demoralizing left-wing activists[31]—all quite 'legal', or at least 'legal' enough.

The really extraordinary thing about this experience is that the policy of 'conciliation', so steadfastly and disastrously pursued, did not cause greater and earlier demoralization on the Left. Even as late as the end of June 1973, when the abortive military coup was launched, popular willingness to mobilize against would-be *putschists* was by all accounts higher than at any time since Allende's assumption of the presidency. This was probably the last moment at which a change of course might have been possible—and it was also, in a sense, the moment of truth for the regime: a choice then had to be made. A choice *was* made, namely that the President would continue to try to conciliate; and he did go on to make concession after concession to the military's demands.

I am not arguing here, let it be stressed again, that another strategy was bound to succeed—only that the strategy that was adopted was bound to fail. Eric Hobsbawm, in the article I have already quoted, writes that 'there was not much Allende could have done after (say) early 1972 except to play out time, secure the irreversibility of the great changes already achieved (how?—R.M.) and with luck maintain a political system which would give the Popular Unity a second chance later . . . for the last several months, it is fairly certain that there was practically nothing he could do'.[32] For all its apparent reasonableness and sense of realism, the argument is both very abstract and is also a good recipe for suicide.

For one thing, one cannot 'play out time' in a situation where great changes have already occurred, which have resulted in a considerable polarization, and where the conservative forces are moving over from class struggle to class war. One can either advance or retreat—retreat into oblivion or advance to meet the challenge.

Nor is it any good, in such a situation, to act on the presupposition that there is nothing much that can be done, since this means in effect that nothing much *will* be done to prepare for confrontation with the conservative forces. This leaves out of account the possibility that the best way to avoid such a confrontation—perhaps the only way—is precisely to prepare for it; and to be in as good a posture as possible to win if it does come.

This brings us directly back to the question of the state and the exercise of power. It was noted earlier that a major change in the state's personnel is an urgent and essential task for a government bent on really serious change; and that this needs to be allied to a variety of institutional reforms and innovations, designed to push forward the process of the state's democratization. But in this latter respect, much more needs to be done, not only to realize a set of long-term socialist objectives concerning the socialist exercise of power, but as a means either of avoiding armed confrontation, or of meeting it on the most advantageous and least costly terms if it turns out to be inevitable.

What this means is not simply 'mobilizing the masses' or 'arming the workers'. These are slogans—important slogans—which need to be given effective *institutional* content. In other words, a new regime bent on fundamental changes in the economic, social and political structures must from the start begin to build and encourage the building of a network of organs of power, parallel to and complementing the state power, and constituting a solid infrastructure for the *timely* 'mobilization of the masses' and the effective direction of its actions. The forms which this assumes—workers' committees at their place of work, civic committees in districts and sub-districts, etc.—and the manner in which these organs 'mesh' with the state may not be susceptible to blueprinting. But the need is there, and it is imperative that it should be met, in whatever forms are most appropriate.

This is not, to all appearances, how the Allende regime moved. Some of the things that needed doing were done; but such 'mobilization' as occurred, and such preparations as were made, very late in the day, for a possible confrontation, lacked direction, coherence, in many cases even encouragement. Had the regime really encouraged the creation of a parallel infra-structure, it might have lived; and, incidentally, it might have had less trouble with its opponents and critics on the left, for instance in the MIR, since its members might not then have found the need so great to engage in actions of their own, which greatly embarrassed the government: they might have been more ready to co-operate with a government in whose revolutionary will they could have had greater confidence. In part at least, 'ultra-leftism' is the product of 'citra-leftism'.

Salvador Allende was a noble figure and he died a heroic death. But hard though it is to say it, that is not the point. What matters, in the end, is not how he died, but whether he could have survived by pursuing different policies; and it is wrong to claim that there was no alternative to the policies that were pursued. In this as in many other realms, and here more than in most, facts only become compelling as one allows them to be so. Allende was not a revolutionary who was also a parliamentary politician. He was a parliamentary politician who, remarkably enough, had genuine revolutionary tendencies. But these tendencies could not overcome a political style which was not suitable to the purposes he wanted to achieve.

The question of course is not one of courage. Allende had all the courage required, and more. Saint Just's famous remark, which has often been quoted since the coup, that 'he who makes a revolution by half digs his own grave' is closer to the mark—but it can easily be misused. There are people on the Left for whom it simply means the ruthless use of terror, and who tell one yet again, as if they had just invented the idea, that 'you can't make omelettes without breaking eggs'. But as the French writer Claude Roy observed some years ago, 'you can break an awful lot of eggs without making a decent omelette'. Terror may become part of a revolutionary struggle. But the essential question is the degree to which those who are responsible for the direction of that struggle are able and willing to engender and encourage the effective, meaning the organized, mobilization of popular forces. If there is any definite 'lesson' to be learnt from the Chilean tragedy, this seems to be it; and parties and movements which do not learn it, and apply what they have learnt, may well be preparing new Chiles for themselves.

1. Had it not been for international pressure and protest, it may well be that Corvalan would have been executed by now (October 1973), like so many others, after the semblance of a trial, or without a trial.
2. *The Times*, 13 September 1973. My italics.
3. *Ibid.*, 20 September 1973.
4. *Le Monde*, 29 September 1973.
5. Quoted by K.S. Karol in *Le Nouvel Observateur*, 8 October 1973.
6. *Le Monde*, 23-24 September 1973.
7. *Ibid.*
8. *Ibid.*
9. *Le Monde*, 13 September 1973.
10. *The Guardian*, 19 September 1973.
11. E.J. Hobsbawm, 'The Murder of Chile', *New Society*, 20 September 1973.
12. *Le Monde*, 29 September 1973.
13. *Ibid.*
14. K. Marx, *The Civil War in France*, in *Selected Works*, Moscow 1950, vol. 1, p.485.
15. Quoted in *The Times*, 5 October 1973. This of course is not an isolated account: *Le Monde*, for instance, has carried dozens of horrifying reports of the savagery of the repression.
16. *The Times*, 5 October 1973.
17. *New Society*, op. cit.
18. Jean-Paul Sartre, *L'Idiot de la Famille. Gustave Flaubert de 1821 à 1857*, Paris 1972, vol. III, p.590.
19. Marcelle Auclair, 'Les Illusions de la Haute Société', *Le Monde*, 4 October 1973.

20. *Ibid.*, 29 September 1973.
21. *Selected Works*, vol. II, p.420.
22. *Ibid.*, vol I, p.468.
23. *Ibid.*, pp.471ff.
24. *Ibid.*, p.22.
25. 'The State and Revolution', *Socialist Register 1970*, reprinted below as essay 8.
26. *Marxism Today*, September 1973, p.226. But see footnote 29.
27. *Le Nouvel Observateur*, 17 September 1973.
28. *Ibid.*
29. *Ibid.* It may be worth noting, however, that Altamirano is also reported as having declared after the attempted coup of 29 June that 'never has the unity between the people, the armed forces and the police been as great as it is now . . . and this unity will grow with every new battle in the historic war that we are conducting'. (*Le Monde*, 16-17 September 1973.)
30. *Le Monde*, 29 September 1973.
31. *Ibid.*, 16-17 September 1973. This is a reference to an article in *Rouge* by J.P. Beauvais, who gives an eye-witness account of one such army raid, on 4 August 1973, in which one man was killed and several were wounded in the course of what amounted to an attack by parachute troops on a textile plant.
32. Hobsbawm. *New Society*.

6

Constitutionalism and Revolution

1978

The following notes are intended to discuss some of the most important characteristics, tendencies and problems of Eurocommunism; and to do this by reference to three of the books which have been published on the subject recently—Santiago Carrillo's *Eurocommunism and the State* (Lawrence and Wishart, 1977). Fernando Claudin's *Eurocommunism and Socialism* (New Left Books, 1978) and the discussion between Eric Hobsbawm and Giorgio Napolitano, published under the title *The Italian Road to Socialism* (The Journeyman Press, 1977). None of them is a weighty publication; but they do offer a useful view of the main lines of thought of Eurocommunism and, in Claudin's case, a qualified critique of its strategy. The focus is on Italy, Spain and France; but the discussion is relevant to all advanced capitalist countries. What is at issue is the elaboration of a strategy of socialist advance which, notwithstanding obvious differences, is broadly applicable to all such countries.

Such a discussion is both important and long overdue; and it is of considerable significance that it should now be occurring inside as well as outside Communist parties. Santiago Carrillo is General Secretary of the Communist Party of Spain and Giorgio Napolitano is a member of the Secretariat of the PCI. But they write in a style very different from that which has by tradition come to be associated with the pronouncements of high Communist officials, and in a manner which invites comment rather than requiring assent. This reflects pressures which cannot be contained or stifled by the suppressive practices of the past, even the fairly recent past. The same pressures are now at work inside the French Communist Party; and these too are unlikely to be easily neutralised. If this is right, the consequences for the left of all advanced capitalist countries will be very large.

As a preliminary, the point needs to be made that Eurocommunism must be sharply distinguished, in theoretical and programmatic terms, from social democracy. There are no doubt definite tendencies towards 'social democratization' in the practice of Eurocommunist parties; and it may be argued that Eurocommunism in the end cannot or will not do more than manage capitalism, if it is given a chance to do so. This is what much of the discussion on the left about Eurocommunism is about. But the Eurocommunist purpose, at any rate, quite clearly goes far beyond that of social democracy. As Carrillo puts it, 'what is commonly called "Eurocommunism" proposes to *transform* capitalist society, not to *administer* it; to work out a socialist alternative to the system of state monopoly capitalism, not to integrate in it and become one of its governmental variants' (p.104). Eurocommunism proceeds from an explicitly socialist purpose. It advocates the thorough transformation of capitalist society; and it proceeds from theoretical premises which social democracy mostly ignores or denies. This is by no means conclusive. But to assimilate Berlinguer to Callaghan, Carrillo to Olaf Palme and Marchais to Schmidt is at this point in time sectarian prejudice. As of now, social democracy and Eurocommunism must be taken as basically different enterprises, in the sense in which Carrillo defines the latter's purpose. The real question is how the transformation is envisaged; and whether the project is politically viable.

The essential and distinguishing feature of Eurocommunism is that it seeks to achieve the transformation of capitalist society in socialist directions by constitutional means, inside the constitutional and legal framework provided by bourgeois democracy; and even though it seeks to effect a great extension of bourgeois democracy itself, the idea is to achieve this also by wholly constitutional and legal means.

There is a sense in which this is an old strategy. After the implantation of the German Social Democratic Party in German political life with the lifting of the anti-socialist laws in 1890, constitutionalism and legality became a major strain in Marxism, and not only in

Germany. Carrillo quotes at length from Engels's famous Introduction of 1895 to Marx's *The Class Struggles in France, 1848-50*; and it is indeed the case that its reliance on universal suffrage and constitutionalism, though somewhat qualified, is unmistakeable, and may legitimately be used to serve as a justificatory text, if such texts be needed, for the stance adopted by Eurocommunist parties. Nor did Communist parties after the revolutionary hopes and upheavals following the Bolshevik Revolution and the end of the First World War, seek to operate outside the framework of constitutionalism, at least in bourgeois-democratic regimes. In those regimes, and with exceptional episodes that were mainly forced upon them, Communist parties have followed the constitutional path of advance, and shunned any other. One of the most spectacular demonstrations of their willingness—indeed their eagerness—to follow that path was of course provided by their entry, where this was permitted, in bourgeois coalitions at the end of the Second World War, notably in Italy and France, and until their expulsion from office with the onset of the Cold War.

This eagerness to join bourgeois coalitions in this period cannot simply be explained by reference to Russian pressure; or to the craving for office by Communist leaders. There was also at work a view of socialist advance, based precisely on constitutional perspectives.

There remained, however, a major ambiguity about this Communist constitutionalism, namely whether it was intended as a means of advance to a point at which an opportunity would offer itself for a revolutionary seizure of power, a 'storming of the Winter Palace', to be followed by the proclamation of the dictatorship of the proletariat, meaning in effect the imposition of a 'monolithic' one-party dictatorship on a pattern which has long been familiar. Engels's Introduction is itself ambiguous, and can certainly be interpreted to suggest that a period of electoral and parliamentary advances would have to be complemented by a revolutionary upsurge on what he called 'the decisive day'; and there is in any case Engels's well-known protests at the emendation of his text in *Vorwärts*, the central organ of the German Social Democratic Party, which was intended, as he put it, to make him appear a 'peaceful worshipper of legality' at all costs, a 'disgraceful impression' which he wanted wiped out.

One of the main concerns of Eurocommunist pronouncements has been to dissipate any such ambiguity and to insist that the commitment to 'normal' politics was total and irrevocable. In this perspective, Communist insertion into the political processes of bourgeois democracy is not the necessary means to an ultimately insurrectionary purpose: there is no such purpose. What is envisaged is the gradual transformation of capitalist society by way of its progressive democratization in all areas and at all levels. Napolitano speaks of giving 'ever newer and richer content to democracy —promoting an effective mass participation in the management of economic, social and political life, transforming economic and social structures, carrying out substantial changes in the power relationship between the classes' (p.29); and Carrillo discusses in some detail the democratization of state structures and of economic and social life in general. Neither Carrillo nor Napolitano suggests that this process will necessarily be smooth. Carrillo evokes the possibility that a government of the left, duly brought to office by constitutional procedures, might 'find itself confronted with an attempted coup', in which case it would be necessary 'to reduce by force resistance by force' (p.76). But the intention at least is to proceed by gradual means, and within a strictly constitutional framework.

Before taking this further, it is worth asking why Eurocommunism should have come to full flowering now.

An answer to this question would obviously have to take account of the failure of the USSR to 'liberalise' or 'democratize' in any significant way in the aftermath of the Twentieth Party Congress in 1956; and of the dramatic demonstration of its opposition to the democratization of Communist regimes provided by its crushing of the Czech reform movement in 1968. There was, after 1956, a hope in Western Communist parties that the denunciation of the 'cult of personality' and of the crimes associated with it (or at least of some of them) would take care of Stalinism, and usher in a new era which would make it possible for these parties to continue to point to the USSR as an exemplar of socialist democracy in practice, much as they had done previously, and with greater plausibility.

With the passage of time, however, it became ever more obvious that this was a vain hope: that the USSR remained a very repressive and authoritarian regime, even if it was less repressive than it had been under Stalin; and that to point to it as an exemplar of socialist democracy must discredit both those who were doing the pointing and the notion of socialist democracy itself. In other words, dissociation from the example of the USSR became a condition of political viability let alone success. The process of dissociation was protracted and halting, as is well documented by Claudin; but it was cumulative and irreversible. It also had the advantage of making possible a renewed emphasis by Communist parties on their national vocation, in full freedom from external dictation and in the defence of national sovereignty, independence and so on.

This assertion of independence from the USSR is a feature of Eurocommunism, but it cannot explain its strategic options: after all, the assertion of independence could easily have been allied to an affirmation of a new 'revolutionary' purpose, using the word in a sense which Western Communist parties have categorically rejected.

The reason for this rejection has to do with much more than the USSR and reaches out to the very nature of working-class politics in advanced capitalist countries, at least under bourgeois-democratic conditions. The point is simply that bourgeois democracy imposes certain definite constraints upon parties which seek to achieve mass political and electoral support: by far the most important of these constraints is the acceptance of 'normal' politics and the categorical repudiation of insurrectionism. This rejection of insurrectionism is the largest and most important fact about the working class in advanced capitalist countries since 1918; and it has been very greatly reinforced by the experience of Soviet Russia and other Communist regimes.

The point has to be handled carefully. The rejection of insurrectionism must not be taken to signify an enthusiastic endorsement of bourgeois democracy, parliamentarism and representative institutions. On the contrary, there is very deep and widespread scepticism about all of this, and the chances are that it has always been so. For the working class in general, it is probably the case that 'politics' has been a term charged with many negative and suspect connotations.

But this scepticism about bourgeois politics has never meant any kind of commitment to its obverse, namely the politics of insurrection and violent revolution. No doubt there has always been a section of the working class, of different proportions from one country to another and from one period to another, which has found such an option and commitment acceptable. But it has always and everywhere been a small section of the whole; and the overwhelming majority of the working class, not to speak of other classes, has always rejected the politics of revolution. In so far as a proletarian revolution of the classic type requires mass support, the conditions for such a revolution have not been present.

It is of course possible to attribute this to poverty of leadership, to opportunism, or to treachery, or whatever. But this is to put far too much weight upon leadership and much too little upon the structures and circumstances in which leadership operates. Lenin was possible (though not inevitable) in Russia but not in Germany. It is no good saying that the German revolution would have been successful in 1918 if only there had been a well-organized German Bolshevik/Communist Party in existence, with proper leadership. This may well be so. But there are reasons why there was no such party or leadership, which have very little to do with will and persons and a great deal with structures and circumstances. There is a dialectic between leadership and organization on the one hand, and structures on the other; but that dialectic cannot possibly produce positive results unless there is a minimal 'fit' between them. There has been no such 'fit' between revolutionary organization and leadership and the structures and circumstances of advanced capitalism and bourgeois democracy. Another way of saying this is that advanced capitalism and bourgeois democracy have produced a working-class politics which has been non-insurrectionary and indeed anti-insurrectionary; and that this is the rock on which revolutionary organization and politics have been broken.

This is not to say that leaderships of working-class movements and parties—in this instance Communist leaderships—could not have done more to further the interests of the working class and the subordinate classes in general, in many different ways. Here the dialectic of leadership and structures does have play, for positive results as well as negative ones. But no leadership, however, inspired, and no organization, however efficient, could have carried mass support for a project whose ultimate purpose was a revolutionary seizure of power.

If failures of leadership are no adequate explanation of this working-class rejection of the politics of revolution-as-insurrection, neither is the invocation of a presumed false consciousness on its part leading to an exaggerated regard for the institutions of bourgeois democracy.

Regard for these institutions varies from country to country (higher say in Britain, lower say in Italy), but it is nowhere very high. But in any case, it is not because of an illusory view of bourgeois democracy and of the power which it confers upon the working class that the latter rejects revolution; it is rather because the fruits of revolution, particularly in the political realm, appear so doubtful and indeed so sour that there is acceptance and endorsement of the kind of institutional framework which has been fashioned, not least as a result of working-class pressure, in the context of advanced capitalism. Claudin makes the point that after 1919, there developed in what he calls 'Comintern ideology' an 'essential conflict between council democracy and representative or delegated democracy' with the implication that 'only the first was suited to proletarian rule; the second was designed exclusively for bourgeois rule'; and he notes that 'the effective workers' democracy of the model was short-circuited (in the Soviet Union—R.M.) by the reality of a system of military, police, economic, administrative, juridical and ideological apparatuses which had escaped all popular control and were now the real power centres—in turn organized and controlled by the central apparatus of the single party.' (p.78) This experience has weighed very heavily upon the socialist project in bourgeois-democratic countries; and it is that experience which has helped to legitimate bourgeois democracy, rather than the latter's own intrinsic virtues. It is not these virtues which robbed the working class of a sense of alternatives, but the repulsive character of the actual, existing alternatives. The *idea* of the dictatorship of the proletariat, out of classical Marxism, is not nearly sufficiently compelling to overcome the impact of these alternatives.

In a broader perspective, it is obvious that conditions in advanced capitalist countries would have to become enormously worse, in ways which it is at present difficult to envisage, for the necessary basis of mass support to be engendered which would significantly advance the prospects of a 'vanguard party' bent on an ultimate seizure of power. Those groupings which see themselves as embryonic (or actual) 'vanguard parties' do in fact work on catastrophist assumptions, and expect that economic collapse, the replacement of bourgeois democracy by some form of authoritarianism and fascism, and even war, will eventually bring about the necessary conditions of revolutionary success and make it possible to repeat the Bolshevik scenario of 1917. On any other basis, the road to power by way of insurrection is blocked. The major difference between Eurocommunists and many—though not all—groupings on the far left which oppose them is that the former believe that it will remain blocked; while the latter believe that it will not. These divergent expectations also naturally produce different strategies: the groupings on the far left do see themselves as potential or actual vanguard parties preparing for the moment of violent confrontation; Eurocommunists for their part see themselves as engaged in what Gramsci called a 'war of position' as distinct from a 'war of manoeuvre', with the purpose of achieving a gradual and ever-greater implantation in capitalist society and in politics, to the point where the achievement of governmental power by the forces of the left becomes possible, on the basis of a majority registered at the polls.

There is of course no way of knowing whether the catastrophist perspectives are mistaken or not; and they may not be. But they do not seem to afford the basis for an adequate political strategy. It is reasonable to suggest that the bourgeois-democratic state, under the pressure of economic, social and political unhingements and crises, may well seek to strengthen further its repressive apparatus and to erode the democratic concessions which it has been forced to make, for instance in the area of labour and trade union law. The process is not uniform: labour may win something inside the factory and lose as much or more on the picket line. The struggle between the forces which seek to constrain and weaken labour and those which seek to reinforce it is a permanent one. But this is obviously a very different perspective from the one advanced by the proponents of the catastrophist thesis. As will be suggested later, Eurocommunism tends to underplay the harsh realities of class struggle. But Eurocommunism's catastrophist critics on the left are forced into far too rigid a mould because of their preconceived view of what socialist transition entails. This, however, should not obscure the problems associated with Eurocommunism.

One such problem has to do with the concept of the dictatorship of the proletariat, and with what its rejection by Eurocommunism entails.

The dictatorship of the proletariat may be taken to have three different meanings: firstly, as the 'dictatorship' which the proletariat exercises over its enemies in a revolutionary period, with a clear denotation of class violence and repression; secondly, as the hegemony which the proletariat is expected to exercise in society in a post-revolutionary period, in the same sense in which the notion is used in regard to the hegemony of the bourgeoisie in a capitalist society; and thirdly, as an entirely new form of government.

Eurocommunism rejects the dictatorship of the proletariat in the first of these meanings, in so far as it rejects a notion of transition in which revolutionary violence plays a major part. The second meaning presents no great problem, at least in this context, in so far as hegemony, meaning the 'domination' of society by the overwhelming majority of the people (an extended version of the working class) is what the whole project is about. The third meaning of the concept, which is also the most important and the one to which Marx was most closely wedded, is much more difficult.

In that meaning, the concept entails an extreme extension of popular rule, almost amounting to direct democracy, with councils and other such institutions as the main form of mediation between people and power; and that mediation was itself expected to be weak and subordinate. The old state was to be 'smashed' and replaced by what Lenin called 'other institutions of a fundamentally different type.' Even though this form of government does involve an element of delegation and representation, the 'Comintern ideology' to which Claudin refers in the remark quoted earlier was right in suggesting an 'essential conflict between council democracy and representative or delegated democracy'. It is the vision of an all-but-direct democratic form of rule, with a state strictly subordinated to society and in any case in a process of 'withering away', which constitutes the essence of classical Marxism's theory of post-revolutionary politics.

I do not believe that this is a viable project in its literal meaning, least of all in a revolutionary period; and that it will not in any case be viable in its literal meaning, under any circumstances, for a long time to come. It represents a leap into a fairly distant future, and leaves the question of the exercise of socialist power unsolved.

But if not the dictatorship of the proletariat in this meaning, what then? The answer which Lenin gave to the question is well known—the dictatorship of the party. Eurocommunism rejects that answer, or at least finds it politically unviable, which is the same thing. What then?

The answer, suggested by Napolitano and Carrillo, is a modified, democratized version of parliamentary or representative democracy, but definitely a version of a familiar system. Carrillo puts it thus:

> 'As regards the political system established in Western Europe, based on representative political institutions—parliament, political and philosophical pluralism, the theory of the separation of powers, decentralization, human rights, etc.—that system is in all essentials valid and it will be still more effective with a socialist, not a capitalist, economic foundation. In each case it is a question of making that system still more democratic, of bringing power still closer to the people.' (p.105)

The idea is to extend still further and very considerably an already existing democratic system. Napolitano speaks of a 'whole series of modifications to be made in the structure and functioning of the state machinery, aiming fundamentally at decentralization, developing regional and local autonomy, popular participation and control'; (p.50) and Carrillo similarly speaks of 'the bringing of the State apparatus closer to the country, to the people', of 'the setting up of regional organs of power', and of 'creating a living democracy at all levels throughout the country—a democracy in which effective power will reside in the organs of popular power (i.e. regional organs—R.M.) so that the vitality of that power is such that no groups installed in the central zone of power could wipe it out at a blow' (p.75).

Carrillo concedes very readily that 'this conception of the State and of the struggle to democratize it presupposes the renunciation of the idea, in its traditional form, of *a workers' and peasants' State*; of a State, that is, built from scratch, bringing into its offices workers from the factories and peasants from the land, and sending functionaries who had hitherto worked in the offices to occupy their places.' This is a very crude characterization of the Marxist vision and Carrillo renounces it all the more readily because, as he goes on to say, 'such a State has never really existed, except as an ideal. Even where the revolution triumphed by an act of force, the bureaucracy, with some exceptions, has continued as such and the new function-aries have rapidly acquired many of the bad habits of the old' (p.76. Italics in text). This being the case, Carrillo is content to advocate a democratized version of existing state structures.

What Carrillo expresses here is representative of Eurocommun-ism in general, and is of great importance. He does not accept the idea of the dictatorship of the proletariat which Lenin put forward in *The State and Revolution*. This, I have indicated earlier, seems to be sensible: that idea is not a realistic blueprint for democracy. But having thus given up the dictatorship of the proletariat, Carrillo then retreats—and so does Eurocommunism in general—to the advocacy of what is in effect another version of radical bourgeois-democratic politics.

Of course, Carrillo and Napolitano and other Eurocommunists do emphasize the importance they attach to further democratiza-tion, to 'participation' and to other features of democratic politics; and the genuineness of their concern is not here in question. But the fact remains—and it is a crucial fact—that this whole perspective amounts, conceptually, theoretically and in practice, to a retreat from the Marxist vision of a disalienated politics as a vital part—perhaps the most vital part—of the socialist project. In its sense of an all-but-direct sort of government, the dictatorship of the prolet-ariat was intended to give form to that vision. To stress its 'utopian' side—as I do—because of its under-estimation of the role of the state in a post-capitalist society and in any relevant future (and to underestimate therefore the *problem* of the state) is one thing. To surrender that vision altogether is another and very different one.

This is what Eurocommunism does, for all its democratizing con-cerns and commitments. Its theorists conceive of democratization as an infinite multiplication of representative bodies at various levels; and this is no doubt required. But they seem remarkably insensitive to the possibilities of enhanced statism and 'officialization' of political life which this *also* opens up. After all, it does not seem unreasonable to think that the multiplication of organs of power, however 'representative' they are intended to be, may not do much to dis-alienate politics; and may simply create an enlarged official-dom of 'representatives' of one sort or another. But even if this danger is averted or attenuated, the difference is obvious between an elaborate structure of officially sanctioned (and controlled) organs of power, however 'representative', and a network of associations, councils, committees and whatever at the grassroots, armed with a genuine measure of power, and operating *alongside* the state and *independently* of it.

The point is a difficult one. It involves breaking with an either/or schema (*either* the dictatorship of the proletariat *or* some version of bourgeois democracy) which has long been firmly fixed, and which has been exceedingly constricting; and it involves breaking with that schema in favour of a search, which is bound to be arduous and problematic, for an adequate relationship between two forms of power—state power and popular power. Marx in *The Civil War in France* and Lenin in *The State and Revolution* made much too light of the former; Eurocommunism is not much interested in the latter where it is not deeply suspicious of it. The socialist project requires a 'dialectical' relationship between both.

Claudin has a strong sense of this requirement, though he mainly refers to it in connection with the struggle for hegemony and the achievement of power. He writes that 'organs of rank-and-file democracy should be developed and . . . co-ordinated with the organs of representative democracy' (p.117). But this is obviously required after the achievement of power as well as before, in the consolidation and extension of a new system as well as in the struggle towards it.

Eurocommunism is not only based on a working-class recoil from violent upheaval in the countries of advanced capitalism and bour-geois democracy. This would hardly constitute the basis for socialist advance of any sort. It proceeds rather from certain assumptions about what the immediate and near future holds for these societies.

The major such assumption, which figures prominently in both Carrillo and Napolitano, is that the large majority of the population of advanced capitalist countries now constitutes a potential con-stituency for socialist transformation; that the 'working class' is no longer an isolated and relatively small part of the population but a section of what Marx called the 'collective worker' of the capitalist mode of production; and that an alliance between the different parts of this 'collective worker', represented by different parties and groupings, is entirely possible, given the massive and growing contradictions of capitalism.

There is nothing inevitable about the coming into being of such an alliance; and neither Carrillo nor Napolitano suggests that there is. On the contrary, they both stress that it has to be forged out of a disparate array of social and political forces.

At this point, however, there occurs a very marked difference in approach and emphasis between Eurocommunist party leaders like Carrillo and Napolitano on the one hand, and a sympathetic critic of Eurocommunism like Claudin. That difference has a number of facets but it essentially consists in the preoccupations of Eurocommunist leaderships with political and electoral gains for their parties; and the preoccupations of their critics on the left with social and political struggles. Neither set of preoccupations need or does exclude the other: but the difference is nevertheless very real.

In effect, Eurocommunist leaders conceive their parties as having a dual vocation—that of both being what Claudin calls 'parties of struggle' and 'parties of government.' In the former role, they want to be the dominant force in the class struggle waged by the subordinate classes. In the latter role, they want to be at the centre of a constellation of forces capable of affirming their hegemony and of translating that hegemony into an effective political presence, whether inside a governmental coalition or outside.

The reconciliation of these two roles is however an exceedingly difficult exercise; and it can easily turn into an impossible one. This is surely the case when a party of the left enters a governmental coalition which is not wholly or predominantly of the left. The following quotation makes the point well:

A proletarian party which shares power with a capitalist party in any government must share the blame for any acts of subjection of the working class. It thereby invites the hostility of its own supporters, and this in turn causes its capitalist allies to lose confidence and makes any progressive action impossible. No such arrangement can bring any strength to the working class. No capitalist party will permit it to do so. It can only compromise a proletarian party and confuse and split the working class.

The quotation is from Karl Kautsky's *The Road to Power*, which was published in 1909, and it seems apposite today. An 'historic compromise' which includes minority participation by the left in an essentially conservative government is most likely to have as its main result the compromising of those on the left who enter into it.

But even where such participation is not involved, the dual vocation of large working class parties with serious socialist purposes is bound to create difficult problems for them in the context of bourgeois democracy; and it is facile for critics on the left to ignore the very real dilemmas which it poses or to pretend that they do not exist or that they can be resolved by the resolute incantation of Marxist-Leninist slogans. On the contrary, the dilemmas are unavoidable and the danger is that party leaders will seek to resolve them by giving in to the pull towards social-democratization, which also requires the stifling of the criticism which the tendency arouses inside the party. Claudin writes that 'between the adventure of extremism and the adventure of the "historic compromise" (understood as collaboration with the forces that constitute the most fundamental block to the kind of change the present situation demands), space must be found for a realistic policy of advance towards the democratic socialist transformation of Italian society' (p.119). The point is of wider application. But to find and occupy such a 'space' may well require party leaders to forego immediate and apparent political advantage for the sake of a longer-term view of what socialist advance entails; and also the acknowledgement that being a 'party of government', in a meaningful and effective sense, is itself a long-term undertaking, which requires not only electoral success but deep and solid popular implantation.

Such implantation, and the popular support which it betokens, is the essential (but not the sufficient) condition for the success of the enterprise which ultimately defines Eurocommunism, namely the achievement of constitutional power for the purpose of socialist change.

Unlike social democracy, Eurocommunism has no illusions about the nature of the capitalist state. 'The State apparatus as a whole,' Carrillo notes, 'continues to be the instrument of the ruling class' (p.13). But unlike classical Marxism, Eurocommunism is also founded on the belief that it is possible to transform the various parts of the state and to apply to them the same democratizing processes that must be applied to all other parts of the social system. In this instance, what is involved is not the kinds of transformation that were discussed earlier in the representative organs of the state, but in the mechanisms of administration and coercion—the civil service, the judiciary, the military and the police.

This derives very logically from the initial premise that it is possible to conceive of a constitutional transition to socialism. But it is surely enough to note this for the ambitiousness of the whole enterprise to be underlined. To transform this or that aspect of capitalist organization is bad enough, but to attempt a profound restructuring of the state apparatus, including, the military and the police, which the project involves, is much worse, or may well so be taken.

On this subject (and on the project as a whole) Eurocommunist writers such as Carrillo and Napolitano leave a strong impression, not of ignoring the difficulties and dangers that are bound to be encountered, but of underestimating them. They repeatedly refer to the internal and external pressures to which a government of the left intent on serious business must expect to be subjected: but what they say about it in no way matches the gravity of the issues.

The reason for this cannot be taken to lie in the personal intellectual merits or political intelligence of either Carrillo or Napolitano. The reason for the weakness of exposition lies rather in the basic approach to the whole question of transition. Given their concern to see their parties integrated into the 'normal' political process, Eurocommunists are necessarily driven to understate the problems of that transition: to do otherwise would compel them to place much greater emphasis than they deem desirable upon the class struggles which are bound to be part of it; and to discuss with much greater precision their parties' role in these struggles.

One of the main features of Eurocommunism is its much reduced claim for the pre-eminence of Communist parties. Thus Carrillo on this subject:

> It continues to be the vanguard party, inasmuch as it truly embodies a creative Marxist attitude. But it no longer regards itself as the *only* representative of the working class, of the working people and the forces of

culture. It recognizes, in theory and in practice, that other parties which are socialist in tendency can also be representative of particular sections of the working population, although their theoretical and philosophical positions and their internal structure may not be ours. It regards as normal and stimulating the competition between different policies and solutions to specific problems, and it has no hesitation in accepting, when circumstances warrant, that others may be more accurate than it in analysing a particular situation. (p.100).

These formulations raise more questions than they solve; and so does Carrillo's view of the relation of the party to the state and society. But there is, in immediate terms, another question relating to the party which is of great importance and interest, yet which he barely touches upon; and which Napolitano altogether ignores; this is the question of the party's internal structure and its organizing principle, democratic centralism.

Carrillo refers to 'organization as a main component of the effectiveness of political action and unity in action and discipline—once the majority has taken a decision at congresses or in leading bodies between one congress and another—as indispensable weapons' (p.101). This is code language for two characteristic features of all Communist parties: the first is a hierarchical organization which permanently ensures that the leadership carries the day at congresses, and is not therefore much troubled between one congress and another; the second and related feature is the famous ban on factions, which Lenin imposed on the Tenth Bolshevik Party Congress at a point of great crisis in 1921, and which has ever since been used by Communist party leaderships to disarm and paralyse opposition. There was a time, not so long ago, when the need for discipline was invoked to silence all criticism inside Communist parties, and to expel the critics. This is no longer the common practice. Criticism is tolerated, so long as the critics do not try to render themselves effective by seeking to come together, and by together pressing their views upon the party.

The simple fact of the matter is that Communist parties have always been exceedingly undemocratic organizations. In this, they have hardly been unique: all parties are in some degree undemocratic. But the degree matters a good deal; and Communist parties have been undemocratic to an extreme degree. Not surprisingly, well-entrenched leaders have little reason to want it otherwise, and find it easy to invoke the need for 'unity in action' to 'protect their supremacy'. On the other hand, the contradiction is blatant between Eurocommunist protestations of commitment to democracy on the one hand, and commitment to undemocratic practices inside Communist parties on the other. That contradiction has now broken surface in the French Communist Party and is a very long way from having played itself out, either in the French or in any other Communist Party. Until it is resolved—and resolved in democratic directions—socialist advance must remain significantly impaired.

Postscript

Three points in this article call for further comment. The first has to do with the differences between Communist parties and Socialist or social-democratic parties in Western Europe. In the article, I say that Eurocommunism 'must be sharply distinguished, in theoretical and programmatic terms, from social democracy'; and that the Eurocommunist purpose 'quite clearly goes far beyond that of social democracy'. These formulations seem rather more emphatic than they should be. For the 'definite tendencies towards "social democratization" in the practice of Eurocommunist parties', to which I also refer, obviously serve to narrow the differences; and these tendencies have increased rather than diminished in recent years. Eurocommunist parties have displayed an ever more pronounced will to being 'parties of government', none more so than the French Communist Party, which has been perfectly willing not only to enter into but also to stay in a government many of whose policies, notably in foreign and defence matters, bear a very marked reactionary stamp. Even so, there remain substantial differences between Communist parties and social-democratic ones: but emphasis on these differences should not occlude the willingness of Eurocommunist parties to support policies which place them very firmly in a social-democratic orbit. The point is particularly relevant in relation to the leaders of Communist and social-democratic parties; and there is consequently rather more to the tendency on the left to 'assimilate' these communist and social-democratic leaders than the 'sectarian prejudice' mentioned in the article.

The second point is of greater importance. I counterpose Euro-communism as a 'constitutionalist' strategy to the strategy of 'insur-rectionism'. But the notion of 'insurrectionism' does not do justice to left positions (for there is more than one) based on the rejection of Eurocommunist perspectives. That rejection for the most part involves many things other than simply support for 'insurrection'. It is, rather, a re-affirmation of the classical Marxist view, first, that a fundamental transformation of the social order is very unlikely to occur without a violent confrontation, even if the socialist forces do not seek such a confrontation; and, secondly, that the working class, in the course of its struggles, will need to create its own organs of power, and that these will eventually form the basis of a socialist democracy far superior to capitalist democracy.

However, the practical significance of left opposition to Eurocom-munism, in situations where revolutionary challenge is in any case a long-term prospect, lies in a different (though related) realm, namely in the different forms of activity which the two perspectives involve. Thus, Eurocommunism may not eschew extra-parliamentary activ-ism, but its emphasis nevertheless falls upon institutions which are, or which are claimed to be, representative of the working class— local and regional bodies, parliament; and great responsibility and power naturally devolve upon the leaders and members of these institutions. Left opposition to Eurocommunism, for its part, may not reject electoral and representative work at local, regional or par-liamentary level, but *its* emphasis nevertheless falls upon the activity of the working class outside representative institutions, and notably upon activity 'at the point of production'. Its main concern tends to be with activism at the grassroots, rather than with the work of rep-resentative bodies. The Eurocommunist perspective has an organ-izational and bureaucratic bias, and proceeds from an essentially traditional view of politics. For its part, the opposition to Eurocom-munism from the left has a bias towards rhetoric and illusionism.

At any rate, the questions at issue here go well beyond any simple notion of 'insurrectionism'.

The third point is closely related to this last one. I say in the article that the 'rejection of insurrectionism is the largest and most import-ant fact about the working class in advanced capitalist countries since 1918'; and while I qualify this by saying that 'no doubt, there has always been a section of the working class, of different proportions from one country to another and from one period to another, which has found such an option and commitment acceptable', I also suggest that 'it has always and everywhere been a small section of the whole', and that 'the overwhelming majority of the working class, not to speak of other classes, has always rejected the politics of revolution'.

This is rather more sweeping than is warranted by the historical experience of the twentieth century: for there have been occasions when much more than 'a small section of the working class' has engaged in what I call 'the politics of revolution'—for instance in Italy in 1919-20 and 1943-45, in Spain in the thirties, and also in Germany in the late twenties and early thirties, by way of mass support for the German Communist Party. It is of course notable that these were countries where capitalist democracy was not very solidly implanted, or where, in the case of Italy in 1943-45, capitalist democracy had been destroyed by Fascism. Nevertheless, the point I was making in the article about the working class needs to be more strongly qualified, in historical terms, than I allowed.

It also needs to be qualified in a different sense. For it is not the case that workers (and others) 'opt', as in a referendum, for the politics of constitutionalism as against the 'politics of revolution'. This is seldom if ever how actual strategic choices present themselves, or are usually presented by the leaders of revolutionary groupings or parties. Much more commonly, specific objectives are at stake, whose pursuit aggravates class conflict to the point of major crisis: it is at some stage in this process that the 'politics of revolution' acquire a literal meaning, insofar as leaders (and followers) engaged in the conflict have to decide whether to move further and seek to gain power, or whether to retreat.

There has only been one important occasion in the decades following the Second World War when such a decision has had to be made in a capitalist-democratic regime—in France in 1968. For the rest, these have been decades when the class struggle has proceeded 'normally' and has posed no major threat to the stability of the social order, however much it might threaten or even topple a government; and given the existence of a capitalist-democratic framework in which the traditional parties of the working class could engage in political competition with their bourgeois rivals and plausibly present themselves as agencies of reform and transformation, it is not really surprising that parties and groupings opposed to 'reformism' and proclaiming their revolutionary objectives should not have obtained much popular support. In this context, the negative example of the Soviet regime may have played a part, as I suggest in the article, in the general alienation from revolutionary politics, though the point has much less bearing on the inter-war years, when there was strong activist sympathy for the USSR, than on the post-war decades of Cold War. But other factors, among which the nature of the political system is in my view pre-eminent, played an incomparably greater role in bringing about the relative political pacification of the post-war years.

This, however, is hardly conclusive (how could it be?) in regard to the political propensities that would be engendered in large sections of the working class (and beyond) in a period of crisis more prolonged and acute, in economic, social and political terms, than has been the case in the countries in question since the end of the Second World War.

II

Marxism
and the Problem of Power

Political Action, Determinism and Contingency*

1979

I

The main concern of this essay is with various questions that arise in relation to 'the role of the individual in history' and the degree to which individuals, singly or in small groups, can significantly affect the historical process.* The subject is obviously crucial for any theory of history and politics. But it is particularly important for Marxism. This is so for at least two related reasons: first, because Marxism has always and pre-eminently been concerned with the forces that determine the historical process: and second, because that question has a direct bearing on political strategy and practice.

Yet, Marxist historical and other work has not paid much attention to 'the role of the individual in history'. Plekhanov's pamphlet bearing this title was published in 1898; and when Marxists have considered the question at all since then, they have tended to rely on a few key concepts and formulations to declare it resolved. On closer examination, however, these concepts and formulations appear to be very inadequate.

In one sense, it is very odd that more should not have been done to meet the challenge which the subject presents to Marxist theory, given the various cults of 'great men' which have been such a pronounced (and awful) feature of 'Marxism-Leninism'—the cult of

* Earlier versions of this article were presented in the Politics Department, Queens University, Belfast; a Philosophy Seminar at the University of Leeds; a History of Ideas Faculty Seminar at Brandeis University; and Boston University's Colloquium for the Philosophy of Science. I am grateful for the comments and criticisms which I received on those occasions.

Lenin after his death, of Stalin, of Mao, and so on. The clear message has been that there were indeed 'makers of history': but there would seem to have been very little attempt to draw out the theoretical implications of the message. Instead, resort has been had to banalities about the indissoluble links which were forged between the 'great man', his party, and the people at large and which made possible the achievement, under his inspired leadership, of revolution, the building of socialism, or whatever. But this belongs to the realm of edification, not theory. The problems remain.

I speak of 'the degree' to which individuals, singly or in small groups, can significantly affect the historical process and intend thereby to exclude from the start two positions that I take to be untenable.

One of these positions is that the whole of human life, past, present and to come, is determined by a force or forces that are not susceptible to modification by human intervention, and of which human actions are only the expression or manifestation. In its extreme forms, this position belongs to a particular form of religious perspective on history, according to which every event and action from the smallest to the largest is a manifestation of the divine will and is altogether predetermined and preordained by that will. Thus, anything that has happened had to happen; nothing else, by definition, could. And what was true of the past will, of course, be true of the future. This is not a view that can be argued with: it can only be accepted or rejected. I reject it, and pass on.

At what might appear to be the opposite extreme, there is a view of history, politics, and life in general, which sees them as altogether contingent, unpatterned, accidental, 'a tale', as Macbeth said when retribution and death were imminent, 'told by an idiot, full of sound and fury, signifying nothing'. In the strong version of this position, there is no historical determination of any kind, only a succession of specific events, produced by a combination of chance and will, whose outcome is altogether uncertain. Accident rules.

In this strong version the accidental view of history, far from escaping determinism, is but another version of it, namely accidental determinism. But what makes it untenable and absurd is its clear implication that anything goes, anywhere, at any time. It is impossible to take this seriously, simply because there is always *some* degree of determination in history, if only in terms of time and place; the French Revolution, whatever view is taken of its 'causes', could not have occurred in the sixteenth century, or in China.

It is in fact a weak version of the role of 'accident' in history that is usually defended. Thus, J.B. Bury, in an essay entitled 'Cleopatra's Nose', once wrote that 'the course of history seems . . . to be marked at every stage by contingencies, some of greater, some of smaller import. In some cases, they produce a situation to which the antecedent situation does not logically lead. In others they determine the form and means of the realization of a logical tendency'.[1]

Whether it is taken to be right or wrong, this is not an absurd view; and it can be situated in a spectrum of historical theories distinguished from each other, in respect of the question of determination and contingency, by the different emphasis they place upon one or the other; and also by the factors to which they attribute greater or lesser importance, or which they deem to be determinant. Great differences between these theories do of course exist, but not on the basis of total predetermination as against total indeterminacy. In all plausible theories of history, there is allowed some degree to which individual intervention can affect the historical process—that indeed may be taken as one of the essential criteria of plausibility. The question is how much.

In classical Marxism the answer is unquestionably: not much. The classical Marxist position is expressed in a number of well-known formulations. One is to be found in *The Eighteenth Brumaire of Louis Bonaparte*:

> 'Men make their own history but not of their own free will; not under circumstances they themselves have chosen but under the given and inherited circumstances with which they are directly confronted. The tradition of the dead generations weighs like a nightmare on the minds of the living . . .'[2]

Another equally, if not even more, familiar formulation occurs in the *Contribution to the Critique of Political Economy*, where Marx states that

> 'in the social production which men carry on they enter into definite relations that are indispensable and independent of their will; these

relations of production correspond to a definite stage of development of their material powers of production. The totality of these relations of production constitutes the economic structure of society—the real foundation on which legal and political superstructures arise and to which definite forms of social consciousness correspond. The mode of production of material life determines the general character of the social, political and spiritual processes of life. It is not the consciousness of men that determines their being, but, on the contrary, their social being determines their consciousness.'[3]

The basic premise which informs historical materialism is not in doubt: it is that men and women, organized in classes, are the collective actors of history, but that the play itself is very largely shaped by forces which are not greatly affected by any single will or by the will of small groups of people. History is the history of class struggles, Marx and Engels said in *The Communist Manifesto*, and many elements—economic, social, political, cultural, historical, and so forth —contribute to the shaping of the form and content of these struggles. Individuals, singly and in groups, can certainly make a difference at a particular moment to the ways in which class struggles work themselves out: but that difference, in classical Marxism, is not very great and certainly should not be taken as being decisive. Marxism is a determinism, though not an economic determinism; and it is a determinism in which individual will and activity, though not to be ignored or dismissed, are only allowed a relatively small part. This is grounded in Marx and Engels's understanding of historical materialism; it also results from their rejection of a certain kind of romantic adventurism, pseudo-revolutionary 'elitism', and sectarian voluntarism, according to which anything is possible at any time, provided a group, sect or brotherhood of sufficiently determined and dedicated individuals wills it. Throughout their political life, and with remarkable consistency, Marx and Engels fought against any such view and against those whom Marx contemptuously called the 'alchemists of revolution', for whom 'the only condition for a revolution is the proper organization of their conspiracy'.[4]

II

In the 1869 Preface to *The Eighteenth Brumaire of Louis Bonaparte*,

Marx noted that he had shown in that work how 'the *class struggle* in France created circumstances and conditions which allowed a mediocre and grotesque individual to play the hero's rule'.[5] On this view, individuals, great or ordinary, mediocre or brilliant, *can* play a 'hero's role', provided that class struggle creates the appropriate circumstances and conditions for it.

This may be entirely reasonable, although I will want to come back to this point later. But the circumstances and conditions, whatever they are deemed to be, which enable the individual to play such a role do not thereby determine specifically what that role will be. The 'hero' could not perform any role without the circumstances and conditions; but what precise role he performs, and with what effect, is not predetermined and settled by the circumstances and conditions in which he acts. At the most, the part of the 'hero' is roughly sketched out, but much that is important about it remains to be filled in. It is clearly not tenable to argue that circumstances and conditions determine in advance every action taken by the 'hero' or their results. To argue this would be to revert to a totally predeterminist 'model', which I have excluded from the start. On the contrary, there is room here for what are rather loosely termed 'accidents'.

Marx's answer to this objection is to be found in a remark he made in a letter to Kugelmann in April 1871, in the midst of the Paris Commune:

> 'World history,' he wrote, 'would indeed be very easy to make, if the struggle were taken up only on conditions of infallibly favourable chances. It would, on the other hand, be of a very mystical nature, if "accidents" played no part. These accidents naturally form part of the general course of development and are compensated for by other accidents. But acceleration and delay are very much dependent upon such "accidents", including the "accident" of the character of the people who first head the movement.'[6]

Engels put the same point somewhat differently when he suggested, more than twenty years later, that

> 'the further the particular sphere which we are investigating is removed from the economic sphere and approaches that of pure abstract ideology, the more shall we find it exhibiting accidents in its development, the more

will its curve run zigzag. But if you plot the average axis of the curve, you will find that this axis will run more and more nearly parallel to the axis of economic development the longer the period considered and the wider the field dealt with'.[7]

These and other such formulations, some of which will be referred to later, are for various reasons unsatisfactory. But before discussing why this is so, reference must be made to Plekhanov's pamphlet on *The Role of the Individual in History*, to which I alluded earlier, and which makes an interesting addition to the interpretation of 'accidents' (in the form of individual intervention) put forward by Marx and Engels.

Like Marx, Plekhanov sought to dispose of the question of 'the individual in history' by suggesting that it is 'circumstances' which 'produce' the required individual, the 'great man', or which turn the mediocrity into the great man. But he then went on to explain why the great man appears unique and providential: this is because of what he called an 'optical illusion'. Plekhanov writes:

'In discussing the role great men play in history we nearly always fall victims to a sort of optical illusion . . . in coming out in the role of the "good sword" to save public order, Napoleon prevented all the other generals from playing this role; and some of them might have performed it in the same way or almost the same way as he did. Once the public need for an energetic ruler was satisfied, the social organization barred the road to the position of military ruler for all the other talented soldiers. Its power became a hindrance to the appearance of other talents of a similar kind. This is the cause of the optical illusion.'[8]

In essence, then, these are the main propositions which Marxist theory has brought to bear on the subject under discussion; and these propositions may be discussed in terms of three distinct problems (or objections) which they raise.

The first of these has to do with the proposition that, where circumstances so demand, they will produce the required individual and that great men are 'invented' when they are needed. Second, it is claimed that, whoever fills the available space, the results will be more or less the same. Third, there is the view that what such intervention does is to 'accelerate' or 'delay' what Marx called the 'general course of development', which is in any case proceeding;

and moreover, 'accidents' of one kind are 'compensated' for by 'accidents' of another kind.

The first of these propositions is exceedingly vulnerable. In the letter to Starkenburg already quoted, Engels had also written as follows:

> 'That such and such a man and precisely that man arises at a particular time in a particular country is, of course, pure chance. But cut him out and there will be a demand for a substitute, and this substitute will be found, good or bad, but in the long run he will be found. That Napoleon, just that particular Corsican, should have been the military dictator whom the French Republic, exhausted by its own warfare, had rendered necessary, was chance; but that, if a Napoleon had been lacking, another would have filled the place, is proved by the fact that the man was always found as soon as he became necessary: Caesar, Augustus, Cromwell, etc.'[9]

The argument, as Sidney Hook points out, is obviously circular: 'Engels tells us that a great man is a necessary response to a social need for him. But how do we know that there is a social need for him? Surely not after the event! That would be viciously circular.'[10]

In any case, the notion of necessity is here much too loose and allows for every kind of self-confirming, *post hoc ergo propter hoc* sort of argument: where a 'great man' was needed, he appeared or was 'invented'; where he did not appear or was not 'invented', there was no necessity for him. This is not only self-confirming but historically arbitrary and restrictive. For there have been periods in history when dominant classes very badly needed a 'great man' to help them meet a revolutionary challenge or a major crisis, but where the need was not met: for instance the *ancien regime* on the eve of 1789 or the tsarist regime in and after February 1917. That no such individual or group of individuals was able to display qualities of 'greatness' at the time can be very adequately explained in terms of a cluster of economic, social, political and ideological conditions that made such a display very difficult.[11] But this is also to say that 'necessity' is not enough, and that there are circumstances where there is a very great 'necessity' for the kind of hero Engels had in mind, yet with no real possibility of that necessity being met. The question is not that there was no one to *save* the *ancien regime* or tsarism, but that there was no possibility for anyone to provide adequate leadership to the forces wanting to save these regimes. It may be assumed that there were many people who, in terms of personal qualities, could have provided that leadership, but that the conditions did not allow them to do so. At any rate, it is not permissible to argue that the 'necessity' for such people was absent.

Nor can it be said that the inability to meet this need is only characteristic of dominant classes in decline and disarray: it clearly applies also to subordinate classes in general and to working-class movements over the course of time. Indeed, it has been a constant theme of much Marxist history of working-class movements in different countries that working-class challenges to the established order were defeated on many occasions because of the absence of the necessary leadership. Here too, the issue is not so much one of absence of leadership as of the inability of would-be revolutionary leaders to intervene effectively. An obvious instance is that of Germany in 1918. At a point of extreme 'necessity', the German working class did not follow the revolutionary leadership that was available; and it is sufficient to evoke the name of Rosa Luxemburg to suggest that it *was* available. Conditions, stretching back over many years, did not allow such people to provide the leadership of which they were capable; or, to put the same point somewhat differently, a complex of conditions led the German working class to reject their leadership. This fact, too, can be explained within the framework of historical materialism. But there is no question of the 'necessity', at least in a revolutionary perspective, of a leadership which circumstances did not allow to be deployed.

In short, and leaving aside the arbitrary and question-begging aspects of the notion of 'necessity', it is clear that there is nothing inevitable or automatic about the emergence of 'great men' at any particular moment. Nor can great men be so readily invented and mediocrities used for the purpose as the argument would have it. There are certainly conditions and circumstances that make the intervention of individuals more likely, and more likely to be effective, than other conditions and circumstances. But nothing is here 'inevitable'.

The second problem concerns the more or less interchangeable nature of the role of individuals, which is suggested in the formulations which I have quoted earlier. Thus, Engels writes that 'if a

Napoleon had been lacking, another would have filled his place'; and Plekhanov similarly says of Napoleon's generals that some of them might have performed his role 'in the same way or almost the same way as he did'. The issue does not, of course, only relate to the case of Napoleon and his generals.

It is perfectly reasonable to think that a military dictatorship in France was very likely indeed in the closing years of the eighteenth century, in the aftermath of the Revolution, Thermidor and the Directoire, and in circumstances which gave military men outstanding opportunities for political intervention. In this case, there is everything to be said for the argument that, if Napoleon had not been there, another 'revolutionary' or *parvenu* general would have attempted a coup which might well have succeeded and installed in power some kind of military dictatorship. But to suggest that any such individual would have played Napoleon's role 'in the same way or almost the same way as he did' is something else altogether, and quite unjustified. Napoleon gave specific and particular forms to the rule he established, and it is obvious that anyone else, having assumed dictatorial power, would have ruled differently, perhaps very differently. What significance this has will be discussed later: the important point here is that the substitution of one ruler for another does make a difference, and can make a very considerable difference.

Other cases readily come to mind. It has been said, very plausibly, that 'the disintegration of the Weimar Republic and the rise of Nazism were two distinct if obviously overlapping historical processes'; and that while 'the collapse of Weimar had become inevitable' by 1932, 'Hitler's triumph had not.'[12] However this may be, it seems to me important not only that it was the Nazis who won, but that it was Hitler who was leading the Nazis—and of course it may be argued that the Nazis won because of Hitler. A different right-wing dictatorship could well have come into being in Germany, with the support of major sections of Germany's dominant class and traditional rulers. But it cannot be said that any such dictatorship would have worked 'in the same way or almost the same way' as did the Nazi dictatorship; and it is further to the point that the Nazi dictatorship was given a particular stamp by Hitler, with enormous consequences both internally and abroad. The notion of interchangeability cannot here be taken seriously.

Another instance is that of Stalin. There seems to me no real question that some kind of dictatorial rule would have prevailed in Russia after Lenin's death, as it had prevailed while he was alive, and that this would have happened whoever succeeded him. It is also very likely—though less certain—that this would have turned into one-man rule rather than 'collegial' or 'collective' leadership. But it is quite arbitrary to claim that any of the individuals other than Stalin who would have filled the role would have filled it as he did, and that they would have given it the same or 'almost' the same stamp as he did. A whole world is concealed in this 'almost', and there *are* cases where 'more or less' is a matter of unfathomable magnitudes. This is one of them. Stalinism was not simply the work of Stalin: the notion is clearly absurd. But it is only in crude propaganda exercises that the forms which collectivization assumed— and the purges, the trials, the camps and all the rest that makes up the whole story of terror and death that has come to be subsumed under the label of Stalinism—were the 'inevitable' or 'logical' or 'necessary' outcome of the Bolshevik Revolution, or of Leninist doctrine, or of Marxism; and that all that happened had to happen, 'more or less'. Here is determinism indeed!

In the utterly unpropitious circumstances of every kind in which the Bolshevik Revolution was made and in which it survived, the regime was bound to have many repressive features and to retain many of them for a long time: and this would have been the case even if Lenin had not been removed by illness and death so early from the scene. But while conditions made dictatorship inevitable (or so I would argue), and made Stalin's dictatorship possible, Stalin himself must be held to have been directly and specifically responsible for many features which the regime assumed. It is impossible to *know* what would have happened if Lenin (or Trotsky, or Bukharin, or Zinoviev, or Kamenev, or a combination of any of them or of others) had led Russia in the twenties and thirties. But it hardly seems eccentric to suggest that much that did happen under Stalin would not have happened under other rulers; and considering the enormities that did happen, this is no small point.[13] Conditions made Stalin possible: but Stalin then added a 'personal' ingredient to the dictatorship, which did make a great difference to its forms. What I call a 'personal ingredient' was itself the product of an endlessly complex numbers of factors which determined Stalin's *persona*. But what he brought by way of this 'personal ingredient' to the history of the Soviet Union was not inscribed in the 'logic' of that history; and what he brought to it did make a difference.

A rather different kind of case must be taken up here, namely where the question is, not the difference which the replacement of one individual by another makes, but rather the actual *irreplaceability* of a particular individual; in other words, the case where there appears to be no 'optical illusion' at work. An obvious and dramatic case in recent history is of course that of Lenin in 1917.

The evidence is overwhelming that there was no substitute for Lenin between April and October 1917; and that without him, the Bolshevik Revolution would not have occurred. In his *History of the Russian Revolution*, Trotsky asked the question ('and this is no unimportant question, although easier to ask than to answer'), 'How would the revolution have developed if Lenin had not reached Russia in April 1917?' He then writes that 'Lenin was not a demiurge of the revolutionary process', and that 'he merely entered into a chain of objective historic forces'; but that nevertheless Lenin 'was a great link in that chain'. Lenin 'was not an accidental element in the historic development, but a product of the whole past of Russian history . . . [he] did not oppose the party from outside, but was himself its most complete expression'; and so on. But Trotsky then goes on to ask: 'Is it possible, however, to say confidently that the party without him would have found its road?' and he answers: 'We would by no means make bold to say that . . . it is by no means excluded that a disoriented and split party might have let slip the revolutionary opportunity for many years.' He adds: 'The role of personality arises before us here on a truly gigantic scale.'[14]

In his biography of Trotsky, Isaac Deutscher noted that he was on other occasions even more definite. In a letter he wrote to Preobrazhensky from exile in Alma Ata in 1928, Trotsky said that 'you know better than I do that had Lenin not managed to come to Petrograd in April 1917, the October Revolution would not have taken place'.[15] Deutscher also quotes from Trotsky's *Diary in Exile* his remark that 'had I not been present in 1917 in Petrograd the October Revolution would still have taken place—*on the condition that Lenin was present and in command*. If neither Lenin nor I had been present in Petrograd, there would have been no October Revolution: the leadership of the Bolshevik Party would have prevented it from occurring—of this I have not the slightest doubt.'[16]

Deutscher notes that 'for a Marxist this is a startling conclusion'; and that 'it accords ill with Trotsky's *Weltanschauung* and with much else besides'. This is certainly true but obviously has no bearing on the argument itself. Nor has the following comment which Deutscher makes upon the point:

> 'If it were true that the greatest revolution of all time could not have occurred without one particular leader, then the leader cult at large would by no means be preposterous; and its denunciation by historical materialists, from Marx to Trotsky, and the revulsion of all progressive thought against it would be pointless.'[17]

Even if the consequences of accepting Trotsky's view of Lenin's indispensable role were as dire as this, this would not invalidate the point itself. But these consequences do not in fact follow: what follows is that there is here a problem that needs to be confronted.

For his part, Deutscher relies on Plekhanov's 'optical illusion' thesis. Thus he writes that

> 'Lenin's influence on events appears to us greatly magnified because once Lenin had assumed the post of leader, he prevented others from assuming it. It is, of course, impossible to say who might have taken his place had he not been there. Not for nothing did revolutionaries as important as Lunacharsky, Uritsky and Manuilsky, discussing, in the summer of 1917, Lenin's and Trotsky's relative merits, agree that Trotsky had at that time eclipsed Lenin—and this while Lenin was there, on the spot; and although Lenin's influence on the Bolshevik Party was decisive, the October insurrection was in fact carried out according to Trotsky's, not Lenin's plan. If neither Lenin nor Trotsky had been there, someone else might have come to the fore.'[18]

The argument cannot by definition be conclusively settled since, as Deutscher also notes, the historian 'cannot re-enact the revolution, keep Lenin out of the spectacle, and see what happens'.[19] Even so, some suppositions are more reasonable than others; and the supposition that Lenin was *not* indispensable, that someone else *could* have played his role in 1917, is very weak indeed. Lenin was by no means alone in advocating the policies which ultimately prevailed and which made the October Revolution possible. As Stephen Cohen has noted in his biography of Bukharin, 'Lenin and the Bolshevik Left, of which Bukharin was the most prominent representative, found themselves in basic agreement on major questions confronting the party in 1917'.[20] But neither of the two groups which he mentions as representing the 'radical' element in the Bolshevik party, the young left-wing Bolsheviks and the Trotskyists, who entered the party in the summer of 1917, were in a position to carry its leadership with them. No one was in a position to do so in 1917 except Lenin, and Lenin himself had a hard enough time of it. There is simply no warrant for the view that Trotsky or anyone else had the standing required for the purpose. An argument based on the 'optical illusion' concept *can* be mounted, but it would have to rely on the proposition that, had Lenin not led the Bolshevik party and shaped it as he did *in the previous years*, there would have been room for someone else to do so and to assume the position of authority and prestige which Lenin achieved over the years. This is not unreasonable, unlike the notion that if Lenin had not for some reason reached the Finland Station, someone else would have taken his place and achieved the same results. It is clearly possible that, had Lenin never been heard of, the people who led Russian Social Democracy at the turn of the century would have found themselves outflanked on their left, that the need to create a party of a more or less 'Leninist' type would have been met, *and* that all the rest would have followed as well. It is possible, but the argument is extremely strained and overburdened with hypothetical clauses. Nor does it affect the point that Lenin *was* indispensable in 1917. Trotsky's own view of the matter appears the more reasonable one; and it does not, as will be argued presently, do nearly as much violence to historical materialism as Deutscher feared.

III

The third and most difficult problem which 'the role of the individual in history' poses to Marxist historiography and to historical materialism concerns the element of 'acceleration' and 'delay' which 'accidents', Marx said, bring to 'the general course of development'; and to this may be related the notion that accidents are 'compensated' for by other 'accidents'. As I noted earlier, the clear implication (and it might even be said the purpose) of these propositions is to devalue the significance of, among other things, individual intervention in the historical process. It is obviously possible to concede the point that individuals can 'make a difference', and that which individual is in charge also 'makes a difference'; and yet to hold that this is not, 'ultimately', 'in the long run' or 'essentially', of really great historical significance, because the effect of individual action can 'only' be to accelerate or delay a given process, or because of the compensation for one 'accident' by another, and so on. It is this which needs discussion.

In his reference to this thesis in *What is History?*, Professor E.H. Carr notes an 'ingenious analogy' which Trotsky once used to reinforce it: 'The entire historical process,' Trotsky wrote 'is a refraction of historical law through the accidental. In the language of biology, we might say that the historical law is realized through the natural selection of accidents.'[21]

Professor Carr describes this theory as 'unsatisfactory and unconvincing'; and while he also suggests that 'the role of accident in history is nowadays seriously exaggerated', he nevertheless goes on to say that 'it exists, and to say that it merely accelerates or retards, but does not alter, is to juggle with words'. Nor, he adds, 'do I see any reason to believe that an accidental occurrence—say, the premature death of Lenin at the age of 54—is automatically compensated by some other accident in such a way as to restore the balance of the historical process'.[22]

This seems to me to be right, and it has the advantage of opening up the issue rather than foreclosing it. Before proceeding further with the implications of the argument, however, I want to discuss briefly the way in which Professor Carr himself deals with the problem. In effect, what he does is to refuse to assess the significance of 'accidents'. He believes that accidents *have* 'modified the course of history' and that 'it is futile to attempt to spirit them away, or to pretend that in some way or other they had no effect'. But he then goes on: 'On the other hand, in so far as they were accidental, *they do not enter into any rational interpretation of history, or into the historian's hierarchy of significant causes'*[23] (my italics); and he gives the following example of what he means, based upon his view of history as 'a process of selection in terms of historical significance':

> 'If you tell the student of history that the struggles in the Soviet Union in the 1920s were due to discussions about the rate of industrialization, or about the best means of inducing the peasants to grow grain to feed the towns, or even the personal ambitions of rival leaders, he will feel that these are rational and historically significant explanations in the sense that they could also be applied to other historical situations, and that they are 'real' causes of what happened in the sense that the accident of Lenin's premature death was not'.[24]

Professor Carr himself notes the dangers that this method holds of 'undue subjectivism'; and the point is emphasized by his reference, as part of his 'rational and significant explanation', to the 'personal ambitions of rival leaders'. For taking these as significant for historical outcomes very definitely reintroduces the 'accidental' factor into the historical process—Trotsky was ill at a critical moment, Zinoviev was vain, Bukharin lacked consistency, and so on.

Still, it may well be that the 'causes' which Professor Carr adduces in the above quotation should be treated as being of a different order than the 'cause' represented by Lenin's premature death: there is only so much that can be done with that fact. But it does seem unduly restrictive to refuse to consider it *at all* as having had some causal significance for the subsequent history of the Soviet Union. That refusal also has a secondary consequence, namely the strengthening of the thesis of the inevitability of Stalinism: not to take account of the possibility that things would have been materially different had Lenin lived is helpful to the view that things were not only as they were but that they could not have been different. Such historical reification is not congruent with a 'rational interpretation of history'.

A better way to proceed with the discussion of this issue of 'accidents' may be to look more closely at Marx's claim that 'accidents' form part of the 'general course of development' and at the notion of 'the general course of development' itself.

The formulation clearly encompasses a view of historical processes which has as its main focus given modes of production and the complex of forces which cause these modes of production to grow, to mature, and to decline and be superseded. In the Preface to the *Contribution to the Critique of Political Economy* from which I have already quoted, Marx also writes that 'at a certain stage of their development, the material forces of production in society come in conflict with the existing relations of production . . . from forms of development these relations turn into their fetters. Then occurs a period of social revolution . . . '.[25]

This is the essence of the Marxist theory of historical change and of historical dynamics. The concept of 'fetters' may be somewhat misleading in so far as it carries the suggestion that a situation has been reached when the mode of production and society at large are tightly bound, unable to move forward, paralyzed. This is clearly not what is involved: it is rather that the discrepancy between the material forces of society and existing relations of production makes it impossible for significant forces in society to achieve their purposes and to fulfil what they deem to be their interests. As for the notion of 'social revolution', it too needs to be interpreted flexibly and must not be taken to mean that at one particular moment discontented classes will move as a man to the assault of a hated system, with a clear perception and a complete programme of alternatives. 'Social revolution' is obviously a much more complex, messy, uncertain, protracted process than this, with many contradictory features in its economic, social, political and cultural manifestations. The actual displacement of the forces which have hitherto held sway in the given system is only one moment—though certainly a crucial moment—in that process.

In this interpretation of historical processes, Marx's view of 'accidents' as forming 'part of the general course of development' may well be justified: this is the kind of history that is concerned with centuries rather than decades and that has as its frame of reference large movements and changes that are the historical equivalents of geological shifts. Thus, to take an obvious example, in the whole debate on the transition from feudalism to capitalism, individual actors and specific events barely figure at all: and so it is with Marxist histories of whole epochs.[26] Large aggregates of people—classes—do figure in 'the general course of development', but mostly as anonymous actors in a vast play which has no genuinely leading actors but only crowd scenes. Such actors as are identified as individuals only make a fleeting appearance and do not make a decisive difference—or even a great difference—to the unfolding and the outcome of the play itself.

What this suggests is that there is *one kind of history* where the role of individuals and the impact of any given event are not large, or at least not decisive and never can be. They may—at the most—be described as 'accelerating' or 'delaying' the general course of development'.

'But there is *another kind of history*, where individuals and events do make a very large and very direct difference, and greatly affect the course of the historical process over a significant period of time —say, for the sake of illustration, something like a hundred years, though it is not necessary to be particularly precise here.

There are no names to differentiate these two kinds of history, but there ought to be. Perhaps the former might be called *transgenerational history*, since its concern is mainly with movements, trends, tendencies, transformations whose duration must be reckoned in centuries rather than decades. The latter kind of history might be called *generational history*, since it deals precisely with a span of time that covers a relatively limited number of generations.

The relationship between these two kinds of history presents a number of problems. There is a banal sense in which it may be said that history is a 'seamless web', and that the decades and the centuries run into one another to form epochs and millennia in an 'uninterrupted' way. But this does not provide any help in explaining the relationship between the 'general course of development' and specific events and interventions.

This relationship is in fact unequal: generational history is very deeply affected by transgenerational history, though in ways that are complex, often indirect, and difficult to identify; while transgenerational history is very little affected and may at a certain level be said not to be affected at all by the actions, episodes and events comprising part of generational history. This requires some further explanation.

Transgenerational history provides a framework, a spectrum, a terrain in which the actions, events and episodes of generational history occur; and it 'determines' to a very considerable degree not only the outcome of occurrences but also, so to speak, the occurrence of occurrences. Certain events will occur at a particular point of time or within a span of time because long-range historical developments—transgenerational history—made them possible (but not inevitable); and the same point roughly holds for their outcome and effects. In *this* history, the play is only written in broad outline; the actors can help shape the plot as they go along, and some may give it an unexpected turn or an unanticipated twist. The play is the whole historical epoch; but within that epoch, there is room for subplays and subplots, which acquire a 'life of their own'. Transgenerational history does affect, shape, influence and situate the occurrence and outcome of generational history, but not so as to foreclose contingencies of every sort and accidents that may be more or less significant, and that are sometimes very significant in terms of that generational history. The issue here, it should also be stressed, is not only determination *and* contingency but the determination *of* contingency. Whether contingency plays a larger or smaller part, what forms it assumes, and the outcomes which it produces, are themselves issues largely 'determined' by a combination of economic, social, political and institutional factors having a different degree of importance at different times. How far in this combination of factors the 'economic' one is primary 'in the last instance' or, as I think more meaningful, 'in the first instance' is an issue that does not concern me here. The point here is that transgenerational history *suffuses* generational history.

If one looks at the question the other way round, on the other hand, the relationship is much more problematic. How far the events of generational history affect transgenerational history is by no means clear. Marx's notion of acceleration and delay of the 'general course of development' may be of some help but cannot be taken very far; and it may indeed be not much more than a convenient way of avoiding a more drastic formulation of the matter, namely that the impact of specific events and interventions upon transgenerational history may be fairly small, possibly not even that. In other words, the impact of specific events, individuals and 'accidents' upon the historical process may be considerable in the relatively short run, but not in the longer run. To push this further, it may even be possible to speak of an historical disjunction between the two histories. This is not intended to suggest that history is a series of unrelated events or epochs, but simply that an event or action, 'accidental' or not, which is of great significance for one period of time becomes less and less significant as time goes on and ultimately ceases to have any significance.

The point may again be illustrated by the case of Lenin and 1917. I have already argued that there was no substitute for Lenin at the time. On this assumption, it seems to me right to advance two seemingly incompatible theses. The first is that Lenin changed the course of world history, given of course the opportunity that was afforded to him by a combination of conditions and circumstances that alone made his intervention possible and effective.

The second thesis is that it is by no means clear how greatly Lenin changed world history *in a transgenerational perspective*. For all its contingent features, the Bolshevik Revolution occurred within a context of developments on a global scale fostered by capitalism over a period of hundreds of years; these developments were making, and are making, for the supersession of capitalism in the more or less long run. The argument by now is what will supersede it and how. The Bolshevik Revolution may have accelerated or delayed this process: the former view has been the more common one, but an equally good case could be made for the latter, and neither is of course susceptible to demonstration. But in any case, the forces and tendencies making for the supersession of capitalism were not created by the Bolshevik Revolution and would have made their way into the twentieth century (or the twenty-first) even if the revolution had never occurred, as it well might not have.

Both perspectives are right. The Bolshevik Revolution *was* an event of massive importance for the twentieth century, and will most likely continue to weigh upon history well beyond it, but with less and less force, to the point where it will have worked itself into the tissue of time; and the link which it created with subsequent history will then disappear.

From this point of view, the element of contingency and 'accident', and the 'role of the individual in history' are of very little consequence. However, the long-range determinism which this entails, even though it so drastically reduces the significance in time of the actions which individuals undertake and of the events in which they

are involved, does not in the least invite the 'fatalism' which opponents of historical materialism have said it must engender. For the
history which individuals live is not that of two centuries hence but
the history of yesterday, today and tomorrow; and the posterity
which enters into their perspective is that of tomorrow and the day
after, and possibly the day after that, but not the posterity represented by twenty generations hence. Nobody really worries about
that. Insofar as individuals are concerned to help shape the future at
all and to 'make a difference', the fact that long-range historical
processes are beyond their control is not very likely to affect their
attitudes and actions in the slightest degree. The *relevant* historical
processes are not 'determined' in such a way as to turn individuals
into mere executants of impersonal forces and into 'bearers' of processes over which they have no influence. On any reasonable
reckoning, there is enough 'openness' in generational history to
make the actions of individuals count and their involvement meaningful and significant. In generational history, individuals always
enjoy a certain degree of autonomy: the constraints upon them are
real enough, but not totally compelling or imprisoning or paralysing.

Nor is the notion of acceleration or delay to be taken, in relation
to generational history, to imply an effect of necessarily minor significance. On the contrary, an intervention which can produce such
results presents a strong inducement to action, which is in no way
dimmed by the knowledge that tendencies are at work which will
ultimately prove irresistible: 'ultimately' is a long time hence, and to
accelerate or delay its arrival by two, three or even more generations
is enough of a challenge and spur.

This is further and very greatly reinforced by the fact that, while
processes may in the long range be 'determined' and irresistible, the
forms in which they manifest themselves at different times in the
course of development are not finally and precisely fixed and are
susceptible to human intervention. Thus, I believe that the forces
which are making for the supersession of capitalism are doing so in
the direction of collectivist systems of one sort or another. But what
sort is by no means 'determined' and matters very greatly. Labels
like 'collectivism' or 'socialism' or any such can be stamped on very
different forms of regime, from socialist democracy at one end of
the spectrum to Stalinism at the other; these forms do comprise part

of the realm of generational history and are capable of modification by human intervention.

The conclusion to be drawn from the argument is as follows: on the one hand, historical materialism, in its classical Marxist version, may well have allowed *too much* room for 'accidents', the 'role of the individual in history', and contingent factors in general, *in the perspective of transgenerational history*. It is understandable that Marx and Engels should have felt driven to make concessions in order to soften the 'determinism' of their position, but these concessions were unnecessary and are in any case unsatisfactory. The idea of 'compensation' of 'accidents' is a good illustration of the kind of off-hand way in which Marx sought to deal with phenomena that were obviously important and that required assimilation into his broad scheme of historical explanation, yet cannot thus be adequately assimilated.

On the other hand, it also seems to me that Marxism, *in the perspective of generational history*, has not allowed *enough* room for 'accidents' and for the 'role of the individual in history'. In that context, the impact of what may be called partially determined contingency has often been much more considerable than classical Marxist and subsequent Marxist historiography has tried to accommodate.

Finally, I want to revert briefly to the question of what 'circumstances and conditions' make it more rather than less likely that 'accidents' and individuals will have a significant impact upon the shape of events; in other words, what it is that produces 'structural opportunities' rather than 'structural constraints'.

As I have already noted, Marx suggested in *The Eighteenth Brumaire* that it was the class struggle in France which enabled Napoleon to play the 'hero role'; and no doubt this was so. But in trying to determine, in broad terms, when contingencies are likely to be significant, I think that class struggle needs to be seen in the broader context of class hegemony; for it is class hegemony and the degree to which it is assured or under threat that matters here.

Class struggle is a permanent feature of all class societies, though the forms it assumes vary greatly from period to period and from country to country. The question is whether it constitutes a challenge to the dominant class or classes and to the social order that marks their dominance. In periods when a class or a combination of classes is more or less secure in its hegemonic hold upon the social order, class struggle will be part of 'normal' politics and such 'accidents' as may occur—or rather as *will* certainly occur—will be fairly easily absorbed. Individual intervention, though by no means negligible, will similarly be of relatively limited scope. Dominant classes will not need or want 'saviours'; and subordinate classes will not want to heed the appeal of would-be revolutionary leaders. Such periods may not be at all peaceful and may in fact witness class conflicts of an acute kind. But the prevailing hegemony will nevertheless prevent 'accidents', however serious, from causing a major conflagration or even from threatening one.

Conversely, it is in periods when such hegemony is no longer secure and when large sections of the subordinate classes have come to believe that great changes are not only necessary but possible that 'accidents' and individual intervention may assume very large significance and impact. In short, and roughly speaking, effective hegemony and significant contingency stand in inverse relation to one another—the more effective the one, the less significant the other.

Postscript

The preceding argument about the relatively small impact of 'generational history' upon 'transgenerational history' needs to be qualified in one very large respect—in relation to the possibility of nuclear war. The advent of the nuclear age, developments in the technology of nuclear weapons, and the possible use of these weapons in a war between the superpowers, all need to be inscribed in the framework of 'transgenerational history'. However, the actual occurrence of a nuclear war between the superpowers, in the course of 'generational history', would have an immense impact upon 'transgenerational history', possibly to the point of decisively changing its course. This unique feature of twentieth-century history does not seem to me to invalidate the general argument: but it is not necessary to insist that it is nevertheless a large qualification.

Political Action, Determinism, and Contingency 153

1. J.B. Bury, *Selected Essays*, Cambridge 1930, p.66.
2. K. Marx, *The Eighteenth Brumaire of Louis Bonaparte*, in *Surveys From Exile*, Harmondsworth 1973, p.146.
3. 'Preface' to *A Contribution to the Critique of Political Economy*, in Marx and Engels, *Selected Works*, London 1968, p.182.
4. Marx and Engels, *Werke*, Stuttgart 1960, vol. 7, p.273.
5. *The Eighteenth Brumaire* p.144, italics in text. See also his remark in *The Class Struggles in France*: 'Every social epoch needs its great men and if it does not find them it invents them, as Helvetius said.' (*Surveys From Exile*, pp. 93-94.)
6. Marx and Engels, *Selected Works*, Moscow 1949, vol. 2, p.421.
7. Marx and Engels, *Selected Correspondence*, Moscow n.d., p.550.
8. G. Plekhanov, *The Role of the Individual in History*, Moscow 1944, p.43.
9. *Selected Correspondence*, p.550.
10. S. Hook, *The Hero in History*, Boston 1943, p.79.
11. Trotsky has a glittering chapter on the English, the French and the Russian monarchies at their time of crisis in his *History of the Russian Revolution*, London 1965, ch. 6, 'The Death Agony of the Monarchy'.
12. F. Stern, ed., *The Path to Dictatorship: 1918-1933*, London 1966, p.xviii.
13. See, for example, R. Medvedev, *Let History Judge*, London 1971, *passim*.
14. Trotsky, pp.343. 344.
15. I. Deutscher, *The Prophet Outcast*, London 1963, p.241.
16. *Ibid.*, p.242, italics in text.
17. *Ibid.*, p.242.
18. *Ibid.*, pp.244-45.
19. *Ibid.*, p.242.
20. S. Cohen, *Bukharin and the Bolshevik Revolution*, London 1974, p.47.
21. E.H. Carr, *What is History*, London 1961, p.96. The quotation is from Trotsky, *My Life*, London 1930, p.422.
22. *Ibid.*, p.96.
23. *Ibid.*, p.97, emphasis added.
24. *Ibid.*, pp.99-100.
25. Marx, *'Preface'*, p.182.
26. See, for example, P. Sweezy *et al., The Transition from Feudalism to Capitalism*, NLB, London 1976, or R. Brenner, 'Agrarian Class Structure and Economic Development in Pre-industrial Europe', *Past and Present*, February 1976, and the debate his article has engendered. See also P. Anderson, *Passages from Antiquity to Feudalism*, NLB, London 1974, and *Lineages of the Absolutist State*, NLB, London 1974.

8

The State and Revolution

1970

The State and Revolution is rightly regarded as one of Lenin's most important works. It addresses itself to questions of the utmost importance for socialist theory and practice, none of which have lost any of their relevance—rather the reverse. And as a statement of the Marxist theory of the state, both before and particularly after the conquest of power, it has, because it was written by Lenin, enjoyed an exceptionally authoritative status for successive generations of socialists, never more so than in recent years, since its spirit and substance can so readily be invoked against the hyper-bureaucratic experience of Russian-type regimes, and against official Communist parties as well. In short, here, for intrinsic and circumstantial reasons, is indeed one of the 'sacred texts' of Marxist thought.

'Sacred texts', however, are alien to the spirit of Marxism, or at least should be; and this is itself sufficient reason for submitting *The State and Revolution* to critical analysis. But there is also another and more specific reason for undertaking such an analysis, namely that this work of Lenin is commonly held, within the Marxist tradition, to provide a theoretical and indeed a practical solution to the all-important question of the socialist exercise of power. My own reading of it suggests, for what it is worth, a rather different conclusion: that *The State and Revolution*, far from resolving the problems with which it is concerned, only serves to underline their complexity, and to emphasize something which the experience of more than half a century has in any case richly—and tragically—served to confirm, namely that the exercise of socialist power remains the Achilles Heel of Marxism. This is why, in a year which will witness so much legitimate celebration of Lenin's genius and achievements, a critical appraisal of *The State and Revolution* may not come amiss. For it is only by probing the gaps in the argument which it puts forward that the discussion of issues which are fundamental to the socialist project may be advanced.

The basic point upon which the whole of Lenin's argument rests, and to which he returns again and again, derives from Marx and Engels. This is that while all previous revolutions have 'perfected' (i.e. reinforced) the state machine, 'the working class cannot simply lay hold of the state machinery and wield it for its own purposes'; that it must instead smash, break, destroy that machinery. The cardinal importance which Lenin attaches to this idea has often been taken to mean that the purpose of *The State and Revolution* is to counterpose violent revolution to 'peaceful transition'. This is not so. The contraposition is certainly important, and Lenin did believe (much more categorically than Marx, incidentally) that the proletarian revolution could not be achieved save by violent means. But as the Italian Marxist Lucio Colletti* has recently noted, 'Lenin's polemic is not directed against those who do not wish for the seizure of power. The object of his attack is not *reformism*. On the contrary, it is directed against those who wish for the seizure of power but not for the destruction of the old state as well.'[1] 'On the contrary' in the above quotation is too strong: Lenin is *also* arguing against reformism. But it is perfectly true that his main concern in *The State and Revolution* is to attack and reject any concept of revolution which does not take literally Marx's view that the bourgeois state must be smashed.

The obvious and crucial question which this raises is what kind of post-revolutionary state is to succeed the smashed bourgeois state. For it is of course one of the basic tenets of Marxism, and one of its basic differences with anarchism, that while the proletarian revolution must smash the old state, it does not abolish the state itself: a state remains in being, and even endures for a long time to come, even though it begins immediately to 'wither away'. What is most remarkable about the answer which Lenin gives to the question of

---

*This description of Colletti requires correction: he has for some considerable time now been strongly anti-Marxist.

the nature of the post-revolutionary state is how far he takes the concept of the 'withering away' of the state in *The State and Revolution*: sò far, in fact, that the state, on the morrow of the revolution, has not only *begun* to wither away, but *is already at an advanced stage of decomposition*.

This, it must be noted at once, does not mean that the revolutionary *power* is to be weak. On the contrary, Lenin never fails to insist that it must be very strong indeed, and that it must remain strong over an extended period of time. What it does mean is that this power is not exercised by the state in the common meaning of that word, i.e., as a separate and distinct organ of power, however, 'democratic'; but that 'the state' has been turned from 'a state of bureaucrats' into 'a state of armed workers' (p.334).* This, Lenin notes, is 'a state machine nevertheless', but 'in the shape of armed workers who proceed to form a militia involving the entire population' (p.336). Again, 'all citizens are transformed into hired employees of the state, which consists of the armed workers' (p.336); and again, 'the state, that is, the proletariat armed and organized as the ruling class' (p.308). Identical or similar formulations occur throughout the work.

In *The Proletarian Revolution and the Renegade Kautsky*, written after the Bolshevik seizure of power, Lenin fiercely rejected Kautsky's view that a class 'can only dominate but not govern'. 'It is altogether wrong, also,' Lenin wrote, 'to say that a class cannot govern. Such an absurdity can only be uttered by a parliamentary *cretin* who sees nothing but bourgeois parliaments, who has noticed nothing but "ruling parties".'[2] *The State and Revolution* is precisely based on the notion that the proletariat *can* 'govern', and not only 'dominate', and that it must do so if the dictatorship of the proletariat is to be more than a slogan. 'Revolution', Lenin also writes, 'consists not in the new class commanding, governing with the aid of the *old* state machine, but in this class *smashing* this machine and commanding, governing with the aid of a *new* machine. Kautsky blurs over this *basic* idea of Marxism, or he does not understand it at all' (p.347). This new 'machine', as it appears in *The State and*

---

*All quotations from *The State and Revolution* are taken from V.I. Lenin, *Selected Works*, London 1969 and the page reference is given in parentheses. Unless otherwise specified, all italics are in the text.

Revolution is the state of the armed workers. What is involved here, to all appearances, is *unmediated* class rule, a notion much more closely associated with anarchism than with Marxism.

This needs to be qualified. But what is so striking about *The State and Revolution* is *how little* it needs to be qualified, as I propose to show.

Lenin strongly attacks the anarchists, insisting on the need to retain the state in the period of the dictatorship of the proletariat. 'We are not utopians,' he writes 'we do not "dream" of dispensing *at once* with all administration, with all subordination' (p.298). But he then goes on:

> The subordination, however, must be to the armed vanguard of all the exploited and working people, *i.e., to the proletariat.* [Emphasis added.] A beginning can and must be made at once, overnight, to replace the specific 'bossing' of state officials by the simple functions of 'foremen and accountants', functions which are already fully within the ability of the average town dweller and can well be performed for workmen's wages. *We,* the workers shall organize large-scale production on the basis of what capitalism has already created, relying on our own experience as workers, establishing strict, iron discipline backed by the state of the armed workers. We shall reduce the role of state officials to that of simply carrying out our instructions as responsible, revocable, moderately paid 'foremen and accountants' (of course, with the aid of technicians of all sorts, types and degree). (p.298)

Clearly, some kind of officialdom continues to exist, but equally clearly, it functions under the strictest and continuous supervision and control of the armed workers; and officials are, as Lenin notes repeatedly, revocable at any time. 'Bureaucrats', in this view, have not been altogether abolished; but they have been reduced to the role of utterly subordinate executants of the popular will, as expressed by the armed workers.

As for a second main institution of the old state, the standing army, it has been replaced, in the words quoted earlier, by armed workers who proceed to form a militia involving the whole population.

Thus, two institutions which Lenin views as 'most characteristic' (p.283) of the bourgeois state machine have been radically dealt with: one of them, the bureaucracy, has been drastically reduced in size and what remains of it has been utterly subdued by direct popular supervision, backed by the power of instant revocability; while the other, the standing army, has actually been abolished.

Even so, Lenin stresses, the centralized state has *not* been abolished. But it takes the form of 'voluntary centralism, of the voluntary amalgamation of the communes into a nation, of the voluntary fusion of the proletarian communes, for the purpose of destroying bourgeois rule and the bourgeois state machine' (p.301).

Here too, the obvious question concerns the *institutions* through which the dictatorship of the proletariat may be expressed. For Lenin does speak in *The State and Revolution* 'of a gigantic replacement of certain institutions by other institutions of a fundamentally different type' (p.293). But *The State and Revolution* has actually very little to say about institutions, save for some very brief references to the Soviets of Workers and Soldiers Deputies.

Lenin reserves some of his choicest epithets for one form of representative institution, namely, 'the venal and rotten parliamentarism of bourgeois society' (p.297). However, 'the way out of parliamentarism is not, of course, the abolition of representative institutions and the elective principle, but the conversion of the representative institutions from talking shops into "working bodies"' (p.296). The institutions which embody this principle are, as noted, the Soviets. On one occasion, Lenin speaks of 'the simple *organization* of the armed people (such as the Soviet of Workers and Soldiers Deputies ...)' (p.329); on another, of 'the conversion of *all* citizens into workers and other employees of *one* huge "syndicate"—the whole state— and the complete subordination of the entire work of this syndicate to a genuinely democratic state, the state of the Soviets of Workers and Soldiers Deputies' (p.334); and the third such reference is in the form of a question: 'Kautsky develops a "superstitious reverance" for "ministers"; but why can they not be replaced, say, by committees of specialists working under sovereign, all-powerful Soviets and Workers and Soldiers Deputies?' (p.346). It must be noted, however, that the Soviets are 'sovereign and all-powerful' in relation to the 'committees' of which Lenin speaks. In regard to their constituents, the deputies are of course subject to recall at any time: 'representation' must here be conceived as operating within the narrow limits determined by popular rule.

The 'state' of which Lenin speaks in *The State and Revolution* is therefore one in which the standing army has ceased to exist; where what remains of officialdom has come to be completely subordinated to the armed workers; and where the representatives of these armed workers are similarly subordinated to them. It is this 'model' which would seem to justify the contention, advanced earlier, that the 'state' which expresses the dictatorship of the proletariat is, already on the morrow of the revolution, at a stage of advanced decomposition.

The problems which this raises are legion; and the fact that they are altogether ignored in *The State and Revolution* cannot be left out of account in a realistic assessment of it. The first of these problems is that of the *political mediation* of the revolutionary power. By this I mean that the dictatorship of the proletariat is obviously inconceivable without *some* degree at least of political articulation and leadership, which implies political organization. But the extraordinary fact, given the whole cast of Lenin's mind, is that the political element which otherwise occupies so crucial a place in his thought, the party, receives such scant attention in *The State and Revolution*.

There are three references in the work to the party, two of which have no direct bearing on the issue of the dictatorship of the proletariat. One of these is an incidental remark concerning the need for the party to engage in the struggle 'against religion which stupefies the people' (p.318). The second, equally incidental, notes that 'in revising the programme of our Party, we must by all means take the advice of Engels and Marx into consideration, in order to come nearer the truth, to restore Marxism by ridding it of its distortions, to guide the struggle of the working class for its emancipation more correctly' (p.310). The third and most relevant reference goes as follows: 'By educating the workers' party, Marxism educates the vanguard of the proletariat, capable of assuming power and *leading the whole people* to socialism, of directing and organizing the new system, of being the teacher, the guide, the leader of all the working and exploited people in organizing their social life without the bourgeoisie and against the bourgeoisie' (p.281).

It is not entirely clear from this passage whether it is the *proletariat* which is capable of assuming power, leading, directing, organizing, etc.; or whether it is the *vanguard* of the proletariat, i.e., the workers' party, which is so designated. Both interpretations are possible. On the first, the question of political leadership is left altogether in abeyance. It may be recalled that it was so left by Marx in his considerations on the Paris Commune and on the dictatorship of the proletariat. But it is not something which *can*, it seems to me, be left in abeyance in the discussion of revolutionary rule—save in terms of a theory of spontaneity which constitutes an avoidance of the problem rather than its resolution. On the other hand, the second interpretation, which fits in better with everything we know of Lenin's appraisal of the importance of the party, serves only to raise the question without tackling it. That question is of course absolutely paramount to the whole meaning of the concept of the dictatorship of the proletariat: what is the relationship between the *proletariat* whose dictatorship the revolution is deemed to establish, and the *party* which educates, leads, directs, organizes, etc.? It is only on the basis of an *assumption* of a symbiotic, organic relationship between the two, that the question vanishes altogether; but while such a relationship may well have existed between the Bolshevik Party and the Russian proletariat in the months preceding the October Revolution, i.e., when Lenin wrote *The State and Revolution*, the assumption that this kind of relationship can ever be taken as an automatic and permanent fact belongs to the rhetoric of power, not to its reality.

Whether it is the party or the proletariat which is, in the passage above, designated as leading the whole people to socialism, the fact is that Lenin did of course assert the former's central role after the Bolsheviks had seized power. Indeed, by 1919 he was asserting its exclusive political guidance. 'Yes, the dictatorship of one party!' he said then. 'We stand upon it and cannot depart from this ground, since this is the party which in the course of decades has won for itself the position of vanguard of the whole factory and industrial proletariat.' In fact, 'the dictatorship of the working class is carried into effect by the party of the Bolsheviks which since 1905 or earlier has been united with the whole revolutionary proletariat.'[3] Later on, as E.H. Carr also notes, he described the attempt to distinguish between the dictatorship of the class and the dictatorship of the party as proof of an 'unbelievable and inextricable confusion of thought',[4] and in 1921 he was bluntly asserting, against the criticisms of the Workers' Opposition, that 'the dictatorship of the proletariat is impossible except through the Communist Party'.[5]

This may well have been the case, but it must be obvious that this is an altogether different 'model' of the exercise of revolutionary power from that presented in *The State and Revolution*, and that it radically transforms the meaning to be attached to the 'dictatorship of the proletariat'. At the very least, it brings into the sharpest possible form the question of the relation between the ruling party and the proletariat. Nor is it even the *party* which is here in question, but rather the party *leadership*, in accordance with that grim dynamic which Trotsky had prophetically outlined after the split of Russian Social Democracy between Bolsheviks and Mensheviks, namely, that the 'party organization [the caucus] at first substitutes itself for the party as a whole; then the Central Committee substitutes itself for the organization; and finally a single "dictator" substitutes itself for the Central Committee.'[6]

For a time after the Revolution, Lenin was able to believe and claim that there was no conflict between the dictatorship of the proletariat and the dictatorship of the party; and Stalin was to make that claim the basis and legitimation of his own total rule. In the case of Lenin, very few things are as significant a measure of his greatness as that he should have come, while in power, to question that identification, and to be obsessed by the thought that it could not simply be taken for granted. He might well, as his successors were to do, have tried to conceal from himself the extent of the gulf between the claim and the reality. That he did not, and that he died a deeply troubled man,[7] is not the least important part of his legacy, though it is not the part of his legacy which is likely to be evoked, let alone celebrated, in the country of the Bolshevik Revolution.

It is of course very tempting to attribute the transformation of the dictatorship of the proletariat, as presented in *The State and Revolution*, into the dictatorship of the party, or rather of its leaders, to the particular circumstances of Russia after 1917—to backwardness, civil war, foreign intervention, devastation, massive deprivation, popular disaffection, and the failure of other countries to heed the call of revolution.

The temptation, it seems to me, ought to be resisted. Of course, the adverse circumstances with which the Bolsheviks had to cope were real and oppressive enough. But I would argue that these circumstances only aggravated, though certainly to an extreme degree, a problem which is *in any case* inherent in the concept of the dictatorship of the proletariat. The problem arises because that dictatorship, even in the most favourable circumstances, is unrealizable without political mediation; and because the necessary introduction of the notion of political mediation into the 'model' considerably affects the latter's character, to say the least. This is particularly the case if political mediation is conceived in terms of single-party rule. For such rule, even if 'democratic centralism' is much more flexibly applied than has ever been the case, makes much more difficult, and may preclude, the institutionalization of what may loosely be called socialist pluralism. This is exceptionally difficult to achieve and may even be impossible in most revolutionary situations. But it is just as well to recognize that unless adequate provision is made for *alternative* channels of expression and political articulation, which the concept of single party rule excludes by definition, any talk of socialist democracy is so much hot air. Single-party rule postulates an undivided, revolutionary proletarian will of which it is the natural expression. But this is not a reasonable postulate upon which to rest the 'dictatorship of the proletariat'. In no society, however constituted, is there an undivided, single popular will. This is precisely why the problem of political mediation arises. The problem need not be thought insuperable, but its resolution requires, for a start, that it should at least be *recognized*.

The question of the party, however, brings one back to the question of the state. When Lenin said, in the case of Russia, that the dictatorship of the proletariat was impossible except through the Communist Party, what he also implied was that the Party must infuse its will into and assure its domination over the institutions which had, in *The State and Revolution*, been designated as representing the armed workers. In 1921 he noted that 'as the governing party we could not help fusing the Soviet "authorities" with the party 'authorities'—with us they are fused and they will be';[8] and in one of his last articles in *Pravda*, written in early 1923, he also suggested that, 'the flexible union of Soviet with party elements', which had been a 'source of enormous strength' in external policy, 'will be at least equally in place (I think, far more in place) if applied to our whole state apparatus.'⁹ But this means that if the party must be strong, so must the state which serves as its instrument of rule. And indeed, as early as March 1918, Lenin was saying that 'for the present we stand unconditionally for the state'; and to the question which he himself put: 'When will the state begin to die away?' he gave the answer: 'We shall have time to hold more than two congresses before we can say, see how our state is dying away. Till then it is too soon. To proclaim in advance the dying away of the state will be a violation of historical perspective.'¹⁰

There is one sense in which this is perfectly consistent with *The State and Revolution*; and another, more important sense, in which it is not. It is consistent in the sense that Lenin always envisaged a strong power to exist after the revolution had been achieved. But it is inconsistent in the sense that he also, in *The State and Revolution*, envisaged this power to be exercised, not by the state as commonly understood, but by a 'state' of armed workers. Certain it is that the state of which he was speaking after the revolution was not the state of which he was speaking when he wrote *The State and Revolution*.

Here too, I believe that simply to attribute the inconsistency to the particular Russian conditions which faced the Bolsheviks is insufficient. For it seems to me that the kind of all-out unmediated popular rule which Lenin describes in the work belongs in fact, whatever the circumstances in which revolution occurs, to a fairly distant future, in which, as Lenin himself put it, 'the need for violence against people in general for the *subordination* of one man to another, and of one section of the population to another, will vanish altogether since people will become accustomed to observing the elementary conditions of social life *without violence* and *without subordination*' (p.328). Until that time, a state does endure, but it is not likely to be the kind of state of which Lenin speaks in *The State and Revolution*: it is a state about which it is not necessary to use quotation marks.

In Lenin's handling of the matter, at least in *The State and Revolution*, two 'models' of the state are contraposed in the sharpest possible way: *either* there is the 'old state', with its repressive, military-bureaucratic apparatus, i.e., the bourgeois state; or there is the 'transitional' type of state of the dictatorship of the proletariat which, as I have argued, is scarcely a state at all. But if, as I believe, this latter type of 'state' represents, on the morrow of a revolution and for a long time after, a short cut which real life does not allow,* Lenin's formulations serve to avoid rather than to meet the fundamental question, which is at the centre of the socialist project, namely the kind of state, without quotation marks, which is congruent with the exercise of socialist power.

In this respect, it needs to be said that the legacy of Marx and Engels is rather more uncertain than Lenin allows. Both men undoubtedly conceived it as one of the main tasks, indeed *the* main task, of the proletarian revolution to 'smash' the old state; and it is also perfectly true that Marx did say about the Commune that it was 'the political form at last discovered under which to work out the economic emancipation of labour'.[11] But it is not irrelevant to note that, ten years after the Commune, Marx also wrote that 'quite apart from the fact that this [i.e., the Commune] was merely the rising of a city under exceptional conditions, the majority of the Commune was in no wise socialist, nor could be.'[12] Nor of course did Marx ever describe the Commune as the dictatorship of the proletariat. Only Engels did so, in the 1891 Preface to *The Civil War in France*: 'Of late, the Social Democratic Philistine has once more been filled with wholesome terror at the words: Dictatorship of the Proletariat. Well and good, gentlemen, do you want to know what this dictatorship looks like? Look at the Paris Commune. That was the Dictatorship of the Proletariat.'[13] But in the same year, 1891, Engels also said, in his 'Critique of the Draft of the Erfurt Programe of the German Social Democratic Party', that 'if one thing is certain it is that our party and the working class can only come to power in the form of the democratic republic. This is even the specific form for the dictatorship of the proletariat, as the Great French Revolution has already shown' (quoted by Lenin in *The State and Revolution*, p.314). Commenting on this, Lenin states that 'Engels repeated here in a particularly striking form the fundamental idea which runs through

---

*This may need qualification in the following sense: *on the morrow of revolution* the problem does often appear to have vanished. The real problems begin to emerge the day after, and the day after that, when the initial impetus and enthusiasm begin to wane and vast new problems and dangers have to be confronted.

all of Marx's works, namely, that the democratic republic is the nearest approach to the dictatorship of the proletariat' (p.314). But the 'nearest approach' is *not* 'the specific form'; and it may be doubted that the notion of the democratic republic as the nearest approach to the dictatorship of the proletariat is a fundamental idea which runs through all of Marx's works. Also, in the Preface to *The Civil War in France*, Engels said of the state that 'at best it is an evil inherited by the proletariat after its victorious struggle for class supremacy, whose *worst sides* the victorious proletariat will have to lop off *as speedily as possible*, just as the Commune had to, until a generation reared in new, free social conditions is able to discard the entire lumber of the state' (quoted by Lenin, *The State and Revolution*, p.320, emphasis added).

It is on the basis of such passages that the Menshevik leader, Julius Martov, following Kautsky, wrote after the Bolshevik revolution that in speaking of the dictatorship of the proletariat, Engels is not employing the term 'to indicate a *form of government*, but to designate the *social structure* of the state power.'[14]

This seems to me to be a misreading of Engels, and also of Marx. For both men certainly thought that the dictatorship of the proletariat meant not only 'the social structure of the state power' but also and quite emphatically 'a form of government '; and Lenin is much closer to them, when he speaks in *The State and Revolution* of 'a gigantic replacement of certain institutions by institutions of a fundamentally different type' (p.293).

The point, however, is that, even taking full account of what Marx and Engels have to say about the Commune, they left these 'institutions of a fundamentally different type' to be worked out by later generations; and so, notwithstanding *The State and Revolution*, did Lenin.

This, however, does not detract from the importance of the work. Despite all the questions which it leaves unresolved, it carries a message whose importance the passage of time has only served to demonstrate: this is that the socialist project is an anti-bureaucratic project, and that at its core is the vision of a society in which 'for the first time in the history of civilized society, the *mass* of the population will rise to take an *independent* part, not only in voting and elections, but *also in the everyday administration of the state*. Under

166

socialism *all* will govern in turn and will soon become accustomed to no one governing' (p.348). This was also Marx's vision, and one of the historic merits of *The State and Revolution* is to have brought it back to the position it deserves on the socialist agenda. Its second historic merit is to have insisted that this must not be allowed to remain a far-distant, shimmering hope that could safely be disregarded in the present; but that its actualization must be considered as an immediate part of revolutionary theory and practice. I have argued here that Lenin greatly overestimated in *The State and Revolution* how far the state could be made to 'wither away' in any conceivable post-revolutionary situation. But it may well be that the integration of this kind of overestimation into socialist thinking is the necessary condition for the transcendence of the grey and bureaucratic 'practicality' which has so deeply infected the socialist experience of the last half century.

1. Lucio Colletti, 'Power and Democracy in Socialist Society,' *New Left Review* 56, July-August 1969, p.19.
2. V.I. Lenin, *The Proletarian Revolution and the Renegade Kautsky*, London 1941, p.24. Italics in text.
3. E.H. Carr, *The Bolshevik Revolution 1917-1923*, London 1960, vol. I, p.230.
4. *Ibid*. p.230.
5. Robert V. Daniels, 'The State and Revolution: A Case Study in the Genesis and Transformation of Communist Ideology,' *The American Slavic and East European Review* (February 1953), vol. 12, no. 1, p.24.
6. I. Deutscher, *The Prophet Armed*, London 1954, p.90.
7. See, e.g., M. Lewin, *Lenin's Last Struggle*, London 1969.
8. Carr, p.223.
9. *Ibid*. p.224.
10. *Ibid*. p.246.
11. K. Marx, *The Civil War in France*, in *Selected Works*, Moscow 1950, vol. I, p.473.
12. K. Marx to F. Domela-Niewenhuis, 22 February 1881, in *Marx-Engels: Selected Correspondence*, Moscow 1953, p.410.
13. *Selected Works*, vol. I, p.440.
14. J. Martov, *The State and the Socialist Revolution*, New York 1938, p.41.

Stalin and After

Some Comments on two books by Roy Medvedev*

Despite their numerous limitations, these two books should be given close attention, particularly by people who think of themselves as part of the Marxist left. Both books deal with matters of crucial importance for socialist theory and practice; and they have been written by a Russian political theorist and historian who, despite his opposition to the Soviet establishment, sees himself as working, so to speak, from within the system. Also, Medvedev writes as a Marxist,[1] and may be taken to represent one tendency in the socialist opposition in the USSR which is of great interest precisely because it seeks reform from within.

How far Medvedev does seek reform from within the system is well indicated by the fact that *Let History Judge*,* which was written between 1962 and 1968, was intended for a Soviet readership and that he tried to get the book published in the Soviet Union. Instead, Medvedev was excluded from the Communist Party and was also soon involved in the organization of a campaign of protest to have his brother, the geneticist Zhores Medvedev, released from a psychiatric hospital where he had been interned for 'personality troubles', as evidenced (obviously) by his book, *The Rise and Fall of T.D. Lysenko*, and by his attack on Soviet bureaucracy in *The Medvedev Papers*. Even so, Roy Medvedev's second book, *De la Démocratie Socialiste*, remains resolutely anchored in the Soviet system: he emphatically proclaims in this book his belief that it is within its

Let History Judge. The Origins and Consequences of Stalinism, London 1972; *De la Démocratie Socialiste*, Paris 1972 (English translation *On Socialist Democracy*, Nottingham 1977). References to *Let History Judge* are indicated by the abbreviation *LHJ*, and to *De la Démocratie Socialiste* by the abbreviation *DS*.

existing framework that reforms must be sought, and that it is perfectly capable of absorbing the kind of reforms which, in his view, would transform the Soviet Union into a 'socialist democracy'.

Of the two books, *Let History Judge* is the more original and important. Stalinism forms an enormous part of the 20th century, one of the forces which have most decisively shaped its history and character. Yet, there have been remarkably few attempts on the left to provide a 'theorization' for it or to work out a political sociology of it. The attempts which have been made to do this mostly derive from or are inspired by Trotsky's own writings on the subject—and they leave much to be explained where they are not positively misconceived. Medvedev does not fill this gap: of course no single man or work could. But he does advance some interesting and suggestive arguments about it—and it should be said that, given the conditions in which his research and writing must have been conducted,[2] his book represents a remarkable intellectual feat as well as a most courageous enterprise.

In effect, the two books address themselves to four main questions: (a) what happened under Stalin? (b) why did it happen? (c) what has happened since Stalin? (d) what is to happen next? It is these questions, as they are dealt with by Medvedev, that I propose to take up here.

Save in some odd quarters, 'Stalinism' has rightly come to stand above all for the massive and arbitrary repression associated with Stalin's rule. This is the sense in which Medvedev uses the term and much of *Let History Judge* is a factual account of Stalinist repression. Although he presents some informative and often very moving documentation which has hitherto remained unpublished, such as extracts from personal depositions, letters and the like, the story which he tells is in essence no longer new. All the same, it is just as well to be reminded of how terrible and monstrous a story it is, the more so since much effort has gone in recent years in trying to blur its horrors.[3]

Three features of the repression may here be highlighted. The first and most obvious is its sheer scale—the fact that millions upon millions of people were subjected to it. Medvedev notes at one point that in the years 1936-39 alone, 'on the most cautious estimates, four to five million people were subjected to repression for political reasons. At least four to five hundred thousand of them—above all the high officials—were summarily shot; the rest were given long terms of confinement. In 1937-38 there were days when up to a thousand people were shot in Moscow alone' (LHJ p.239).

Of course, these were the years of the Great Terror, when pre-war Stalinist repression reached its paroxysm, its moment of extreme hysteria, the years of the great trials and of the great confessions. But repression on a huge scale had begun much earlier[4]—with the 'liquidation' of the *kulaks* and the great upheaval of forced collectivization, and repression on a huge scale proceeded well-beyond the thirties, right up in fact until the death of Stalin in 1953.

In this connection, it is worth noting that Medvedev quotes figures which suggest that for three years of the Civil War, 1918-20, fewer than 13,000 people were shot by the Cheka (ibid., p.390). The source is suspect and the figures may be an under-estimate; and 13,000 people is 13,000 people. But the difference in scale remains nevertheless obvious, and matters greatly.

A second (and related) feature of Stalinist repression is that the overwhelming majority of those whom it struck were innocent of any crime. Speaking of the political trials of the late twenties and early thirties, Medvedev notes that they 'produced a chain reaction of repression, directed primarily against the old technical intelligentsia, against former Cadets who had not emigrated when they could have, and against former members of the Social Revolutionary, Menshevik and nationalist parties'; and he adds that 'not all the repression of those years was unjustified' (ibid., p.137). In other words, some of the people subjected to repression were actually guilty of some of the crimes of which they were accused. It is very likely that this is also true of the repression of later years: in so huge a conglomeration of people imprisoned or shot, it seems reasonable to suppose that *some* must have been guilty of acts against the Soviet regime, and even of the offences of which they were accused. But as Medvedev notes, 'by 1968 all the defendants in the Moscow political trials had been rehabilitated as citizens, and seventeen had also been posthumously restored to Party membership' (ibid., p.181). At any rate, the main point is that the repression for the most part hit entirely innocent people.

Thirdly, and crucial to an appraisal of the nature and meaning of Stalin's rule, there is the fact that those whom the repression hit hardest of all were Party members at all levels of the Soviet system of power. This is one of the features of Stalinism which is probably unique as an historical event: for it devastated all ranks of official-dom in every sphere of Soviet life—political, administrative, managerial, military, scientific, cultural, even the repressive apparatus itself. As Medvedev puts it in regard to the military, 'never did the officer staff of any army suffer such great losses in any war as the Soviet army in this time of peace' (ibid., p.213) i.e. during the late thirties. But the point also applies to all other areas of official life. Stalin 'liquidated' most of the old Bolsheviks: but he also 'liquid-ated' vast numbers of newer Bolsheviks who had come to occupy positions of greater or lesser power and responsibility by the late twenties and thirties, or for that matter by the forties. In Medve-dev's striking formulation, 'the NKVD arrested and killed, within two years, more Communists than had been lost in all the years of the underground struggle, the three revolutions and the Civil War' (ibid., p.234). Among them, incidentally—or rather *not* incident-ally, given what it is likely to have meant for post-war Eastern Europe—were many of the most dedicated and experienced cadres of foreign Communist parties, in exile in the USSR.

All this, and much else which is incredibly tragic or gruesomely bizarre,[5] is well recounted by Medvedev. But important though it is to tell it as it happened, the really big question is why it happened and was allowed to happen.

The main argument which Medvedev is concerned to oppose in explaining why it happened is that Stalinism was the inevitable result of the need to wrench Russia out of her desperate backwardness, and to do this in the most desperately adverse conditions—the human losses of the Civil War, including the loss of so many of the best revolutionaries; the physical devastation of the struggle; the isolation of the USSR; external hostility soon reinforced by the menace of Nazism. In such circumstances of backwardness, priva-tion, isolation and danger, the familiar argument goes, it was idle to expect anything resembling a socialist democratic order to come into being. On the contrary, it was inevitable that, if the Revolution was to be saved and consolidated, a harsh and dictatorial regime must come to prevail, in which many 'excesses' would be committed, and in which the weaknesses of one man or of a group of men, possessed of great power, would be given free play.

In any case, the argument also goes, the Stalin years were not by any means only years of repression, purges and executions. Alongside the excesses and the mistakes, and much more significant because more enduring, there was the enormous development of the Soviet Union, its industrialization, its progress in the economic, social and educational fields, which made it possible for it to withstand the Nazi onslaught which Stalin had predicted ten years earlier when he had spoken of the urgent need to prepare the defence of the USSR by its modernization; and it was also on the foundations laid in those grim pre-war years that it was possible to make good the fearful ravages of the war, and to turn the Soviet Union into the second industrial nation in the world.

The argument is very familiar and it also appears very plausible. This, however, does not mean that it is right, and Medvedev very usefully helps to expose some of its fundamental flaws. These are of critical importance for the whole evaluation of the Soviet experience, and possibly for much else as well.

We must begin by noting that Medvedev does not deny the achievements: indeed, he sometimes tends to overstate them, as when he writes: 'The Communist Party and its chiefs are supposed to educate the masses to independence and a sense of responsibility, to conscious discipline, to democracy and love of freedom, to hatred of injustice and arbitrary rule. And the Party accomplished much in that direction even in the thirties and forties' (ibid., p.537). This and similar judgements, though usually given some additional qualification, seem hardly warranted by the evidence. But however this may be, the point is that what Medvedev denies is not the achievements, but the notion that Stalinism was their necessary pre-condition. On the contrary, what he does say is that Stalinism, far from being such a pre-condition for the development and defence of the Soviet Union, was a frightful encumbrance upon it, and that the achievements occurred *despite* Stalin and the regime to which he gave his name. Nor in any case does he accept the notion that Stalinism, whatever it may or may not have achieved, was inevitable in Russian circumstances.

'I proceed from the assumption,' he writes, 'that different possibilities of development exist in almost every political system and situation. The triumph of one of these possibilities depends not only on objective factors and conditions, but also on many subjective ones, and some of these factors are clearly accidental' (ibid., p.359). This is obviously right, though within certain limits about which Medvedev, in the case of Russia, is rather undecided. Thus, he writes in *Let History Judge*: 'The contest between various alternatives began under Lenin and was bound to grow more intense. But if he had not died in 1924, the victory of genuinely democratic and socialist tendencies would have been more probable than the victory of Stalinism' (ibid., p.360). In *De la Démocratie Socialiste*, on the other hand, he expresses the view that 'administrative methods, a severe centralism and other elements of a "tough" leadership were certainly necessary in the twenties and thirties. But these methods had not been invented by Stalin. They had come into being ever since the time of Lenin' (DS, p.333).

This last quotation seems to me to indicate a much more realistic alternative to Stalinism than that referred to by Medvedev as 'the victory of genuinely democratic and socialist tendencies'. In the circumstances prevailing in Russia after the Revolution and the Civil War, the chances of victory of such tendencies were slim indeed, whether Lenin had lived or died. But the important point which Medvedev is making is that, between this on the one hand and Stalinism on the other, there did exist the possibility of a third alternative, that which he describes as a 'severe centralism and other elements of a "tough" leadership'. A regime with such features (but which could also have included *some* features of socialist democracy) may well have been 'inevitable': but there would have been a very large difference indeed between *such* a regime and the Stalinist regime that actually came into being. The former would have been a long way removed from a socialist democracy; but neither would it have been the monstrous tyranny of Stalinism; and those years of unavoidable storm and stress would in consequence have left a very different imprint upon the Soviet Union, and upon the world socialist movement as well.

Of course, there is no way of 'proving' that there was an alternative. But to insist that Stalinism, with all that it entailed, was the *only* possibility is to give way to the crassest and narrowest kind of retro-dictive determinism; and it is also to fly in the face of the historical evidence. For there *is* proof in plenty that Stalinist repression, quite apart from its human cruelties, retarded Soviet development and actually crippled every area of Soviet life, beginning with Soviet agriculture which has yet to recover from Stalinist collectivization. Nor does it seem particularly extravagant to suggest that, had the Soviet military cadres not been gratuitously decimated on the eve of the war, and had Stalin been willing to heed the many warnings of a coming Nazi attack in the months which preceded it, the war that was won at the cost of 20 million lives might have been won at a rather lower cost—no small matter both for those who died and also to those who survived. As Medvedev puts it, 'Stalin was for thirty years the helmsman of the ship of state, clutching its steering wheel with a grip of death. Dozens of times he steered it onto reefs and shoals and far off course. Shall we be grateful to him because he did not manage to sink it altogether?' (LHJ p.564).

All this obviously brings into very sharp focus Stalin himself, and Medvedev certainly devotes a large amount of attention to Stalin's personal contribution to Stalinism. No doubt, it is very necessary to avoid engaging in an inverted kind of cult of personality, but the focus and the emphasis are nevertheless absolutely justified. For one thing, Stalin did hold absolute personal power and Medvedev is not exaggerating when he says that, though 'he was already called a dictator, a one-man ruler, and not without reason' by the end of the twenties and the early thirties, 'the unlimited dictatorship that he established after 1936-38 was without historical precedent. For the last fifteen years of his bloody career Stalin wielded such power as no Russian tsar ever possessed—indeed no dictator of the past thousand years' (ibid., p.355). Moreover, Medvedev also notes that 'many new documents have confirmed beyond any doubt that Stalin not only knew about all the main acts of repression; they were done on his direct instructions' (ibid., p.293). One example of this is the fact that Stalin (with Molotov) signed some four hundred lists of 'condemnations of the first degree' (i.e. execution by shooting) which bore 'the names of 44,000 people, mostly Party and govern-ment officials, military personnel and cultural leaders' (ibid., p.294). The notion that Stalin was not a central element, indeed *the* central element of the repression is untenable: he was its prime source, its first inspiration.

This is *not* to argue that Stalinism was the work and the responsibility of one man: that too is untenable. But it is nevertheless entirely reasonable, indeed inescapably necessary, to see Stalin as having played a crucial role in the particular character which the Soviet system assumed during the years of his rule: in other words, the system would have functioned very differently without him— even though it would not have been an entirely different system.

By this I mean that Stalinism enormously exacerbated, and pushed to its most extreme and most cruel possibilities, a situation which in any case precluded the establishment of a socialist democracy in a Soviet Union both saddled with a heritage of terrible backwardness *and* left isolated (as well as devastated) in a hostile capitalist world.

All that the notion of 'inevitability' can be taken to mean here (and it is certainly no small matter) is that this combination of circumstances was most likely—was indeed all but certain—to result in the drastic subordination of civil society to political power, as represented by the party, and by the state as the instrument of the party, or rather of the party leaders. The big question, which Stalin resolved in his own way, but which could have been resolved differently, is how far that subordination would go, and what forms it would assume.

It seems to me helpful to stress that there was nothing historically unique in the phenomenon itself. As far as Russia was concerned, it represented no more than the continuation, and the accentuation, of a situation which had been historically typical of Russia, where, as Gramsci put it, 'the State was everything, civil society was primordial and gelatinous'.[6] More widely, Marx's description of the phenomenon of 'Bonapartism' as applied to France in *The Eighteenth Brumaire of Louis Bonaparte* and in *The Civil War in France*, fits here remarkably well, for all the vast differences between the countries concerned. Thus, in the first work, Marx was at pains to emphazise a feature of 'Bonapartism' which was obviously present in the post-revolutionary system in Russia as well, and which may be taken as a critical characteristic of both regimes, namely the vast strengthening and increase of executive and bureaucratic power at the expense of all other elements in society—'this executive power with its enormous bureaucratic and military organization, with its ingenious state machinery, embracing wide strata, with a host of officials numbering half a million, besides an army of another half million, this appalling parasitic body, which enmeshes the body of French society like a net and chokes all its pores'.[7]

As to *why* 'Bonapartism' came to prevail, there is Marx's famous formulation in *The Civil War in France* that 'it was the only form of government possible at a time when the bourgeoisie had already lost, and the working class had not yet acquired, the faculty of ruling the nation',[8] a formulation which, whether valid for France or not, provides a critical clue for an explanation of Russian developments subsequent to the Revolution and the Civil War. For it is precisely the fact that the Russian working class had 'not yet acquired the faculty of ruling the nation', even though it had played a key role in making and defending the October Revolution, which opened the way to that 'substitutism' against which people like Trotsky and Rosa Luxemburg had issued prophetic warnings many years previously. However, it is not enough, and it is indeed misleading, simply to speak of 'substitutism', as if all that was involved was the assumption by an entity called 'the Party' of the role which ought to have been played by the working class. The point is that the Party itself was crippled by the weakness of the working class, a weakness greatly aggravated by the decimation of its best elements in the years of the Civil War. Medvedev quotes Lenin's warning in 1922 that 'the insignificant percent of Soviet and Sovietized workers will drown in this sea of chauvinistic Great Russian riffraff like a fly in milk' (LHJ, p.414); and he himself notes that 'the transformation of the Bolshevik Party from an underground organization to a ruling party would greatly increase petty-bourgeois and careerist tendencies among old Party members and also bring into the Party a host of petty-bourgeois and careerist elements that had previously been outside' (ibid., p.414).

It would in any event have been hard enough to remedy this situation. But as noted earlier, Stalin enormously accentuated all the negative tendencies that were already present before his rise to power. Stalinism in this sense was the product of a situation which it in turn vastly aggravated.

On the other hand, Stalin's personal and peculiar contribution to this situation also included as one of its paradoxical ingredients the extermination of wave after wave of the situation's beneficiaries, as well as of many others. On this, I can do no better than quote Isaac Deutscher, who notes that Stalin 'raged against his own bureaucracy and, on the pretext of fighting Trotskyism and Bukharinism, decimated it in each of the successive purges. It was one of the effects of the purges that they prevented the managerial groups from consolidation as a social stratum. Stalin whetted their acquisitive instincts and wrung their necks . . . While on the one hand the terror annihilated the old Bolshevik cadres and cowed the working class and the peasantry, it kept, on the other, the whole of the bureaucracy in a state of flux, renewing permanently its composition, and now allowing it to grow out of a protoplasmic or amoeboid condition, to form a compact and articulate body with a socio-political identity of its own.'[9]

In this connection, Medvedev refers to a 'strange explanation' of the purges which he first heard in the late fifties, namely that 'many of the people Stalin destroyed had stopped being revolutionaries by the mid-thirties' and that he had 'to get rid of those who were interfering with the further development of the socialist Revolution; he had to push up young officials who were capable of leading the revolution forward' (LHJ, p.313). This thesis, which according to Medvedev, 'has wide currency among Party and State officials, both active and retired' (ibid., p.314), is of course nonsense, not only because, as he suggests, of the indiscriminate and arbitrary nature of the purges, or because the replacements were no better than their predecessors—more important is the fact that the terror, though it killed off vast numbers of 'bureaucrats', as well as many other people, did nothing to weaken the *system* that produced the luxuriant growth of 'bureaucracy'. On the contrary, Stalin greatly strengthened that system in many different ways, and indeed had to do so, since it is impossible to exercise repression on so great a scale and against so many different areas of society without an apparatus adequate to the task: it took a very large number of people's participation to exclude the people from participating in political life or, as far as vast numbers were concerned, from life itself.

Nor was Stalin grudging in his bestowal of advantages and privileges to the 'bureaucrats'. As Medvedev notes, 'in 1937 the pay of

NKVD employees was approximately quadrupled. Previously a relatively low pay scale had hindered recruitment; after 1937 the NKVD scale was higher than that of any other government agency. NKVD employees were also given the best apartments, rest homes and hospitals. They were awarded medals and orders for success in their activities. And, in the latter half of the thirties, their numbers were so swollen as to become a whole army, with divisions and regiments, with hundreds of thousands of security workers and tens of thousands of officers.' (LHJ, p.392). The privileges of which Medvedev speaks were not of course confined to the NKVD: Stalinism *was*, among other things, a system of privileges for 'bureaucrats' in all areas of Soviet life, including intellectual and cultural life, with extraordinary chances of promotion by virtue of the sudden disappearance of superiors: the only major drawback was the extreme insecurity which, under Stalin, attached to all positions of power, at all levels. In Medvedev's words, 'Stalin was not simply a dictator, he stood at the peak of a whole system of smaller dictators; he was the head bureaucrat over thousands of smaller bureaucrats' (ibid., p.416). This incidentally does not mean that Stalin 'represented' this bureaucratic element or was its instrument, as has sometimes been argued. Stalin 'represented' only himself and it was the 'bureaucrats' who were *his* instruments. It was only with his death that they were released from their bondage and that they were able to come into their own as the inheritors of the system he had consolidated, but whose fruits he had so brutally snatched away from so many of them during the years of his rule.

The fact that, for all its fearful attendant risks, Stalin's rule was of such great direct advantage in terms of position and privileges to such a large number of people is one reason why it endured as long as it did. Another is the scale and ruthlessness of the repression, which obviously paralysed most of the potential opposition. But there is another factor, which is an essential part of the whole story, namely that Stalin was able to interweave inextricably his own rule, and the terror that went with it, with the building of 'socialism' in the Soviet Union. Medvedev writes of the 'frightful paradox' that 'thousands upon thousands of people, arrested in 1937-38 on charges of plotting against Stalin and his aides, could be reproached today for insufficient resistance to evil and for excessive faith in their leaders' (ibid., p.401). But then, he also speaks of 'this complex mixture of contradictory feelings—incomprehension and panic, *faith in Stalin* and fear of the terror—[which] fragmented the Party and made it fairly easy for Stalin to usurp total power' (ibid., p.405, my italics).

Matters would no doubt have gone rather differently if Stalin really had sought to pave the way for or been the architect of that Russian 'Thermidor' which Trotsky and the Opposition so greatly feared.[10] Medvedev quotes Trotsky as issuing the warning in 1926, i.e. during the period of the New Economic Policy, that 'the ruling circles are increasingly growing together with the upper strata of Soviet-nepmen society' and that 'the Soviet state could become an apparatus through which power could be moved from its proletarian base and put into the hands of the bourgeoisie, which would then kick aside the Soviet "footstool" and convert its power into a Bonapartist system' (ibid., p.56). Such developments would indeed have deserved the name of a 'Thermidorian' restoration. But instead of moving in directions which would have made this possible, Stalin in 1928 adopted, in however crude and caricatural a form, some of the basic elements of the Opposition's platform, namely the radical speeding up of industrialization and the struggle against the *kulaks* by way of massive collectivization. As Deutscher rightly notes, 'at a stroke the Opposition's dilemmas were immensely aggravated. It became almost ludicrous for its members to chew over old slogans, to clamour for more industrialization, to protest against the appeasement of rural capitalism, and to speak of the threatening Neo-N.E.P. The Opposition either had to admit that Stalin was doing its job for it or it had to re-equip itself and "rearm" politically for any further struggle. Trotsky, Rakovsky, and others were indeed working to bring the Opposition's ideas up to date. But events moved faster than even the most quick-minded of theorists'.[11] The same story was repeated time and again in subsequent years, not because events moved too fast, but because Stalin, whatever else he might or might not be doing, was not preparing a 'Thermidorian' restoration, in any meaningful sense of the notion, and therefore deprived the opposition, outside Russia as well as inside, of its essential argument against him.

Indeed, Stalin and his propaganda machine had little difficulty in turning the argument against the opposition. Not only were the foundations of the Soviet system, the collective ownership of the means of economic life, *not* being undermined: they were being extended into the countryside. Upon these foundations, the propagandists insisted, 'socialism' was being built, and built in the shadow of the ever-growing threat of external aggression—it is of course impossible to underestimate the importance of the fact and threat of Hitler's Germany in this whole story. Yet, here was this ill-assorted band of renegades and traitors (most of the leaders self-confessed ones too) who dared to denounce Stalin (the man who was now described as Lenin's closest and most trusted collaborator) in the name of socialism. The tune is familiar, and needs no extensive rehearsal here. The point to note is its *plausibility*; and the basic element of that plausibility was precisely that the foundations of the system *were* being safeguarded. As to what was being built upon these foundations, it was conceded (though not at all willingly) that mistakes sometimes occurred: but then, was it not Stalin himself who (in circumstances which turned his words into the blackest of humour) insisted repeatedly on the need for criticism and self-criticism?[12]

In the same vein, the fact that the terror struck at so many Party and other cadres was not, as far as popular support was concerned, to Stalin's disadvantage. On the contrary, it made him appear as the ever-vigilant defender of the Revolution against its enemies; and, in a different perspective, Medvedev also cites a *Samizdat* article which suggests that for many workers, Stalinism represented *their* revenge against a host of bureaucratic oppressors: 'such a "Stalinism" is an expression of the hatred of bureaucracy' (DS, p.69). It may well be that this is how it was for many people, themselves unable to organize any means of self-defence.

It was not, in short, by terror alone that Stalin kept himself in power. Nor, as far as the cadres were concerned, was his support based on a simple appeal to careerism and greed. No doubt, there was plenty of that—but there was also much else as well. To reduce the matter to terror on the one hand and to careerism on the other (which Medvedev himself does not do) is to miss some of the basic reasons for the enormous catastrophe which, in the form of Stalinism, blighted Soviet society and the cause of socialism throughout the world.

Let History Judge ends on a relatively optimistic note: notwith-standing the dreadful ravages of Stalinism, 'a solid foundation was laid for a truly socialist democracy' (p.549). In *De la Démocratie Socialiste*, Medvedev discusses what he means by this and shows in the process how great are the reforms that would be needed in the existing regime in order to achieve anything even remotely approxi-mating to it.

The reason for this, as Medvedev occasionally notes with refer-ence to specific aspects of the regime's functioning, is that the Soviet political system, as a system, has not basically changed since Stalin's death. What his successors inherited might perhaps best be des-cribed as a regime of *tyrannical collectivism*: 'collectivism' to denote the fact that his regime was based on collective ownership; and the old-fashioned world 'tyrannical' will do as well as more modern inventions to denote the unbridled power wielded by one man, though that power was expressed through a set of Party and state institutions. Stalin's successors have turned this into a regime of *oligarchical collectivism*, in which a relatively small minority of people rather than one man exercise power through more or less the same set of Party and state institutions, and without any effective check or control from below.

This is by no means to underestimate the vast changes which have occurred since Stalin's death in the operation of the system—most obviously the elimination of mass terror and of wholesale 'liquida-tion' from Soviet life, which is a change indeed, and the consider-able reduction in the power wielded by the apparatus of repression. In this sense, 'de-Stalinization' has a clear and specific meaning; and the changes which have occurred may well justify the applica-tion to the process of 'de-Stalinization' of the notion of 'liberaliza-tion' in a somewhat wider sense—in the sense of a 'loosening up' in the texture of Soviet life.

In another sense, however, the notion of 'de-Stalinization' has always been misleading, insofar as it has been held to include basic changes in the nature of the political system, in the direction of its 'democratization'. But 'liberalization', in this context, and 'democratization' are not synonymous terms, nor are they even necessarily inter-related; and whatever there has been of the former process in the twenty years since Stalin died, there has been very little that is significant of the latter.

The 'democratization' of the Soviet system would require not merely this or that element of reform at the edges, but a fundamental change in what has always been the central feature of the system, namely the absolute and exclusive monopoly of political power exercised by the people in command of the party and state apparatus, or more properly and to avoid confusion, of the party-and-state apparatus. That they have claimed to hold their mandate from the Soviet people and to have its interests at heart, not to speak of the cause of socialism in the world, is neither here nor there. The fact remains that 'democratization' *would* require the end of this kind of monopoly—*either* by the reform of the Communist Party in ways that would introduce into its functioning at all levels what it now so conspicuously lacks, namely a genuine measure of democracy, with the acceptance of open debate between recognized tendencies and factions, which could not only be confined within the party but would find quite naturally its echo outside; *or* it would require an even more drastic 'pluralization' of Soviet political (and intellectual) life, with the acceptance by the Communist Party of competition with other political groupings, and the existence of institutions and organizations that would not be under its control.

In *Let History Judge*, Medvedev, while noting the 'negative tendencies' that result from the 'prolonged existence' of a one-party system, nevertheless suggests categorically that 'of course in the Soviet Union today a change to any sort of multi-party system is not possible or feasible'. But this very fact, he also adds, 'reinforces the needs to create specific safeguards against arbitrary rule and bureaucratic distortions, safeguards built into the structure and working methods of the ruling Party itself' (LHJ, p.384). In *De la Démocratie Socialiste*, on the other hand, the question of one party or more is treated much more tentatively. Medvedev notes that the attempt in 1968 in Czechoslovakia to reconstitute a social-democratic party was denounced in the Soviet press and in part of the Czech press as 'anti-socialist' and 'counter-revolutionary'. But this approach to the question, he suggests, is unrealistic and fails to take into account the difficulties and complexities involved in the building of socialism (p.132). 'One should not,' he wryly notes, 'over-estimate the social and political monolithism of present-day Soviet society' (ibid., p.132). Different political tendencies and currents do exist and could form the basis of new political groupings, organizations and even parties.

What Medvedev is doing here, however circumspectly, is to attack the most sacred of all Soviet cows, namely the 'leading role' (i.e. the political monopoly) exercised by the Communist Party over all aspects of Soviet life. 'We believe', he writes, 'that a certain political "pluralism" would be normal, given the situation in our country' (ibid., p.135). By this, he does not necessarily mean the coming into being of new political parties, but the acceptance, at the very least, of the existence of organizations in which the Communist Party would *not* play the 'leading role'; and he also advocates the publication of newspapers and journals run by representatives of different currents ('I would even say by non-communists', ibid., p.228). Similarly, his programme for the 'democratization' of Soviet life involves a clear demarcation between different elements of the structure of power, based on the belief that 'the continued exercise of legislative and executive power by one organ engenders the hypertrophy of the executive power and transforms the representative organisms into mere appendages of the executive ones' (ibid., p.176). He recognizes that this runs counter to Lenin's own perspectives on the matter (themselves based on Marx's reading of the experience of the Paris Commune), but is persuaded by Soviet experience of the need for the kind of separation of which he speaks.[13]

The 'democratization' which Medvedev wants is not confined to the functioning of the political system and to the liberation of intellectual activity: it reaches out to every area of life, including the process of production. He wants Soviet trade unions to play a much stronger role ('the role of the trade unions in enterprise remains insignificant, the more so as bureaucracy continues to dominate the trade union apparatus', ibid., p.298): he advocates more workers' 'participation'; and he favours experiments to determine the possibility of creating workers' councils, presumably to take charge of production, 'even if only in a few enterprises' (ibid., p.299). But what he has to say on these crucial matters is perfunctory and banal: after all, *everybody* is now in favour of greater workers' involvement in the productive process, including the Soviet leaders, one of whom, and he no less than Prime Minister Kosygin, Medvedev quotes to this effect. But the question, it is fair to say, does not appear to be central to his preoccupations.

'Socialist democracy', as it may be taken to have been understood by Marx, and as it was understood by Lenin (at least by the Lenin of *The State and Revolution*) entails in the economic as well as in all other realms of life a degree of self-government which goes very far beyond anything envisaged by Medvedev in *De la Démocratie Socialiste*. What his proposals and perspectives amount to is the further transformation of Soviet political life into a regime which, to continue along the line of classification adopted earlier, might be described as *democratic collectivism*, the counterpart, in a society in which the means of production are under collective ownership, to bourgeois-democracy in a society where these means are predominantly under private ownership and control. 'Socialist democracy', on this view, would represent a much more advanced social and political system, of which history so far offers no example and of which there is unlikely to be an example for some time to come.

To speak of Medvedev's proposals as amounting to democratic collectivism rather than to the Marxist concept of socialist democracy is in no way to denigrate or belittle these proposals. What was said earlier about the positive nature of the change from tyrannical to oligarchical collectivism applies here with even greater, indeed with very much greater, force; the achievement of something like democratic collectivism, with the new political and civic life this would inject into every area of Soviet society, would in the given context represent an enormous advance on the present—and an advance too, in due course, on capitalist democracy.

There have always been critics of the USSR on the left for whom nothing less than a total upheaval would do, with a workers' revolution establishing a dictatorship of the proletariat based on a resuscitated Soviet system and accompanied by a clear beginning of the withering away of the state. To those possessed of such a vision, Medvedev's perspectives must appear intolerably reformist, gradualist and so on—and they do in fact have these characteristics. For that matter, Medvedev himself explicitly repudiates that current of thought among others in the Soviet opposition which he describes as 'anarcho-communist' and which seeks the immediate replacement of existing state institutions by new organs of 'popular power'.[14] The tragic irony of his own position, however, is that the circumstances in which he writes turn his own proposals, for all their would-be gradualism and moderation, into demands for changes so far reaching as to have distinctly 'revolutionary' overtones.

This might have been much less true if 'liberalization' and 'democratization' had already made substantial inroads into the system. But not only does Medvedev have no illusions on this score—on the contrary, he repeatedly suggests in *De la Démocratie Socialiste* that after an initial period of 'liberalization' following Stalin's death (presumably the Khrushchev period) the current has been flowing the other way—in other words that there has been regression rather than advance; and it is quite clear that he genuinely fears and takes as a real danger the growth in influence and even the possible predominance of 'neo-Stalinist' elements, of the people who are fighting 'not for the widening but for the restriction of socialist democracy, for the hardening of censorship and for the "bringing back into line" of the social sciences, literature and art, for the strengthening of bureaucratic centralism in all domains of public life' (DS, p.71).

However, 'neo-Stalinism' is only one current in the Party, and its predominance is not an accomplished fact but one possibility amongst others. True, the 'bureaucratic' style pervades Soviet society: 'By the power which they have at their disposal, by their standard of living and the privileges which they enjoy, those who belong to the upper layers of the state and party apparatus, of the economy and of the army, are still a long way removed from the workers at the lower and intermediate levels, and this affects their behaviour, their habits and their psychology' (DS, p.335). But Medvedev sees most of these people as representing a 'conservative', rather than a frankly reactionary, 'neo-Stalinist' element in the political system. He rejects the thesis that they form a 'new class', though he refers to the possibility that by a slow (and still reversible) evolution, such a new class may be in the process of formation. (ibid., p.340). However, he believes that the 'bureaucrats' are much more vulnerable than is often suggested, and so is their susceptibility to pressure from below. What is needed is for the pressure to be applied; and he hopes that the tendency of which he is a declared member, that of the 'Party democrats',[15] will in the coming years help to supply that pressure and even turn it into a mass movement. In any case, even though this tendency has until now remained practically unrepresented in the higher circles of the Party, it is not, he suggests, without a fair measure of support in various sections of the party and governmental apparatus (ibid., p.81).

To a large extent, Medvedev's qualified optimism is based on the fact that the dynamic of Soviet economic development is revolutionizing the productive process, and therewith the producers themselves. Thus he writes that 'by the end of the 20th century, there will certainly no longer be in the Soviet Union either peasants or workers or employees or intellectuals in the old meaning of these terms. The population of our country will be made up of highly educated and cultivated workers, whose activity will be both manual and intellectual, and who will participate in industrial production, in agricultural work, in the management of industry and in public affairs' (ibid., p.355).

The question here is not whether Medvedev exaggerates the pace of the changes that he sees coming; nor even whether he is right about the picture he presents of its results. Much more important is his insistence—which is undoubtedly right—that the great changes which are occurring and will go on occurring in the productive process will have vast consequences for Soviet society. Medvedev does not argue that these consequences are *bound* to be in the direction of the 'democratization' of Soviet political and civic life—only that the changes cannot but sharpen the multitude of problems which the present 'bureaucratic' order is unable to resolve: and he is also saying that while a hardening of the regime as a response to this is one possibility,[16] its 'democratization' is another.

Furthermore, Medvedev believes that if radical change is to come, it must be envisaged as coming through the reform of the existing system rather than through a revolutionary upheaval whose nature is as vague as its prospects are remote. This is also the view which Isaac Deutscher, writing immediately after Stalin's death, expressed in *Russia After Stalin* and which he continued to express in later works;[17] and Deutscher himself was only echoing a hope which had been held in the ranks of the Opposition long before Stalin died.

It can hardly be said that the last twenty years have been particularly kind to these perspectives. But this does not mean that, if there is to be 'democratization' at all, these perspectives of 'reform from within', of course brought about or furthered by pressure from outside, namely from workers and others, do not remain the most likely (or the least unrealistic) of the ways in which it can occur. Naturally, there are people on the left who *know* that these perspectives are absurd. But then, one remembers that, in 1967, there were also people on the left who *knew* that the idea of reform from within in Czechoslovakia was just as absurd, and that wherever else it might occur, it couldn't occur there, since Novotny and his people had the whole system under impermeable control. Yet there *was* a Czech spring; and it took Soviet intervention to crush the flowering of its promise. Of course the Soviet Union is not Czechoslovakia, and there is at present no sign whatever of the coming of a Soviet spring —rather the reverse. Medvedev and those who, like him, want a socialist alternative for their country are struggling against enormously powerful and deeply-entrenched interests, forces and traditions. They may not succeed in a relevant future. But if or when a Soviet spring does come, there will be no 'Brezhnev doctrine' and no Soviet tanks to stop it; and the long and tortured pre-history of Soviet socialism will then at last have come to an end.

1. In this Preface to *De la Démocratie Socialiste*, Georges Haupt suggests that 'Medvedev's philosophy is that of a moralist in Leninist clothes whose mind recalls tha of R.W. (sic) Tawney, one of the Christian theoreticians of British socialism in the 20th century' (p.30). This is inaccurate. There may be argument as to what kind of a Marxist Medvedev is; but he proclaims himself as one and his thinking is miles apart from Tawney's.
2. These conditions may also help to account for the blots which sometimes mar his work—see, for instance, his misrepresentation of Isaac Deutscher's work (LHJ, pp.559-60).
3. So much so that Medvedev is able to write that 'most of our students and senior school-children know nothing of Stalin's crimes' (DS, p.71). He gives many examples of the ways in which attempts have been made, particularly in recent years, to qualify the condemnation of 'the cult of personality' and of Stalin's contribution to the horrors of Stalinism. It was actually possible for two historians to write in 1966 that, in the years of the terror, 'the Party and its local organs lived their own active, autonomous life. In continuous conflict with the unhealthy tendencies engendered by the cult of personality, *the genuinely Leninist principles* on which the Party was founded invariably won out' (LHJ, p.355. Italics in text).
Medvedev is also understandably and rightly bitter about the Chinese attitude of broad approval for Stalin, notwithstanding his 'mistakes' which are grudgingly

acknowledged. For a recent example of the Chinese evaluation of Stalin, see S. Lee 'Conversation with Premier Chou-En-Lai', *Social Praxis*, 1973, Vol. 1, No. 1, in which the latter is reported as 'evaluating' Stalin as '70% good, 30% bad' (p.6).

Nor of course is this a Chinese quirk. Many 'anti-revisionists', including some who are members of Communist Parties, have tended to see the defence of Stalin as part of their struggle against their party's 'revisionism'. The notion is grotesque, but not particularly surprising; and it emphazises the need to continue the exposure of the reality of Stalinism.

4. As early as 1933, the Leningrad Branch of the Communist Academy was able to report that it had rooted out 'Trotskyism, Luxemburgism and Menshevism, not only on the historical but also on the economic, agrarian, literary and other fronts' (LHJ, p.143). But the authors had obviously underestimated the magnitude of the task.

5. Such as the fact that the wife of Kalinin, the President of the Soviet Union, was kept in prison for seven years. In Medvedev's words, 'the epoch of the cult is epitomized in that situation: the country had a President whose wife was kept in a concentration camp' (LHJ, p.349). Something like this also happened to Molotov's wife after the war. There are endless examples of individual and collective repression which convey this element of the bizarre (not to speak of the gruesome) in Stalinism. Thus, 'in 1938 I.A. Akulov, one-time procurator of the USSR, fell while skating and suffered an almost fatal concussion. On Stalin's suggestion, outstanding surgeons were brought from abroad to save his life. After a long and difficult recovery, Akulov returned to work, whereupon he was arrested and shot' (LHJ, p.291).

6. A. Gramsci, *Selections from the Prison Notebooks*, London 1971, p.238.

7. K. Marx, *The Eighteenth Brumaire of Louis Bonaparte*, in K. Marx and F. Engels, *Selected Works*, Moscow 1950, Vol. I, p.301. 'Bonapartism' is here used without military connotations: it is as well to remember that, while the first Bonaparte was a great military figure, Louis Bonaparte hardly qualifies at all. 'Bonapartism' here means above all the extreme inflation of executive power at the expense of all other organs of the state, and the subordination of society to the state.

8. K. Marx, *The Civil War in France*, in *Ibid.*, Vol. I, p.470.

9. I. Deutscher, *The Prophet Outcast*, London 1963, p.306.

10. For a discussion of the manner in which Trotsky and the Opposition envisaged a Russian 'Thermidor', see *ibid.*, passim; and also *The Prophet Unarmed*, London 1959, pp.314-16.

11. *The Prophet Outcast*, p.66.

12. See, for instance, LHJ, p.548.

13. Even if the one-party system is maintained, Medvedev notes, representative institutions could be given vigour, particularly the Supreme Soviet of the USSR (DS, p.173).

14. See his sharp criticism of P.G. Grigorenko: 'Grigorenko proposes the immediate and total liquidation of the State apparatus whose representatives have always belonged to the class of exploiters...Even though he calls himself a Marxist, his theses are those of an anarchist and have nothing to do with Marxism' (DS, p.111). At the same time, Medvedev pays tribute to Grigorenko's 'admirable courage and honesty' and describes his internment in a psychiatric hospital as 'an arbitrary and illegal act' (*ibid.*, p.111).

15. Medvedev describes this tendency as a 'complex movement. It includes a large number of sub-groups with the most diverse political tendencies. Some are moderates; others propose more radical solutions and sometimes commit unnecessary excesses. As a general rule, the representatives of this current struggle both for the

188

re-establishment and the widening of Leninist norms in the life of the Party and the State. They demand that the cult of Stalin should be completely rejected and that its painful consequences should be done away with at all levels. For them, Marxism-Leninism remains the foundation of ideology and social science, but must be adapted to the changes which have occurred in the world and to the developments in science and technology. One of the essential demands of this current is the thorough democratization of the Party and of our society in general' (*ibid.*, p.79).

16. 'In the future, when the conflict between diverse tendencies will extend to the leading organs of the Party, the security services may again escape from the control of the Communist Party and become an institution independent of the Party and the State' (*ibid.*, p.199).

17. 'Lenin proceeded to restrict inner party democracy, and Stalin abolished it. The reverse process can begin only with the infusion of democracy in the Communist Party. Only from there can freedom of expression spread to other bodies, covering an ever wider range, until a fully fledged Soviet democracy comes into being, backed by a high industrial civilization and an up-to-date socialist system' (*Russia after Stalin*, London 1953, p.174). See also *The Prophet Outcast*: 'On the face of it, the chances of revolution are still as slender as they were in Trotsky's days, whereas the possibilities of reform are far more real' (p.312). For a similar 'optimistic' view, see Deutscher's last book, *The Unfinished Revolution*, London 1967.

10

Bettelheim and Soviet Experience

In the preface to *Les Luttes de Classes en URSS 1917-1923*, Charles Bettelheim notes that he has been studying the USSR for some forty years; and that until some time after the Twentieth Party Congress of 1956, he saw no reason, as he puts it, why the USSR should not pursue what he had always believed to be its progress towards socialism and communism, notwithstanding the 'difficulties and contradictions' on the way.[1] Indeed, he thought that the Twentieth Party Congress itself showed that the CPSU had the capacity to engage in the self-criticism which the rectification of 'mistakes' required. He has since then changed his mind; but it is worth stressing how thorough the change has been. For he now believes that the USSR is a capitalist country of a particular kind (though not all that particular, e.g. 'it is the laws of capitalist accumulation, therefore of profit, which determine the use of the means of production'[2]); and that this 'state capitalist' country is ruled by a 'state bourgeoisie' whose purpose is domination at home and imperialism abroad. He does not, however, suggest that this is the result of some dramatic counterrevolutionary change which has occurred in the last twenty-odd years, but rather that it marks the extreme accentuation of certain tendencies which were already present at the very inception of the Russian Revolution. He therefore intends to provide us with a series of volumes, of which this is the first, which will chronicle and explain this historical process.

Of course, the view that developments in the USSR following the first years of the Revolution were the logical or inevitable result of early tendencies is not at all new: in one form or another, it has been the underlying theme of much if not most writing on the subject, particularly from sources hostile to the Bolsheviks and for whom Stalinism, with all its horrors, was the 'inevitable' outcome of Leninism, or even of Marxism. Bettelheim for his part writes from the opposite end of the spectrum, from what may be described as a Chinese or Maoist perspective. The categories which he uses are also and specifically those which the Chinese Communist leaders use to depict the Soviet Union today. Bettelheim makes it quite clear that his present views on the USSR and its evolution over time were largely formed under the influence of Chinese experience, or what he reads that experience to be. His enterprise is in effect the most ambitious and comprehensive 'Western' attempt to apply Maoist categories to an elucidation of Soviet history—in the present volume to an elucidation of the first years of Soviet experience. This indeed is the main interest of the book, since it contributes nothing new to the actual history of these years, and is in fact extremely perfunctory about that history. It is as an essay in one kind of socialist theory and interpretation that the book must be judged; and I might as well say at the outset that, as such, it strikes me as a very bad piece of work. But this too is not without its interest. For Bettelheim is a respected socialist writer; and the fact that his book has so many crippling weaknesses may tell us something about the categories he uses, and which have come to enjoy fairly wide currency. Moreover, the issues involved are of considerable contemporary importance, and their discussion by Bettelheim therefore needs careful attention.

Economism

Bettelheim starts from the now familiar proposition that the cardinal error of the working-class movement, from the days of the Second International right through the history of the Third, and pervading the whole Soviet experience, was 'economism'. The term has come to be used in an exceedingly loose and arbitrary way, but it is interpreted by Bettelheim to mean three different things: firstly, the belief that public ownership of the means of production is synonymous with, or at least necessarily followed by, the socialist transformation of the relations of production. Secondly, there is the (related) belief in the 'primacy' of the development of the productive forces, in other words the assumption that socialist relations of production depend on, or must be preceded by, the achievement of a certain level of development of the productive forces. The third error of economism, in this version of it, is the belief that, with the abolition of private ownership and the disappearance of capitalists, the power apparatuses, and notably the state, altogether change their character and come to reflect or even incarnate the dictatorship of the proletariat.

In asserting that these are grave deformations of Marxism, Bettelheim is obviously right. In fact, the point may be taken more generally: taken literally, economism is a form of historical and sociological reductionism which dooms to failure any explanation or project which rests upon it. Nevertheless, two qualifications need to be entered in regard to Bettelheim's presentation of the issue. For one thing, it is very doubtful if the economistic deformation of Marxism was ever quite as crude and extreme as he makes out, even where it came to be most prevalent, namely in the stance adopted, largely for manipulative purposes, by the Third International under Stalinist direction or compulsion. Economism should not be turned into a catch-all explanation for phenomena which require deeper probing than the denunciation of it allows. In regard to the working-class movement before Stalinism, the economistic deformation, though real, can easily be exaggerated. The second and more important point is that the denunciation of economism, in the Bettelheim version of it, can easily turn into a very serious *under-estimation* of the weight of economic factors (which are, of course, never purely 'economic', whatever that could mean). One obvious result of this under-estimation is the obverse of economism, which has sometimes been called voluntarism.

In the present context, this under-estimation proceeds from an over-optimistic reading of Chinese experience. Thus, Bettelheim claims that 'the example of China shows that it is not necessary (and indeed that it is dangerous) to want to construct *"first"* the material bases of a socialist society and to put off *until later* the transformation of the social relations which would then be made to correspond with the higher productive forces'.[3] But it is not true that the Chinese example 'shows' anything as conclusive as Bettelheim suggests. What it shows is that the margin of innovation is much larger than Stalinist dogma prescribed; and that much more, in different fields, is possible under highly unfavourable economic conditions than a crudely economistic perspective would indicate. But the Chinese themselves, to their credit, have been rather less prone than many of their worshippers to under-estimate let alone ignore the weight of 'economic' factors—as indeed how could they, in a country still dominated by pervasive under-development? Bettelheim himself is well aware of the meaning of under-development; and he therefore tries to integrate it into his framework by saying that the development of the productive forces and the socialist transformation of the relations of production must be seen as 'joint tasks'. This, he says, is what the Chinese Communist Party expresses in the formula 'Make the revolution and promote production'.[4] But such formulations and slogans do not resolve the theoretical, not to speak of the practical, problems which a low level of productive forces presents for the creation of a socialist society, as distinct from the rhetorical proclamation that such a society *has* been created, or is well on the way to being created, here, there or wherever. Bettelheim regretfully notes that Marx and Lenin were not always and altogether free from what he considers to be economistic thinking. But it is not economism, in the sense in which he means it, to see the level of productive development as a major *limiting* factor. Economism means fixing the limits so narrowly as to exclude the possibility of socialist innovation; and it has an even more definite meaning in so far as it denotes a belief that a high level of productive forces under collective ownership necessarily and automatically produces socialist relations of production. *Beyond* these meanings, 'economism' is a healthy corrective to incantation and triumphalism, though it would not be called economism.

Some doubt may also be expressed on the wisdom of Bettelheim's insistence, in the same vein, that the transformation of the juridical forms of property is not sufficient to bring about a transformation in the relations of production. True enough. But the currently fashionable dismissal, even among Marxists, of 'mere' measures of nationalization runs the risk of devaluing the importance of such measures as a necessary condition for the achievement of anything else. Nationalization is not socialization. But socialization, if it is to have any chance at all, does require the transformation of the juridical forms of property.

Still Bettelheim is right to lay stress on socialist relations of production. But what, it may well be asked, does he actually *mean* by this? One major weakness of his book is that he is so remarkably imprecise on this score. At one point, he defines these relations as consisting in 'the form of the social process of appropriation' (presumably meaning who gets what and why) and 'the place which the form of this process assigns to the agents of production', i.e. 'the relations which are established between them in social production' (presumably who does what and under what conditions).[5] But this, obviously, does not do more than point to the questions which need to be tackled. Moreover, Bettelheim situates these relations of production inside a totality of social relations, all of which are interdependent and need to be 'revolutionized' for the purpose of creating a socialist society.[6] What this entails, he also notes, is the achievement of a social order whose major characteristics are the abolition of the social division between the 'directing function' and the 'executive function', the separation between manual and intellectual labour, the difference between town and country and workers and peasants.

So be it. But as Bettelheim repeatedly and rightly insists, this is bound to be a long, difficult and painful process (even assuming its complete realization to be possible). Meanwhile, there remains the question of socialist relations of production which have to be seen as part of that long, difficult and painful process. The crucial problem is to be able to determine what are the criteria which make it possible to judge whether advances are or are not being made, and the more specific the criteria the better. But on this, Bettelheim is entirely unhelpful and in fact has nothing to say that would suggest what the criteria are. He tells us that 'by establishing its class power and by nationalizing some factories (*sic*), the proletariat acquires the possibility—but only the *possibility*—of revolutionizing the real process of production and thus bringing about new relations of production, a new social division of labour and new productive forces. In so far as this task has not yet been accomplished, the former relations of capitalist production endure, as well as the forms of representation and the ideological forms in which these relations appear. In so far as this task is on the way to being accomplished, the former relations are partially transformed, the *socialist transition* is under way, and one may speak of a "socialist society".[7] Why we should be able to speak of this 'process of transition' as designating a 'socialist society' is not clear. But leaving this aside, it must be obvious that the question posed earlier has in no way been answered, namely what, in institutional or any other terms, is actually involved in the 'process of transition'? Who gets what? Who directs? Under what conditions? Bettelheim does not know or does not tell. What he does say is that this process of transition involves a new 'class struggle', whose discussion in the book does not answer any of the questions raised by 'socialist relations of production', but which raises a set of different questions.

The 'State Bourgeoisie'

Very early on in his book, Bettelheim notes that 'the existence of the dictatorship of the proletariat and of state or collective forms of property is not sufficient for the "abolition" of capitalist relations of production and the "disappearance" of the antagonistic classes: the proletariat and the bourgeoisie. The latter may undergo changed forms of existence and assume, notably, the form of a state bourgeoisie.'[8] Despite the fact that this concept of state bourgeoisie is clearly of key importance for his analysis, he does not discuss it in any detail, and specifically states that he 'cannot develop it' in this book—why is not made clear.[9] But he does say that the concept 'designates the agents of social reproduction other than the direct producers who—by virtue of the system of existing social relations and the dominant social practices—have the *effective disposal of the means of production and of the products* which formally belong to the state'.[10] In a later footnote he also explains that, when it has been consolidated, the state bourgeoisie is distinguished by its relation to the means of production; its role in the social division of labour; the share it takes of the wealth produced; and its 'class practices'.[11]

In these formulations as in so many others, Bettelheim takes for granted what has to be demonstrated, or at least argued—in this case the actual *existence* of a 'state bourgeoisie', a concept which conjures up *a very definite class formation* whose exact nature *demands* specification. But it demands in vain. Bettelheim appears to have taken over a rather extreme version of the 'new class' thesis, and he also appears to date the emergence of such a class from the earliest days of the Bolshevik revolution. What he seems to be suggesting is that, where there exists a division of labour according to which some people, located in the state or party apparatus, exercise a 'directing function', they constitute a 'state bourgeoisie' engaged in 'class struggle' with 'the proletariat'. As a sociology of the complex processes of stratification and domination which are part of the consolidation of collectivist regimes, in this instance of the Soviet Union, this will hardly do. Nor is the 'model' much improved by the qualifications which may be drawn from various parts of the text, and which may be itemized as follows.

Firstly, 'it would be quite erroneous', Bettelheim writes, 'to consider that all those who occupied directing posts in industry or in the economic and administrative apparatuses (in the years after the Revolution) formed part of the state bourgeoisie'. For some of these posts were occupied 'by communists who developed proletarian practices as much as possible in these posts, helped the workers to the maximum extent to free themselves from bourgeois relations and to give free rein to their initiatives'.[12] These cadres, who generally refused to receive a salary higher than that of workers, were not part of the state bourgeoisie but of the proletariat 'to which they were ideologically and materially integrated and from which they often stemmed'.[13] *What* these proletarian practices are remains unspecified. But the picture presented here is one where some cadres, lodged in one or other apparatus of power, are members of the state bourgeoisie; while others, *lodged in the same apparatuses of power*, are not. But this clearly deprives the notion of state bourgeoisie of any but the most arbitrary and subjective meaning. Except for the matter of salary, which can easily be got round by various perquisites and other devices, membership of the state bourgeoisie depends on entirely unspecified criteria. Or it may be that the criteria are laid down by higher authority, in which case it is obviously possible to be a communist today, a member of the state bourgeoisie tomorrow, or retrospectively, or whenever.

This impression of subjective or external designation is strengthened by Bettelheim's second qualification, namely that constituted by the revolutionary party, or rather some elements of the revolutionary party. For the 'proletarian character' of the party 'can only be enduringly maintained if the *ideological unity of the party is established in the principles of revolutionary Marxism and if the party functions in accordance with these principles*, thus constituting a revolutionary vanguard supported by the working masses'.[14] However, since Bettelheim does not trouble to say what this involves, we are not much advanced. But what he does tell us is that the 'definition of a revolutionary proletarian line cannot depend on a simple "majority vote" either in a popular or workers' assembly or in a Party Congress or in a meeting of its Central Committee. Experience shows that *in the face of a profoundly new situation*, it is in general only a minority which finds the right way, even in an experienced proletarian party'.[15] Given this, it is no great wonder that Bettelheim has a rather elastic notion of the dictatorship of the proletariat; and that he has no great difficulty in identifying it, in the years following the Bolshevik revolution, with the dictatorship of the party, notwithstanding the latter's growing isolation, its 'autonomization', of which more in a moment, and the emergence of a state bourgeoisie. Once 'the right way' is located in a minority, all else becomes easy, provided of course that one belongs to it, or approves of it.

But it is not really on a minority as such that Bettelheim relies as a means of countering the formation and consolidation of that state bourgeoisie. It is rather—and this is the third qualification to his 'model'—on the great leader. Though it is not so explicitly stated, this is what is involved in the manner of Bettelheim's apotheosis of Lenin after 1917, when Lenin is described as the all but omniscient guide, equipped with a self-correcting mechanism for the rare occasions on which he made what might be called mistakes. Most if not all the real mistakes were made, need one add, by other people, and because of a wrong application of Lenin's right policies and views.[16] In this perspective, Lenin is quite consciously cast as an exact prototype of Chairman Mao, in terms which are copied from the descriptions often applied to the latter's leadership. Unfortunately, the forces against which Lenin was fighting were too strong for him, as they were for all other counter-tendencies, with the result that the state bourgeoisie developed and consolidated its hold. Before we pursue this further, it is worth noting that there is one other 'counterforce' which Bettelheim mentions, namely the workers' resistance, 'which constitutes one of the obstacles that limit the possiblities of consolidation of the state bourgeoisie'. But this is an 'elementary' form of class struggle, which cannot really affect the issue.[17] It is very remarkable and very revealing that, for all his constant references to proletarian practices and the like, Bettelheim is seized by extreme circumspection and suspicion when he comes upon *this* kind of 'class struggle'. Nor has he anything to say on the way in which democratic practices may be institutionalized—which is absolutely crucial. His whole cast of thought leads him to rely rather on 'communists' in the power apparatuses, on a minority which knows 'the right way', and on an inspired leader who can 'swim against the current'.

From Leninism to Stalinism

Like every other writer on the Russian Revolution, of whatever disposition, Bettelheim notes the shrinking basis of Bolshevik support once the first flush of revolutionary euphoria was over. But it has to be said that his presentation of that phenomenon not only fails to add anything to our knowledge of it—in a number of important respects it tends to subtract from our understanding of its meaning. Three features of his presentation may be singled out here as being particularly important.

To begin with, the apotheosis of Lenin is so pronounced as to cast into deep shadow all other Bolshevik leaders during the period under discussion. The point is not that this is 'unfair' or bad history, though it is both. Much more important is that it devalues very greatly the significance of the debates that went on in those years, and the fact that intense and *genuine* debates, with opposing sides actually being *heard*, occurred at a time of extreme revolutionary crisis and over matters of crucial importance. Much if not most of the meaning of this tremendous fact is lost in Bettelheim's account, and with it a proper appreciation of the character and temper of Bolshevik party life between 1917 and 1921, and even for a little while beyond 1921. Yet it is essential, for a proper appreciation of *later* periods, to remember the debates of those years; and also that the sharp tightening up of 1921 was viewed as a temporary measure, required by conditions of great crisis, and *not* acclaimed as a great triumph of party unity.

It is not very surprising that the significance of these debates should be lost in Bettelheim's account, and that he should accord very little interest to the different tendencies in the party. After all, if Lenin was always right, then everybody else who opposed Lenin, or who failed to give him instant and wholehearted support, must have been always wrong. Any such opponent must have been guilty of a rightist deviation, or of a leftist one, or of a rightist-leftist one, and/or represented petty-bourgeois elements, or anarcho-syndicalist ones, or economistic tendencies, or whatever—in any case, cannot have been of serious account. In Bettelheim's index, Trotsky has half a dozen references and Bukharin a few more, and practically no other revolutionary figure save Stalin qualifies for inclusion at all. In fact, no figure other than Lenin makes more than a fleeting appearance in the story, and when one does, it is only as a member of the supporting (or opposing) cast in a drama in which Lenin is the only distinct individual. It is in no way to detract from Lenin's pre-eminence to say that this is an absurd and misleading way to write the history of those years.[18]

Secondly, and related to this way of writing, there is Bettelheim's characterization of the phenomenon of 'autonomization' of Bolshevik power in the years immediately following the revolution. He refers to the dreadful ravages of those years, to the famine, disease, destruction, civil war, invasion, which resulted in the death of seven and a half million people from epidemics, hunger and cold, and of another four million in war. These circumstances were all but certain to produce a drastic shrinkage of support for the Bolsheviks, now that they were in power, a strong centralization of such power as they commanded, and a related disappearance or destruction of the organs of popular initiative—notably the soviets—which had sprung into being in 1917. Nor is it surprising that this situation should also have produced a vast inflation of bureaucracy, both in terms of numbers and of power.

This whole process is by now well documented. But Bettelheim has a particular view of it. For him, there was already at this time a state bourgeoisie in the process of formation. At the end of his book, he notes that most Bolsheviks used the notions of bureaucracy and bureaucratic deformation as a substitute for what he calls a class analysis, and thereby helped to mask 'the bourgeois political and ideological relations of which the "bureaucratic" phenomena were only the manifestation'. There are two points here. The first, which is valid, is that 'bureaucracy' and 'bureaucratic deformation' *have* been over-used in the analysis of the Soviet experience, and have served as a convenient escape from a serious sociology of that experience. The second point, however, does not follow. For Bettelheim is asking us to adopt the notions of state bourgeoisie and class struggle instead of bureaucracy and bureaucratic deformation, without advancing a shred of justification for it. It may be that we should adopt that 'model': but there is nothing in the work which justifies doing so, least of all in relation to the early years of the revolution.

This brings me to the third and in some ways the most important point of all. By locating a state bourgeoisie in the process of formation in the earliest period of the revolution, Bettelheim's suggests a link of a direct kind between that early history and the later one, a steady development, an unbroken line, stretching from 1917 onwards and encompassing both Leninism and Stalinism as part of a single, evolving process.

But this is a perniciously misleading perspective. For there is a world of difference between the Leninist years and the Stalinist ones; and there are few things more important in socialist historiography than to mark very clearly *the break* between Leninism and Stalinism, not because it happens to be politically convenient but because it happens to be historically true. Bettelheim's account does precisely the opposite, for reasons which are made clear in the Introduction to his book, and which concern his view of Stalin's role.

In this Introduction, Bettelheim tells us that Stalin 'persevered with inflexible rigour in the application of measures called for by perspectives which were not only his but those of the quasi-totality of the party, including most of its members who opposed this or that concrete measure'.[19] So much for the various and conflicting elements of the anti-Stalin opposition: with the exception of this or that 'concrete measure', they *really* agreed with him. Moreover, the 'quasi-totality' of the party agreed with him because he was in fact applying the 'Leninist thesis' of socialism in one country and thus renewing the self-confidence of the party and the workers.[20]

This sort of language is very familiar indeed: it once served to lull the political and moral sensibilities of successive generations of socialists. Bettelheim provides other and equally telling examples of its use. Thus, Stalin, by taking up the 'Leninist' positions he did, 'contributed to setting in motion a process of transformation of gigantic scope, which was to create the necessary condition for the defence of the USSR and the aggravation of the divisions of the imperialist camp, which enabled the Soviet Union to make a decisive contribution to the defeat of Hitlerism', and so forth.[21] There is nothing whatever here to suggest that Bettelheim has considered the possibility that Stalin might have been a major contributory factor to the disasters which befell the Soviet Union, and the world socialist movement, and indeed the rest of the world, in the years of his absolute power. No doubt, 'serious mistakes' were made. But 'in the situation in which the Soviet Union was at the end of the twenties and in which the Bolshevik Party found itself, the mistakes that were made were probably historically inevitable'.[22]

It is not the vulgar apologetics of Stalinism which matter most here; nor the fact that Bettelheim appears to believe that the USSR has gone from bad to worse *since* Stalin died. Much more serious, in the present context, is the conflation, referred to earlier, of the early years of the revolution and the years of Stalinism. Bettelheim notes that the 'mistakes' committed by Stalin provided an 'exemplary lesson for the world proletariat'. But it is instructive to discover what he believes this exemplary lesson to have been: the mistakes in question 'finally showed that some forms of attack against capitalism were illusory and only served to reinforce the bourgeoisie inside the political and economic apparatuses'.[23] It might have been thought that the Stalinist cataclysm provided a few other 'exemplary lessons'. But here comes the main point: 'The lessons drawn by Lenin from the *analogous* but limited experience of "war communism" were thus confirmed'.[24]

The notion that there is anything analogous between the experience of war communism and Stalinism is a gross perversion of the truth. Much that was damaging was done in those early years, including much that was cruel and unjust; and some of it is directly attributable to Lenin. But there is nothing in the period in which Lenin was at the head of the revolution which begins to resemble the ater experience. Nor can it be seriously argued that the early years 'paved the way' for the later ones. In regard to the issue of concern here, that notion is very misleading. Obviously, the centralization of power which occurred and the 'military style' which came to dominate the way things were done were of help to Stalin in his ascent to power. But to make much of this is to blur the enormity of the difference in kind between the two periods, and the fact that it took a qualitatively different state of affairs to make possible the 'liquidation' and incarceration of millions upon millions of people, the creation of an all-pervasive police regime based on fear and delation, the total suppression of any vestige of criticism of Stalin and his policies. *This* was Stalinism; and it was *not* inscribed in either Leninist theory or practice. Whatever judgement may be passed on Leninism, it must not, as a matter of simple historical accuracy, be turned into the progenitor or early version of Stalinism. In so doing Bettelheim renders a great disservice to the elucidation of Soviet experience, which socialists badly need and which he wants to provide. He does not provide it: he has only exchanged one set of blinkers for another.

1. Charles Bettelheim, *Les luttes de classes en URSS 1917-23*, Paris 1974. An English translation was published in 1977 by Harvester Press. Two further volumes, dealing with later developments have also appeared.
2. *Ibid.*, p.42.
3. *Ibid.*, p.40. Italics in text.
4. *Ibid.*, p.397.
5. *Ibid.*, p.19.
6. *Ibid.*, p.118.
7. *Ibid.*, p.117. Italics in text.
8. *Ibid.*, p.19
9. *Ibid.*, p.41, n.l.
10. *Ibid.*
11. *Ibid.*, p.146, n. 2. He also uses 'state bourgeoisie' later as meaning the developed element of which 'the bureaucracy' of the state and the party were the embryo in the early days of the Revolution; and he further defines it as that 'directing fraction' which '*disposes of the whole or the essential part of the means of production*, and where these are activated on the basis of *capitalist relations of production* (particularly the capitalist division of labour)' (pp.279-80, italics in text).
12. *Ibid.*, p.147.
13. *Ibid.*
14. *Ibid.*, pp.368-9. Italics in text.
15. *Ibid.*, p.371. Italics in text.
16. *Ibid.*, pp.49, 309-10, 464-5 and *passim*.

17. *Ibid.*, p.147.

18. For an instructive comparison with Bettelheim's treatment, see the second part of Marcel Liebman's *Leninism Under Lenin*, London 1975.

19. *Ibid.*, p.36.

20. *Ibid.*, p.37.

21. *Ibid.*, pp.37-8.

22. *Ibid.*, p.38.

23. *Ibid.*, p.39.

24. *Ibid.* My italics.

A Commentary on
Rudolf Bahro's Alternative
1979

At the time this is written (July 1979), Rudolf Bahro is still in prison in the German Democratic Republic, purging an eight-year sentence for 'treason' which he received in June 1978*. His real crime was that he, a functionary of the East German state and party apparatus and a party member since 1952 (he was then seventeen), wrote a book which was published in West Germany in 1977 and which is deeply critical of the 'actually existing socialism' he has served in different capacities and in different spheres for more than two decades. His imprisonment and his sentence have provoked a campaign of protest in a number of countries, notably West Germany but also France, Britain and Italy. This is all to the good, and must go on until Bahro is released; and what is done on his behalf is also helpful to other 'dissidents' in East Germany who suffer pressure and persecution.

However, it would be no service to Bahro if the fact that he is a 'cause', and a very good cause, were to inhibit critical consideration of his book. It is an important work, which well deserved the award of the Isaac Deutscher Memorial Prize for 1978. Its English title, *The Alternative in Eastern Europe* (New Left Books, 1978) may suggest a more restricted compass than is warranted. It does mainly deal with Eastern Europe and Soviet-type regimes: but many of the problems with which it is concerned are of a more general character and are directly relevant to basic issues of socialist theory and practice, and notably to the general issue of the distribution and control of power under socialism. Whole-hearted support for Bahro is obviously compatible with a stringent appraisal of his book.

---

* He was released in October 1979.

A preliminary point about it is that Bahro proceeds from the premise that there does exist a desirable *socialist* alternative to 'actually existing socialism'. Unlike so many 'dissidents' in and from Eastern Europe and the USSR, whose bitter experiences have led them to reject socialism altogether and often to turn into fierce reactionaries and apostles of the Cold War, Bahro remains in this book the uncompromising advocate of a socialist vision of the future, and above all concerned to explore how the obstacles to its realization may be overcome. So much is he concerned with a socialist future that much which he says about it has occasionally been dismissed as 'utopian' even by Marxists and other sympathetic readers. But if by 'utopian' is meant constructs which belong to the realm of fantasy, Bahro is not guilty of the charge: he may well underestimate the difficulty of achieving many of the objectives he believes to be central to the socialist project. But that is something else. It is only if one believes that *any* socialist vision is utopian that Bahro qualifies for the label: but that is more of a comment on those who apply the label than on Bahro. In many respects, he is if anything rather 'anti-utopian' and very hard-headed, even possibly too much so.

Bahro begins with a fundamental postulate, namely that socialism, in so far as it entails what he calls the 'overcoming of subalternity' and the free association of equal citizens, is incompatible with economic backwardness and the requirements of industrialization. He goes very far in suggesting that the incompatibility is absolute. In the Russian case, he notes, it was inevitable that backwardness should 'levy an institutional tribute on the Bolsheviks' (p.90). Indeed, 'the more one tries to think through the stations of Soviet history . . . the harder it becomes to draw a limit short of even the most fearsome excesses, and to say that what follows on the other line was absolutely avoidable' (p.90).

This is an 'economic determinism' pushed to extremes. There is obviously no way of disproving that all that happened in Stalinist Russia, including the 'most fearful excesses', was inevitable. But the claim is nevertheless unreasonable, in that it leaves no room whatever for any element of contingency, whereas such an element must be presumed always to exist. In this context, this makes an enormous difference. Bahro writes that 'it was not only on account of the constant threats to it, but rather because of the positive tasks of driving the masses into an industrialization which they could not immediately desire, that the Soviet Union had to have a single, iron, "Petrine" leadership' (p.116); but also that 'if a more gifted man than Stalin had managed to adapt himself to this aim, then the *ideological* resources that the old party tradition already possessed would have stretched somewhat further, and the most extreme expressions of the terror would have been avoided. Russia would have been spared the Caesarian madness, but hardly more' (*ibid*.). But 'hardly more' is not an adequate description of the difference which another outcome to the struggles of the twenties could have made.

The point is not purely historical. Bahro writes that 'the peoples of the backward countries' require not only revolution, but also 'a strong state, often one that is in many respects despotic, in order really to overcome the inherited inertia' (p.58). But the 'inherited inertia' is in any case being overcome, not least because of the fierce pace of super-exploitation to which many 'backward countries' are being subjected by multi-national capitalist enterprises; and a 'strong state' can mean different things, and may be strong in different ways and in different degrees. It is surely dangerous not to make distinctions here and to underestimate what 'more or less' can mean in practice.

On the other hand, Bahro is right to point to the exceedingly unpleasant fact that countries whose people 'are just in the process of organizing themselves for industrialization' do need a strong state; and he is very probably and unfortunately right in also saying that 'their state can be nothing other than bureaucratic' (pp. 128-9). It was often said, until not very long ago, that the Chinese had conclusively disproved the latter point in their own process of 'organizing themselves for industrialization': recent convulsions, 'revelations' and about-turns confirm that such claims were exaggerated or spurious. Still, the point holds that 'bureaucracy' has many different facets and degrees, and that some forms of it are less stifling and arbitrary than others.

In any case, it is not with countries in the early stages of industrialization that Bahro is concerned, but with societies that have made the big industrial leap under the auspices of 'actually existing socialism' or where it at any rate prevails—countries such as the

USSR, the German Democratic Republic and Czechoslovakia. His starting-point in regard to all of them is that they are in a state of deep and structural crisis:

> 'It has gripped all countries of the Soviet bloc, affecting all areas of life, and it is ultimately based on the contradiction recognized by all Marxists, between the modern productive forces and relations of production that have become a hindrance to them, coming to a head. The abolition of private property in the means of production has in no way meant their immediate transformation into the property of the people. Rather, the whole society stands property-less against its state machine.' (pp.10-11.)

'Relations of production' here stands for a political order dominated by a state/party apparatus which has monopolized all power and which is stifling the vitality of the social and economic order as well as the political one. As he also notes somewhere else,

> 'the oligarchy at the top of the pyramid decides the goals for which the surplus product should be used, and subjects the *entire* reproduction process of economic, social and cultural life to its regulation. As in the case of all earlier systems of domination, the steady reproduction of its own monopoly, and when possible its expanded reproduction, goes into the overall calculation of social development and has to be paid for by the masses' (p.241, italics in text).

The contradiction, for Bahro, squarely resides in the political realm, which stifles the 'surplus consciousness' generated by industrial development: whatever was impossible at the beginning of the industrializing process because of the retarded state of the productive forces and society in general, has now become possible because of economic development, and is being repressed by a rigid, self-regarding and bureaucratic state/party apparatus. Bahro also clearly places the *source* of power in the political realm. It is not economic power which produces or determines political power, but the other way round: it is their location in the state/party apparatus which makes it possible for leaders to exercise economic and ideological as well as political control. It is also this location which ensures the economic privileges of the dominant groups ('exploitation in our system is a *political* phenomenon, a phenomenon of distribution of political power', p.97); and the more favourable the location, the greater the privileges.

The privileges with which Bahro is most concerned are not the obvious material ones, but those that have to do with the exercise of power, and from which the others derive. Again and again, it is to the concentration of power at one end and its atrophy at the other that he returns:

> 'Do the working masses of the "socialist" countries,' he asks, 'have even the least positive influence on the decisions that bear on their material fate, and ultimately therefore on their overall fate? On decisions as to the proportions between accumulation and consumption, between production for war and for peace, between building of homes and building of monuments, between expenditure on education and expenditure on the propagandist self-portrayal of the power structure, between the costs of liberating women from domestic slavery and the cost of security for those "in charge of society"? Of course not.' (pp.151-2).

It is this 'division of labour' between rulers and ruled which is for Bahro the cancer of 'actually existing socialism': 'we must thank Edward Gierek', he also writes, 'for the forthright way in which he summed up the problem of our societies after the Polish December (1970) crisis, with the slogan: "You work well, and we will govern well"' (p.176). This is what Bahro rejects; and that rejection is at the core of his vision of a socialist alternative to 'actually existing socialism'. For he believes that the pain and suffering of the process of industrialization have at last produced the conditions in which it is possible for the people to take an ever-larger share in the determination of all aspects of their own lives. His first premise is that the 'overcoming of subalternity' is possible and is one of the great defining elements of the socialist project. What he wants and believes possible is at least the beginning of a 'cultural revolution' that would break down a functional fetishism which condemns most people to permanently fixed and subordinate tasks, and which effectively robs them of self-determination: the first condition of this 'cultural revolution' is the 'de-bureaucratization and genuine socialization of the activity of management, the participation of all individuals in disposal over the reproduction process'; its second condition 'bears on the elevation of the collective worker to the level of the given principles of science and technique of the time, which are at work in the production process' (p.276). But the 'cultural revolution' of which

Bahro speaks reaches out much further even than this and encompasses all aspects of existence.

The most difficult questions concerning Bahro's work do not lie in his reaffirmation of socialist ideals, but rather in his views of the ways in which progress is to be made in realizing them in the countries with which he is mainly concerned.

The first such question has to do with the social class or stratum which is to initiate and lead the movement for change. On this, Bahro is honestly and resolutely forthright: 'New and higher cultures are never created without the masses, without an essential change in their condition of life, nor without their initiative, at a definite stage of maturity of the ongoing crisis. But in no known historical case did the first creative impulse in ideas and organization proceed from the masses; the trade unions do not anticipate any new civilization' (p.149).

This is a somewhat different way of advancing a proposition similar to the Leninist view of what could be expected from the working class, and what could not—a view which largely determined the kind of party which Lenin and the Bolsheviks brought into being. In so far as the working class cannot by its own efforts be the agent of its own emancipation, the vanguard party must assume a major historical role; and the less advanced and prepared the working class, the greater must be the role of the party. This being the case, frantic efforts must then be made to obscure and deny the gap that separates class and party, which leads to illusionism and myth-making. Bahro rejects this: but he also rejects, as I have noted, the notion that all that is required is to place back the emphasis on the working class and to declare it to be the subject of its own and society's emancipation. Those upon whom he relies to constitute the leading element, in social terms, of the movement for change are the people who exercise managerial and 'intellectual' functions in the societies of 'actually existing socialism' and who form the middle and higher echelons of the 'collective worker'. 'The initiative for fundamental change', he writes, 'can only proceed from those elements who are most bound up with the developmental functions and tendencies of the forces and relations of production'; and he believes that it is the 'intellectualized strata of the collective worker' who will 'for the time being inevitably set the tone' of a transformed socialist society (pp.328-9).

Of course, Bahro knows perfectly well that there are many people in this stratum who are themselves 'reactionary and bureaucratized' and are part of the privileged and parasitical order that has to be changed. But he also believes that there are many others who are well aware of the need for change, and for an end to 'the permanent tutelage of society by the state' and to 'the permanent treatment of people (individuals and collectives) as infantile subjects of education' (p.313). He derives this belief from different sources: from the Czech Spring of 1968, which showed that many of the people whom he has in mind were prepared for change, and were prepared to take great risks to see it brought about; from a 'structural' analysis, which leads him to think that 'Soviet scientists, technicians and economists will come up more obstinately than ever, and ever more frequently, too, against the fundamental incompatibility between the old superstructure and the new productive forces' (p.335); and it is difficult to believe that he does not draw from his own experience as well in thinking that there are many people in the stratum to which he himself belonged who want change in progressive directions.

> 'Those ideologists of all kinds,' he writes, 'who are pressed into the roles of party and state officials, from social scientists through to journalists, from artists to their censors, from the strategists of natural science to teachers of history—these are all continuously demeaned, both directly and indirectly, by proscriptions, by the reprimands and the praises of the arrogant politbureaucrats (the petty ones still more than the great ones). In order to follow the norms and rituals of official 'intellectual life', they must mostly learn to present the public image of pathetic cretins' (p.324).

The changes which are inscribed on the agenda of the countries of 'actually existing socialism', and which nothing can remove from their agenda, will tell whether Bahro's expectations are realistic or not. But his hopes must not be misunderstood: he neither underestimates the role of the working class in the process of change; nor does he seek to present scientists, technicians, managers and 'intellectuals' as the new 'universal class' in place of the working class. On the contrary, he is concerned to stress both the importance of the 'intellectual' stratum *and* the limited nature of its demands, from the socialist perspective that Bahro holds. Although he attaches importance to demands for 'liberalization' and the exercise of democratic freedoms, this, he also says, does not reach deep enough and touch the heart of the matter, the heart of the matter being for him a society in which a structured, functionally sanctioned system of authority relations prevails and must be overcome.

I think that Bahro rather underestimates the significance and reach of democratic demands in the societies of 'actually existing socialism'—or for that matter anywhere else: now as always, the battle for democratic freedoms everywhere is not simply a prelude to the battle for socialism, but an intrinsic part of it; and he is unduly dismissive of what he calls a 'superficial and impatient radicalism' which erupted in Czechoslovakia in 1968 alongside the Action Programme of the Czech Communist Party 'and which ultimately served the purpose of securing the uninhibited and uncontrolled development of these privileged forces [i.e., 'intellectuals, economists and technicans'—R.M.] on the TV screen, in culture, in the state apparatus and in the leading positions of economic management' (p.307).

Whether appropriate to the Czech Spring or not, Bahro's suspicion (or qualified suspicion) is consistent with the argument that runs like a thread throughout his book, namely that socialism does not mean the replacement of one oligarchy by another, but the dissolution of oligarchy: the 'tendency' to which he objects in the Czech Spring is that which was leading, as he sees it, to the 'appropriation of political power on the basis of "competence", i.e., of the effective socio-economic status that its representatives had acquired in the two decades since 1948' (p.308). What Bahro has in mind is perhaps best expressed in the following quotation: 'Political revolution or reformation only has meaning if it improves the conditions for the technical and at the same time cultural revolution that liberates people step by step from the chains of the traditional division of labour and the state, and ensures them the preconditions for the free development of all, right down to the primary cells of society' (p.182).

It is an obvious exaggeration to say that political revolution or reformation *only* has meaning if it achieves the purposes which Bahro stipulates; but it is nevertheless salutary, not least for an 'intellectual' stratum engaged in more or less acceptably creative work, to be reminded that, in socialist terms, the notion of democracy has to go far beyond political arrangements if it is to erode effectively and ultimately dissolve the 'subalternity' in which other parts of the 'collective worker' are permanently located. In this respect, Bahro speaks in the most authentic socialist voice and cannot be faulted.

But if neither the 'working class' nor the 'intellectual' stratum can be expected to represent the 'universal' interest, how is that interest to be expressed, and by whom?

It is here that Bahro is least convincing and that his perspectives are most clouded. He does not believe that ruling Communist parties, as they now function, can serve as agencies of socialist emancipation. On the contrary, 'the party leadership is working not to overcome this late class society of ours, but rather to consolidate and perpetuate it, and would like to confine social and economic progress to their necessary limits' (p.242). In fact, the state and the party in this system are the main constitutive elements of a single apparatus of power and domination, each reinforcing the other.

On the other hand, he categorically rejects party pluralism as an 'anachronistic piece of thoughtlessness, which completely misconstrues the concrete historical material in our countries' (p.350). Parties, he seems to believe, must represent distinct and antagonistic social classes and elements. In so far as such classes and social elements do not exist in the countries of 'actually existing socialism', except for the 'class' conflict between the people and the party/state apparatus, there is no basis for a plurality of parties.

This is unconvincing. The notion that independent political groupings and parties can only have a meaningful existence if they are based on clearly defined classes is much too simple and reductionist, in stipulating that political activity can only be significant as a reflection of 'pure' class representation; and that the alternative 'political fragmentation of the workers' movement is only a phenomenon of groups of intellectuals, with their claims to power and their rivalries' (p.350). The experience of capitalist societies shows the matter to be much more complex than this; and Bahro provides no good reason for thinking that it is simpler in post-capitalist societies—unless it is forced into simplicity, by a system which he rejects.

This is not to say that a plurality of parties is a sufficient condition for the achievement of socialist democracy; and it may even be the case that it is not a necessary condition for radical changes to occur in the countries of 'actually existing socialism'. To fasten on such plurality as paramount or critical may well be unduly rigid: much would depend on the alternative. For Bahro, the alternative consists in a new form of party or political organism, a League of Communists, to which he devotes considerable attention and which is inspired by Gramsci's concept of the party as a 'collective intellectual'.

The League of Communists is intended to give expression to all the 'emancipatory interests' in society and to 'inspire the system of social forces and organizations in the name of a constructive but substantially transforming counter-force, which puts the state hierarchy in its proper place . . . this means a division of social power, the installation of a progressive dialectic between state and social forces, and not just temporarily as within the party process itself, but rather for the whole duration of the transition. The result will be a situation of dual supremacy, in which the statist side gradually becomes less dominant' (p.361).

The absolutely key question here is the relationship of the party or league to the state. Bahro wants his League of Communists to stand outside the state apparatus, so that there may be a possibility of 'bringing contradiction into the government apparatus' (p.370). Communists, he also says, 'must organize the social forces in such a way that these confront the apparatus on a massive scale as autonomous powers, and can force it into progressive compromises' (p.371). Again, he makes the point that the League will have different tendencies and fractions (which is interesting in relation to the discussion of party pluralism); but he then immediately adds that the existence of tendencies and fractions in the League of Communists 'naturally presupposes that the state and administration are not directly dependent on the League and its internal debates' (p.366).

But this separation of the party or league from the state raises more questions than it solves: for it leaves *the state* in a position of *independent power*, which is precisely what needs to be overcome. Bahro is eloquent and convincing in outlining the role of the League, namely 'the unification, coordination and direction of intellectual and moral efforts for elaborating a strategy and tactics of cultural revolution' (p.376), on the basis of inner-party democracy and equality; and it might be argued that the very fact that it was possible for such an organization to come into being would mean that the problem of the control of the state was already much less acute: a state that would enable a League of Communists, such as Bahro has in mind, to operate freely would be a different state from any that we know in the countries of 'actually existing socialism'. There is something to this argument (which is not incidentally Bahro's argument), but not enough. For it would still be essential—and it will remain essential for any foreseeable future—to find ways and means of controlling the state in its policies and actions. The trouble with Bahro's League of Communists is that there is no obvious mechanism whereby it would be able to constrain the state apparatus and compel it to enter into the 'progressive compromises' of which he speaks, let alone impose new policy directions upon it.

The independence of the state in relation to society is the greatest of all political problems in Soviet-type regimes. This is as true for China as for the USSR and for Vietnam as for Cuba or Hungary: policy is made at a level which leaves out the people altogether, and the more important the decisions, the less say do the people have. Not only are such decisions not subject to determination by the people: they are not even subject to genuine discussion and debate in society. It is symptomatic of a general state of affairs in these regimes not only that the people of Vietnam should have had no say in that country's invasion of Cambodia, or the people of China in that country's invasion of Vietnam, but that there should have been no debate on these acts of state policy. Genuine debate, with effects on the outcome, is not part of the political culture of the countries of 'actually existing socialism'. Capitalist democracy hardly shines in this respect either: but its political practice is much superior to that of Soviet-type regimes. So long as this remains the case, socialists everywhere will be in great trouble.

Bahro wants to remedy this state of affairs; but the means he proposes are not adequate to the purpose. However, I do not wish to conclude this commentary on a negative note. Bahro may not answer the questions he poses: but he does pose them, with great courage and honesty, in the name of a humanism without sentimentality which embodies the values and aspirations that make socialism the hope of mankind. In an epoch like the present, so ravaged by cynicism, doubt, disillusionment and despair, his voice reaches out from his jail and speaks of better days to come, or rather of better days to be made, East and West.

12

Kolakowski's Anti-Marx*

1981

Leszek Kolakowski describes his history of Marxist thought as a 'handbook', but the description is not very accurate. His three volumes do provide a remarkably comprehensive survey of the writings which have contributed to form the 'main currents' of Marxism. But a handbook is supposed to be an explanatory guide, in which the author's opinions do not obtrude too insistently. Kolakowski could not have written such a book, on this subject. He is much too deeply engaged; and his account is in fact very strongly coloured by his extreme hostility towards Marxism. This seems to me to have had a very adverse effect on the work. However, this is by no means the main ground on which these volumes are to be criticized: the much more serious ground for criticism is that Kolakowski's whole approach to Marxism and to much of its history is fundamentally misconceived. His knowledge of the literature, as shown in all three volumes, is truly prodigious; and much that he says in the course of these fifteen hundred pages is penetrating and challenging. Yet, and notwithstanding the validity that there may be in his criticism of this or that thinker or concept, the work as a whole is, I believe, badly flawed. Kolakowski's history has been described as monumental; and it is undoubtedly that. However, the monument rests on unsound foundations and is full of cracks.

What is in question here is firstly the character of Marxism; and

* L. Kolakowski, *Main Currents of Marxism*, Vol. 1, *The Founders*; Vol. 2, *The Golden Age*; Vol. 3, *The Breakdown*. Translated from the Polish by P.S. Falla (Oxford, Clarendon Press, 1978). This review appeared in *Political Studies*, vol. xxix, no. 1, March 1981. A reply by Kolakowski appeared in the same issue.

secondly its relation to Leninism and Stalinism. I propose to show in what follows that Kolakowski is basically wrong on both issues.

Kolakowski's account begins with a discussion of such unlikely figures as Plotinus, St. Augustine, Eriugena and others who do not usually make an appearance in histories of Marxism and of its antecedents. But their appearance is justified by Kolakowski's particular understanding of Marxism, and provides an important clue to his interpretation of it in these volumes.

The early philosophers and mystics of whom he writes, and others who came later, have in common the search for an answer to what Kolakowski calls 'basic, immemorial questions',[1] namely how to account for human misery, wickedness and imperfection; and how to overcome human alienation from a world constituted by God or Nature or Reason or man/woman's 'essential' nature. Both the formulation of the question and the answer to it differ from thinker to thinker, but the question itself remains—how to reconcile contingent human existence to an essence from which it is estranged. The quest to overcome this duality, Kolakowski notes, is not only to be found in religious thought: on the contrary, 'the theory of man's return to himself . . . together with the paradigmatic image of a lost paradise, is an unchanging feature of man's speculation about himself, assuming different forms in different cultures but equally capable of finding expression within a religious or a radically antireligious framework.'[2]

Kolakowski's view of Marxism is that it is fundamentally about the same quest, and that Marx was in his own way seeking the same resolution of duality as were a host of religious and anti-religious thinkers who preceded him. Here, for Kolakowski, is the core of Marxism, its essential thread, the definition and thrust of the whole project. Thus, in a 'Recapitulation' of Marx's thought up to 1846, he writes that 'from 1843 onwards, he developed his ideas with extreme consistency, and all his later work may be regarded as a continuation and elaboration of the body of thought which was already constituted by the time of *The German Ideology*.'[3] At the heart of this body of thought, Kolakowski suggests, there is the belief that 'the transcendence of alienation is another name for communism—a total transformation of human existence, the recovery by man of his species-essence';[4] and again, Marx 'did not regard socialism merely as a new system that would do away with inequality, exploitation, and social antagonism. In his view it was the recovery by man of his lost humanity, the reconciliation of his species-essence with his empirical existence, the restoration to man's being of his "alienated" nature'.[5] 'These,' says Kolakowski, 'are the fundamental principles of Marx's theory, from which he never departed. The whole of his work, down to the last page of *Capital*, was a confirmation and elaboration of these ideas.'[6]

There is a broad sense in which this is true; and another, much more important sense, in which it is very misleading and indeed false. It is true in the sense that Marx never lost the vision of a free society, in which men and women, liberated from all forms of human domination, would be able fully to develop their individual self in harmony with their social being, and with nature. The expression of this hope is to be found scattered in Marx's post-1848 work as well as in his earlier writings, for instance in famous passages of *Capital* and the *Critique of the Gotha Programme*.[7]

Even so, there is a great difference in this respect between the early Marx and the later one, which has nothing to do with an Althusserian 'epistemological break', but with the concrete historical, social and economic analyses which occupied Marx from the mid eighteen forties onwards, and which were mostly absent from the earlier, 'philosophical' writings. Passages such as those I have noted from the later works retain in full the vision of a free society: this is the constant and ultimate point of reference. But the later works turn the vision into a concrete project, rooted in social and economic analysis and controlled by a sharp awareness of prerequisites to be fulfilled and of obstacles to be overcome. Quite naturally, 1848 and the years of exile and of the British Museum left their deep mark.

There is hardly any sense of this in Kolakowski's account. 'There can be no doubt,' he writes, 'that Marx laid more weight on the purely scientific, objective, deterministic aspect of his observations in the sixties than in the forties.'[8] But even this passing reference to the shift in Marx's preoccupations from the mid-forties onwards is virtually qualified out of existence, so that Marx is made to appear as a more or less unchanging philosophical visionary who spent the thirty-five years between 1848 and his death merely trying to fill in the details of an early vision arbitrarily plucked out of a philosophical construct, and only producing a 'confirmation and an elaboration' of it. This is an unhistorical and inaccurate view. It is significant for his whole perspective on Marx that Kolakowski should open his history with the words 'Marx was a German philosopher', by which he means that Marx must be seen as part of a philosophical tradition, of which Hegel was the dominant figure. But Marx was not, in fact, a 'German philosopher': he was, if any label is to be used, an economic and social theorist whose intellectual concerns cannot be assimilated to those of 'German philosophers', or any other philosophers for that matter. No 'philosopher' of the kind Kolakowski has in mind could have written *Capital*, or would have felt any need to write it.

Kolakowski's insistence on Marx-the-German-philosopher is crucial to his whole work; for it supplies him with his main theme, namely that Marxism was born out of Marx's quest for absolute solutions to the 'human predicament', and was fatally marked by these origins. This is the basis for Kolakowski's claim that 'Marxism has been the greatest fantasy of our century . . . a dream offering the prospect of a society of perfect unity, in which all human aspirations would be fulfilled and all values reconciled'.[9] This is of course an absurdly overdrawn formulation of the Marxist purpose, and is contradicted by Kolakowski's own observation that 'the fulfilment of humanity is not, in Marx's view, a matter of attaining some final, imagined perfection, but of freeing man for ever from conditions that hamper his growth and make him the slave of his own works'.[10] This is a more reasonable view of the matter, and it applies not only to Marx but to most if not all Marxists after him.

On the other hand, the more reasonable formulation, in so far as he takes account of it at all, does not find more favour with Kolakowski than the extreme one. In his first volume, he also notes that 'salvation, for Marx, is man's salvation of himself; not the work of God or Nature, but that of a collective Prometheus who, in principle, is capable of achieving absolute command of the world he lives in. In this sense, Man's freedom is his creativity, the mark of a conqueror overcoming both nature and himself.[11] What, it may well be asked, is wrong with this project? It is easy to imagine the answer which some religious thinkers, or secular sceptics or cynics could return to this question. Yet very remarkably, considering his wholesale condemnation of Marxism-as-fantasy, Kolakowski does not offer any reasoned answer to the question. He asks at one point whether Marx's 'vision of social unity' can be imagined 'in any other way than that of a totalitarian state',[12] and clearly believes that it cannot; and in the concluding words of his third volume he tells us that 'the self-deification of mankind, to which Marxism gave philosophical expression, has ended in the same way as all such attempts, whether individual or collective: it has revealed itself as the farcical aspect of human bondage'.[13] However, these and similar observations hardly constitute the sustained argument which an indictment as relentless as Kolakowski's requires.

He also suggests, with obvious disapproval, that 'Marx did not believe in the essential finitude and limitations of man, or the obstacles to his creativity. Evil and suffering, in his eyes, had no meaning except as instruments of liberation; they were purely social facts, not an essential part of the human condition.'[14] Marxist writing less sloppy than this gets severe treatment from Kolakowski. Marx would have had to be exceedingly shortsighted not to perceive the 'essential finitude and limitations of man'; and he would have had to be a very twisted fellow indeed to believe that 'evil and suffering had no meaning except as instruments of liberation'. Marx believed nothing of the sort. However, he did hold that there were many obstacles in man/woman's path which were social in character, and therefore remediable, as was much of the suffering and evil to which men and women were subject; and that the removal of these obstacles would very greatly reduce man/woman's 'essential finitude and limitations', and enable them to reach heights of achievement which could scarcely be imagined at the present time. Such 'optimism' is deeply offensive to many people who do not believe in the possibility of infinite human progress, and perhaps even more so to people who once believed in it but no longer do; but the fact that they do not like it is hardly sufficient ground for accepting the view that the belief is a mere 'fantasy' or for intoning after them the familiar conservative cry: *'Pas trop de zèle!'*

One of the purposes which the notion of Marxism as a 'utopian' construct serves is to explain something which would otherwise, within Kolakowski's terms, be very puzzling, namely its appeal. Here, for him, is a doctrine whose every tenet is either blatantly inadequate, or plainly false, or merely trivial. He occasionally acknowledges Marx's stature; but on the strength of what he has to say about Marx's work, it is difficult to see what the acknowledgement is worth. His discussion of historical materialism illustrates the point, and illustrates also a device to which he is prone (while condemning it in Marxists), whereby what is granted with one hand is taken back with the other: 'No reasonable person,' he writes, 'would deny that the doctrine of historical materialism has been a valuable addition to our intellectual equipment and has enriched our understanding of the past.' 'True,' he hastens to add, 'it has been argued that in a strict form the doctrine is nonsense and in a loose sense it is a commonplace.' 'Still,' he goes on, 'if it has become a commonplace, this is largely thanks to Marx's originality.' But this 'originality' is soon disposed of, for, Kolakowski tells us a dozen lines later, 'the sociological approach to the study of civilization was expounded by writers before Marx, such as Vico, Herder and Montesquieu, or contemporary but independent of him, such as Michelet, Renan and Taine.' However, 'none of these expressed his ideas in the extreme, one-sided, dogmatic form which constituted the strength of Marxism'.[15] So, what we have is a set of ideas which many others than Marx put forward; but which he helped to disseminate by his extreme, one-sided and dogmatic mode of expression.[16] None of Marx's other main ideas fares any better—if anything rather worse. Nor do those of any Marxist after Marx. Why then has Marxism made such a powerful appeal, not least to so many extremely gifted people?

Kolakowski's explanation of this phenomenon is remarkable only for its superficiality: 'The influence that Marxism has achieved, far from being the result or proof of its scientific character, is almost entirely due to its prophetic, fantastic and irrational elements. Marxism is a doctrine of blind confidence that a paradise of universal satisfaction is awaiting us just round the corner.'[17] This is miserable stuff. Are we seriously expected to believe that Marxism has been taken up by successive generations of intellectuals and others because it provided them with 'blind confidence' that a 'paradise of universal satisfaction' was just round the corner? If Kolakowski were to search his own memory, would he not find that some of the Marxists he once knew, say in wartime or post-war Poland, were moved by rather different impulses and expectations?

There are many people, including Marxists, who crave for certainty; and there are no doubt Marxists who find it in Marxism, or at least in a debased version of it. Marx himself did not find certainty in the body of thought which he brought forth and which he significantly never once called Marxism—not out of modesty but because the notion of a completed system that could once and for all be labelled was altogether alien to his ways of thought. Nor would Marx's most able successors have wrestled so hard with the problems they encountered in Marxism if it had so easily satisfied their alleged craving for certainty. The lengths to which Kolakowski is driven by his excessive partisanship and hostility are well exemplified by his strictures on Rosa Luxemburg. Here, it appears, is 'an outstanding example of a type of mind that is often met with in the history of Marxism and (which) appears to be specially attracted by the Marxist outlook'. This 'type of mind' is 'characterized by slavish submission to authority, together with a belief that in that submission the values of scientific thought can be preserved. No doctrine was so well suited as Marxism to satisfy both these attitudes, or to provide a mystification combining extreme dogmatism with the cult of 'scientific' thinking, in which the disciple could find mental and spiritual peace. Marxism thus played the part of a religion for the intelligentsia.'[18]

As a description of Rosa Luxemburg—and the passage is related to her—this is plain character assassination. For where is the evidence of her 'slavish submission to authority'? In fact, the evidence is all the other way. And where is the extreme dogmatism? Or is this no more than Kolakowski's way of describing Luxemburg's willingness to risk and eventually to incur death for her beliefs? Where is the evidence for the gratuitous assertion that Luxemburg was seeking or found 'mental and spiritual peace' in Marxism? Had he been concerned to explain rather than to denounce, Kolakowski would have paid more attention to reasons of a very different order for the appeal of Marxism: for instance, that people who wanted to understand the world and also to change it found that Marxism provided them with a more reasonable explanation of historical and contemporary structures and processes than any available alternative; and that the attraction was enhanced by Marxism's call to oppose great evils and to create conditions for a different kind of world, from which such evils would be banished.

The call to fight against great evils is here crucial. It is only very fleetingly that Kolakowski refers to the actual historical circumstances which, it is clear, led people to Marxism. Exploitation, poverty and crisis, war and the threat of war, imperialism and fascism, the crimes of ruling classes—these are not figments of fevered Marxist imaginations; they form the essential context for the history of Marxism in the twentieth century. Kolakowski does not give to that historical context anything like its proper due; much is thereby missed, and much is thereby distorted.

Kolakowski declares at the beginning of his work that he intends it to be 'not only an historical account but an attempt to analyse the strange fate of an idea which began in Promethean humanism and culminated in the monstrous tyranny of Stalinism'.[19] The formulation is highly loaded, since it takes as settled what is in fact a very controversial question, namely whether it *was* Marxism which 'culminated' in Stalinism; in other words, whether it it possible to speak of Stalinism as a 'version' of Marxism. Kolakowski says at one point that 'thanks to an unusual combination of circumstances, power in Russia was seized by a party professing Marxist doctrine. In order to stay in power the party was obliged successively to revoke all the promises contained in its ideology, which had no doubt been sincere in the mouths of its first leaders'.[20] This would have been a promising line of thought for Kolakowski to pursue. Instead, he qualifies it out of existence with the remark that Marxism 'contained essential features, as opposed to accidental or secondary ones, that made it adaptable' to its becoming the 'ideology of the self-glorifying Russian bureaucracy'.[21] His basic view is that what he calls the 'Leninist-Stalinist version of socialism' was indeed 'a possible interpretation, though certainly not the only possible one, of Marx's doctrine'.[22]

This is obviously a point of fundamental importance for the history of Marxism, and for much else as well; and I think that Kolakowski has got it wrong, because he badly underrates the degree to which so much that came after Marx directly contradicted his ideas at crucial points, and cannot therefore reasonably be taken to be in any way congruent or compatible with Marx's Marxism, or to be a 'possible interpretation' of it.

In regard to Leninism, Kolakowski mis-states its divergence from Marx on an issue of critical importance for the whole Marxist project, namely the role of the party. It was one of Marx's most fundamental convictions that 'the emancipation of the working classes must be conquered by the working classes themselves';[23] but it was also one of Lenin's strongest convictions—which may indeed be taken as a defining element of Leninism—that the working class by itself could not make a revolution but must be led by a vanguard party, closely related to the working class but also clearly separate from it.

The point is not here that Marx was right and Lenin wrong, or vice-versa: I think that, although Marx did not reject all forms of organization, he nevertheless greatly underestimated how much organization a socialist movement—let alone a socialist revolution —required; and that Lenin, for his part, altogether underestimated the problems that the organization which he wanted and brought into being must in all circumstances produce. The point, however, is that there is no way in which it is possible to reconcile Marx and Lenin on this central issue. Kolakowski only discusses this in relation to the production of revolutionary consciousness; and, having noted Lenin's belief that 'the party alone could and must be the initiator and source of revolutionary consciousness', he goes on to say that 'although Marx himself never put the matter in these terms, there is insufficient ground for holding that Lenin's opinion on this point was a "distortion" of Marxism'.[24] I believe, on the contrary, that there is ample ground in Marx's work for holding that Lenin's prescriptions in regard to the party, whatever view may be taken of them, are a fundamental departure from Marx and in direct contradiction with his views.

The invention of something called 'Marxism-Leninism' in the Soviet Union after Lenin's death was intended to blur this and other contradictions and contrasts between Marx and Lenin; and endless reiteration of that formula has given an appearance of solidity and substance to a conflation which is in reality quite arbitrary and question-begging. Kolakowski, for his own reasons, accepts the conflation as perfectly legitimate and reasonable; but it is much more reasonable and accurate to stress how much there is of crucial importance that separates Marx from Lenin. The implicit granting of equal theoretical status to Marxism and Leninism in the formula 'Marxism-Leninism' is in any case unjustifiable: Marxism is a vast theoretical contruct, extraordinarily rich and many-sided; Leninism is primarily a theory and a strategy of revolution. And as such, it stands in clear contradiction to Marx's own perspectives on the process of revolutionary change.

Kolakowski is also emphatic in his linking of Leninism and Stalinism. 'The Soviet regime as it developed under Stalin,' he writes, 'was a continuation of Leninism', and again, 'the state founded on Lenin's political and ideological principles could only have maintained itself in a Stalinist form'.[25]

There is much to be said against this view. I would certainly want to argue that the Soviet Union could not have become a socialist democracy after the Bolshevik revolution. But in no way can this be taken to mean that the regime installed by that revolution was therefore *bound*, as Kolakowski suggests, to become a Stalinist tyranny, and that it became one because of Lenin's 'political and ideological principles'. Dictatorships are abhorrent forms of government, but there can be a lot of difference between one sort of dictatorship and another, for instance the difference between millions of people being destroyed in one way or another by the state, and their not being destroyed. 'The thirties,' Kolakowski says, 'were only an intensification and consolidation of the process which began in Lenin's lifetime and under his direction'.[26] But the 'only' in this sentence covers and conceals a world of difference between the twenties and what followed. Kolakowski himself notes that 'the mass slaughter of Communists in 1936-9 cannot be called a "historical necessity", and we may suppose that it would not have taken place under a tyrant other than Stalin himself'.[27] Yet, the significance of this qualification does not seem to be apparent to him. The mass slaughter of Communists in 1936-9 (and after) was not a detail; and the question which Kolakowski's qualification immediately invites is what *else* was not a 'historical necessity' which forms part of Stalinism? And on the assumption, which is surely reasonable, that there *was* much else which occurred between 1928 and 1953 and which was not a 'historical necessity', what does it mean to say that the state founded by Lenin could only have maintained iself in a Stalinist form?

Stalinism was not merely an extension of the regime that came into being with the Bolshevik revolution. It was, as has often been said, a 'revolution from above', which marked a momentous shift from a relatively repressive dictatorship to an absolutely repressive one, with a rapid clamping down on every manifestation of independent activity in every area of life. This Stalinist regime was, to use Kolakowski's own formula, which in this instance he repudiates, *one* of the possibilities which the Revolution and its aftermath had created. It was not the only one. He believes that the 'totalitarian character of the regime . . . increased without interruption between 1924 and 1953';[28] and he also believes that 'the system that prevailed until 1953 has not been effected in any essential way by the changes of the post-Stalinist era'.[29] On this view, 'Stalinism' has prevailed in the Soviet Union more or less throughout its existence. This is to deprive the term of its specific meaning and to obliterate its unique characteristics. On Kolakowski's own showing, there was much about the twenties that was very different from what followed;[30] and while it may be argued that 'the system has not essentially changed since 1953, the fact remains that there is much about the Khruschev and Brezhnev eras that is very different from the years in which Stalin held absolute power, for instance, and not least, the ending of mass terror as an intrinsic part of government.

To speak of Stalinism as following naturally and ineluctably from Leninism is unwarranted. However, to speak of Stalinism as 'one possible interpretation of Marx's doctrine' is not only unwarranted but false. Kolakowski describes the whole period from 1924 onwards as 'the progressive destruction of civil society and absorption of all forms of social life by the state'.[31] Leaving aside the question of continuity versus discontinuity, this is precisely the reverse of what Marx intended: it was, after all, he who said that 'freedom consists in converting the state from an organ superimposed on society into one thoroughly subordinate to it'.[32] Nor will it do to argue, as Kolakowski does, that whatever Marx intended or said or thought, he can be 'interpreted' as legitimating Stalinism. There is nothing in Marx's work which provides a reasonable justification for the notion that Stalinism was anything but the absolute contradiction of Marx's project. Kolakowski suggests that Marx's 'dream of unity' could 'take the form of despotic party oligarchy, while his Prometheanism would appear in the attempt to organize economic life by police methods, as Lenin's party did at the outset of its rule'.[33] This is a perverse travesty of Marx's thought.

Kolakowski proceeds throughout from the view that, in political terms, Marxism leaves no choice on the left except between extreme alternatives of his own choosing. He refers at one point to a 'polarization' which occurred in the First World War, and which led 'to a state of affairs that still exists: on the one hand reformist socialism bearing only a tenuous relation to Marxism, and, on the other hand, the monopolization of Marxism by Leninism and its derivatives'.[34] However, the 'reformist socialism' which he has in mind is much more a form of adaptation to capitalism than a challenge to it; and it is a gratuitous assumption that the only alternative to it is 'Leninism and its derivatives'. It is of course a very convenient and fashionable view, for it forecloses any possibility for the left other than, on the one hand, acceptance of a barely modified status quo and, on the other, adherence to organizational principles and forms which, at least in the conditions of advanced capitalism and capitalist democracy, condemn their devotees to ineffectual sectarianism. This, however, is only an arbitrarily restrictive view of what is possible.

Kolakowski is a man of great talent. But his history of Marxism is not worthy of that talent, or of its subject. It is a work of great erudition, but written with so much animus as to warp the author's perspective and judgement. It will no doubt serve well enough as one more weapon in the already extensive arsenal of anti-Marxism; but it will not serve much else, and least of all a proper understanding of what has for so long given Marxism so great an appeal and influence.

Postscript

This review of Leszek Kolakowski's history of Marxism calls for some further comments. The first one concerns the sharpness of tone of the review. I think this is in part attributable to a strong personal sense of disappointment at Kolakowski's political evolution. I have known Kolakowski since the fraught days of 1956 and have always thought him to be a man of outstanding integrity and courage, with a brilliant and original mind. His turning away from Marxism and, as I see it, from socialism has been a great boon to the reactionary forces of which he was once the dedicated enemy, and a great loss to the socialist cause, of which he was once the intrepid champion. I felt that loss very keenly as I was reading his history and writing my review.

Secondly, I must make some brief comments on my references in the review to Lenin and Leninism. To say as I do that 'Leninism is primarily a theory and a strategy of revolution' may be accurate, but the formulation is nevertheless a serious undervaluation of Lenin's contribution to the development of Marxism. Also, I seem at one point to endorse Kolakowski's view that, for Lenin, 'the party alone could and must be the initiator and source of revolutionary consciousness': this is a very partial interpretation of Lenin's position on this issue. Finally, I say in the review that Leninism, as a theory and a strategy of revolution, 'stands in clear contradiction to Marx's own perspectives on the process of revolutionary change'. As I explain in the preceding paragraphs, this refers to the role of the party. Crucial though this is, it nevertheless ought to be said that there is also much in Leninism's theory and strategy of revolution which *accords* with Marx's own views, notably Lenin's insistence that the working class, in Marx's own words, could not 'simply lay hold of the ready-made state machinery, and wield it for its own purposes', but must 'smash' it, and create its own organs of power.

1. *Main Currents of Marxism* (henceforth MCM), Vol. 1, p.10.
2. MCM, 1, p.39.
3. MCM, 1, p.117.
4. MCM, 1, p.178.
5. MCM, 2, p.41.
6. MCM, 1, p.181.
7. 'The realm of freedom actually begins only where labour which is determined by necessity and mundane considerations ceases; thus in the very nature of things it lies beyond the sphere of actual material production . . . Freedom in this field can only consist in socialized man, the associated producers, rationally regulating their interchange with Nature, bringing it under their common control, instead of being ruled

228

by the blind forces of nature; and achieving this with the least expenditure of energy and under conditions most favourable to, and worthy of their human nature. But it nonetheless remains a realm of necessity. Beyond it begins that development of human energy which is an end in itself, the true realm of freedom, which, however, can blossom forth only with this realm of necessity as its basis. The shortening of the working-day is its basic prerequisite.' (Karl Marx, *Capital*, Moscow 1962, Vol. 3, pp.799-800).

'In a more advanced phase of communist society, when the enslaving subjugation of individuals to the division of labour, and thereby the antithesis between intellectual and physical labour, have disappeared; when labour is no longer just a means of keeping alive but has itself become a vital need; when the all-round development of individuals has also increased their productive powers and all the springs of cooperative wealth flow more abundantly—only then can society wholly cross the narrow horizon of bourgeois right and inscribe on its banner: From each according to his abilities, to each according to his needs!' (Karl Marx, 'Critique of the Gotha Programme' in *The First International and After: Political Writings*, Vol. 3, London 1974, p.347.)

8. MCM, 1, p.416.
9. MCM, 3, p.253.
10. MCM, 1, p.265.
11. MCM, 1, p.414.
12. MCM, 1, p.171.
13. MCM, 3, p.530.
14. MCM, 1, p.413.
15. MCM, 3, p.524.
16. For other and similar comments on historical materialism, see also MCM, 1, pp.363ff.
17. MCM, 3, p.526.
18. MCM, 2, pp.94-5.
19. MCM, 1, p.5.
20. MCM, 3, p.161.
21. MCM, 3, p.161.
22. MCM, 1, p.418.
23. These are the first words of the Preamble to the Provisional Rules which Marx drafted for the First International. See also, among other things, Marx's bitter denunciation of the 'alchemists of revolution' who believed that 'the only condition for a revolution is the proper organization of their conspiracy'. (K. Marx and F. Engels, *Collected Works*, London 1978, Vol. 10, p.318.)
24. MCM, 2, p.398.
25. MCM, 3, p.2.
26. MCM, 3, p.7.
27. MCM, 3, p.3.
28. MCM, 3, p.7.
29. MCM, 3, p.2.
30. Kolakowski writes that, from 1924 to 1929, the period of the New Economic Policy, 'there was considerable freedom of private trading; political life no longer existed outside the Party, but there were genuine disputes and controversies within the leadership; culture was officially controlled, but different trends of opinion and discussions were allowed within the bounds of Marxism and of political obedience. It was still possible to debate the nature of "true" Marxism; one-man despotism was

not yet an institution and a fair proportion of society—the peasantry, and 'Nepmen' of all kinds—was not yet wholly dependent on the state from the economic point of view'. (MCM, 3, p.8.)

31. MCM, 3, p.7.
32. *Critique of the Gotha Programme*, p.354.
33. MCM, 3, p.418.
34. MCM, 2, p.30.

13
Military Intervention
and Socialist Internationalism*
1980

I

Soviet military action in Afghanistan has once again served to underline the need for socialists to clarify their positions on the issue of military intervention by the USSR and other Communist states in other countries—including of course intervention against other Communist states. Before the USSR's intervention in Afghanistan, there was Vietnam's intervention in Kampuchea and its overthrow of the Pol Pot regime; and there was also China's intervention in Vietnam. Before that, there was Cuba's intervention in Angola and also in Ethiopia. Other instances from the less recent past readily come to mind—for instance Soviet intervention in Czechoslovakia in 1968 and in Hungary in 1956; and so on back to the overthrow by the Red Army of the Menshevik regime in Georgia in 1921 and its abortive march on Warsaw in 1920.

These very different episodes—or at least some of them—have raised much more difficult questions for socialists than does American and other Western military intervention all over the world. Insofar as such Western intervention has been intended to shore up reactionary regimes against revolutionary movements of very diverse kinds, socialists have had no problem in opposing it. But Russian, Chinese, Vietnamese and Cuban military intervention has produced no such easy unanimity on the left. On the contrary, it has generated great uncertainty, confusion and division; and it has commonly led

* An early version of this article was presented to a private seminar in London in May 1980. The discussion that followed was very helpful and I am grateful to the participants.

to the adoption of positions which are not based on any obvious socialist principle but rather on antecedent sympathies or antipathies, according to which a particular intervention is approved or condemned. Empirical justification comes later; and given sufficient selectivity and a strong will to believe, it comes quite easily.

That there should be much uncertainty and confusion over military intervention by Communist states is not surprising: the issues, for socialists, are often full of difficulties and dilemmas. To recognize that this is so is perhaps the first rule to be followed in discussing them. But the difficulties and dilemmas make it all the more necessary to clarify the principles on which judgements are made. This is what the present article tries to do.

II

It may be best to begin with the one set of conditions in which military intervention poses no problem in terms of socialist principles. This is where a more or less progressive government (the use of the formula will be justified presently), enjoying a large measure of popular support, is seeking to repel a counter-revolutionary internal movement, in conditions of civil war or approximating to civil war; or where such a government is seeking to repel a military attack from abroad which is clearly designed to overthrow it. Both internal and external attack may of course be combined. Military help to a threatened government is obviously justified in such circumstances in terms of socialist internationalism. What precise form the help should take must remain for the requesting government to decide, just as states being asked for help must take many different considerations into account, including the larger international implications of the giving of help, particularly if it is to assume the form of military intervention.

Even in these circumstances, it is crucial that the requesting government should remain in charge, and that it should not surrender its destinies to another power, however friendly. This may raise problems, even serious problems, for instance of military command, or of strategic decision-making. But to the greatest possible extent, the requesting government must remain in charge and seek to preserve ultimate sovereignty; otherwise, there is a great danger that military intervention will soon come to bear a disturbing resemblance to military domination and even occupation.

The classic case of justified external military help is (or perhaps more accurately should have been) that of the Spanish Civil War, where a liberal-left government was faced with a military rebellion of fascist inspiration, backed by Fascist Italy and Nazi Germany. The International Brigade that was then formed, mostly at Communist initiative, was the most remarkable example of international socialist solidarity and of 'proletarian internationalism' in history. And for all the many foul features of Soviet help to the Spanish Republic, that help also falls under the rubric of international solidarity. What was wrong with Soviet intervention is that there was not enough of it; and that one of the forms it took was the liquidation of large numbers of anti-Stalinists who were fighting for the Republic.

Another more recent example is that of Cuban intervention in Angola. Whether initially prompted by the USSR or not, Cuban military intervention there was clearly justified on the criteria advanced earlier. For it contributed to the survival of a revolutionary government just emerging from a long anti-colonial war against Portugal, enjoying a large measure of popular support, and faced with internal enemies backed by South Africa, the United States, Zaire, China, and so on.[1] In the same line of thought, Soviet and Chinese help to Vietnam was similarly justified, and there would have been every justification, in principle, for more such intervention, had the Vietnamese asked for it—although larger considerations of war and peace would obviously have had to be taken into account.

I have referred here to 'more or less progressive' governments and regimes, and use this formula in order to take some necessary distance from the rhetoric which is the usual accompaniment of discussions of intervention, where the regime which is being helped tends to be accorded every conceivable socialist virtue and is painted in the most brilliant colours. Yet, such governments are not, and in the circumstances cannot be, as pure and praiseworthy as they are said to be by their internal representatives and external apologists. Whatever they may say about themselves, and whatever may be said on their behalf, the conditions in which they have come to power and in which they function, are bound to affect adversely—often very adversely—the 'socialism' which they proclaim. One of the many blights that Stalinism cast on socialist thinking was the habit—indeed the requirement—to view favoured regimes (beginning with Stalin's own) as unblemished examples of socialist construction; and the habit at least did not die with Stalin. The craving to believe is very strong; but it surely ought to be resisted. Governments do not have to be perfect in order to be supported—and *critical* support is the most that *any* government ought to be accorded. The legitimacy of intervention does not rest on the (always illusory) socialist perfection of the government that is being supported: it rests rather on a judgement that its survival is in peril; and that, for all its imperfections and shortcomings, it deserves to survive, because of the hopes it offers and because of the reactionary nature of the forces which are threatening its survival.

A second set of conditions is where a movement of opposition or liberation, with a substantial measure of support, is waging a military struggle, from its own liberated bases, against an authoritarian and reactionary regime representing landed, commercial and financial oligarchies, foreign concerns, multinational corporations, and is backed by the United States and other Western powers. It is worth stressing that such governments and regimes have since the Second World War enjoyed the backing of the United States and other Western powers because, however repressive and corrupt they may be, they are part of the Free World, meaning in effect the Free Enterprise world. This being the case, defending these regimes against their own people is an instrinsic part of the logic of imperialism. This logic requires such defence for a number of different but related reasons: as long as they are part of the Free World, they are available for the operations of free enterprise; they may also have strategic importance; and they may have resources—for instance, oil or uranium—which enhance their value to their protectors. The overthrow of reactionary and repressive regimes by popular movements, of whatever kind, is therefore unacceptable or at least unwelcome, because all the advantages that these governments offer to imperialism risk being extinguished; and there is also the risk that successor regimes may be sympathetic to Communist powers, or that they will at least be less easy to handle than hitherto; and their success in achieving power in any case strengthens the anti-imperialist cause. The coming into being of successor regimes may not always be prevented; but they must then be subverted and co-opted back into the Western camp.

Clearly, movements of opposition and liberation require and deserve international socialist solidarity and support. But military intervention is a different matter: and as a matter of fact, such movements very seldom ask for it. The reason for this is obvious, namely that, if they did, they would run the very grave risk of being swamped and taken over by the intervening power, or at least of losing effective control over the struggle they are conducting; and its leaders would at the same time be bound to incur the accusation of being puppets or agents of that power. Liberation struggles, however inspired and whatever they call themselves, have almost by definition a strong nationalist ingredient. Very often, the movement is impelled by the will to rid the country of a regime which has brought it into subordination to another state: all other aims, including the achievement of economic, social and cultural advances, are seen to pass through the achievement of national independence or statehood. Given this, acceptance of foreign protection by way of foreign military intervention cuts across this national—and nationalist—emphasis, or at least runs the very great risk of doing so. This is presumably why leaders of liberation and guerrilla movements do not usually seek military aid beyond the supply of weapons, or training assistance, or military advisers.

Governments are a different matter. For they can at least claim sovereign authority, and are therefore better able to control the foreign intervention they require and may ask for. A group of revolutionaries in the field is likely to find such control more difficult to achieve. Also, the intervening power, being by definition 'friendly', is likely to be more inhibited in its relations with a formally independent government, able to claim sovereign authority, than with a revolutionary movement. But even in the case of governments, the risk of being swamped, of being taken over, or of suffering a serious reduction of authority, may be considerable, and is bound to weigh in the calculations that government leaders must make whether to invoke external military help or not.

The third set of conditions is the one the left has most commonly had to confront, and which it has found the most difficult. This is where military intervention has occurred without it being requested by a government enjoying any measure of popular support, or indeed by anyone at all except some individuals without authority (Hungary, 1956; Afghanistan, 1979); or where military intervention has occurred *against* a government enjoying a large measure of popular support, and at the behest of some individuals again without authority or support (Czechoslovakia, 1968). A rather different case, which falls however within the same spectrum, is that of Vietnam's intervention in Kampuchea: what might be called a frontier war between the two countries was taken further by Vietnam, to the point of overthrowing the Pol Pot regime and installing another regime in Phnom Penh, acceptable to the Vietnamese. The military intervention of China against Vietnam is of a different order, and must be treated separately.

In such cases as Hungary, Czechoslovakia, Kampuchea and Afghanistan, the claim that foreign armies had some legitimate ground for intervention because they were 'invited' is evidently spurious. But this is not of course the only ground on which intervention is defended. It is in fact defended on one or other of three different grounds (or on all three), each of which requires consideration: unlike the claim about intervention being 'invited', these other arguments raise precisely the issues that socialists have to confront.

One such argument is that, in case after case, there existed a grave and imminent threat of counter-revolution, backed by Western imperialism and indeed instigated by it, against a socialist regime and its revolutionary achievements. Even in Czechoslovakia in 1968, it was claimed, and still is, that whatever the intentions of Alexander Dubcek and the Czech Government might have been, there was a clear and immediate threat of 'things getting out of control', of the 'restoration of capitalism', of 'counter-revolution', of Czechoslovakia pulling out of the Warsaw Pact, and so on.

Such claims cannot by definition be conclusively proved or disproved, which is why it is possible for endless controversy to go on about them, without anyone's positions being much affected either way. It may be that a better way to proceed is to ask first of all what some of the key terms—notably counter-revolution—actually mean in this context. Misunderstanding of what the argument is about may thereby be avoided. For some, 'counter-revolution' is more or less synonymous with the replacement of a government wholly sub-servient to the USSR by a government not thus subservient. But this —typically Stalinist—definition is clearly not adequate. When Tito broke with Moscow in 1948, Communist parties everywhere—not to speak of the Soviet government—denounced him as an 'authentic Fascist' and as, in the terminology of the French Communist Party at the time, a 'Hitlero-Trotskyist', who was indeed leading a counter-revolution. Without a doubt, if Russian armies had intervened in Yugoslavia then, had succeeded in overthrowing Tito, and had installed a 'pro-Soviet' government in Belgrade, there would have been many to say that the Soviet Union has rescued the Yugoslav people from counter-revolution. This should perhaps serve to induce some caution in the making of statements about what would have happened in this country or that if the Russians had not inter-vened. For whatever else may be said about Tito's rule after 1948, it can hardly be said that he pushed through a 'counter-revolution' in Yugoslavia; and it is now said that the denunciations of him as a 'Fascist', 'counter-revolutionary', or an 'agent of the West' were part of the history of Stalinist aberrations and are best forgotten. But the aberrations ought not to be forgotten, for they have important lessons to teach, and there is much evidence that the danger of repeating these aberrations or similar ones is still very much alive. Less dramatically than Yugoslavia by far, Romania has managed to achieve a considerable degree of independence from the USSR in regard to both internal but particularly external affairs (which does not prevent the regime from being as repressive as any in Eastern Europe); but no one has so far claimed that President Ceausescu has engineered a 'counter-revolution' in his country.

Properly speaking, a counter-revolution may be said to have occur-red when a regime of the left, Communist or not, has been overthrown (or for that matter replaced by legal means) and where the successor regime pushes through a series of economic, social and political mea-sures designed to assure or restore the power, property and privileges of landlords, capitalists and other segments of the ruling class who have been threatened with dispossession or who have actually been dispossessed by the regime which the counter-revolution has replaced. This involves the return to landlords and capitalists of their land and factories and banks, and of property in general, where it has been taken from them. It also involves the reaffirmation of their power and preponderance by the suppression of the defence organizations of the subordinate classes—parties, trade unions, cooperatives, clubs and associations. It further involves the suppression or drastic curtailment of civil rights; the physical suppression of opposition leaders, of agitators, subversives and enemies of the state; and the political restructuring of the state in authoritarian directions.

Many counter-revolutions of this kind have occurred throughout Europe since 1918, sometimes against a newly implanted Communist regime, but also against non-Communist left ones, or even against liberal and conservative ones when they were thought to be inadequate in opposing the left: Hungary in 1919, Italy in 1921 and after, Germany in 1933, Spain in 1936, France with the Vichy regime in 1940, and, outside Europe, Chile in 1973 are all examples of such counter-revolutions; and the list could easily be stretched out. It is not essential for a revolution actually to have occurred for a counter-revolution to be mounted: the apparent illogicality is purely in the semantics, not in the reality.

If counter-revolution is taken to involve the sort of changes that have been mentioned here, it would seem reasonable to say that in none of the cases where Soviet armies have intervened since the Second World War, with the doubtful exception of Afghanistan, has there been a clear and compelling threat of counter-revolution. As noted earlier, this is not susceptible to proof; but neither in the case of Hungary in 1956 nor certainly of Czechoslovakia in 1968, to take two major instances of Soviet intervention, is there evidence that counter-revolution was about to succeed, or likely eventually to succeed. Of course, there were, particularly in Hungary, people who had counter-revolutionary intentions: but that is obviously not the same thing. Nor is it my argument that the Communist monopoly of power would have been maintained intact in either country: on the contrary, it would have been loosened; indeed, the process had already gone some way in Czechoslovakia. In both countries, there might well have come into being a coalition regime in which the Communist Party would not have been assured of an automatic preponderance; and other such variations can easily be conceived. The point is that, whatever may be thought of these possibilities, they cannot, on any reasonable assessment, be equated with 'counter-revolution', or anything like it.

This must be taken a little further. Had the processes at work in Hungary and Czechoslovakia not been crushed out of existence by military intervention, it is likely that there would have occurred a measure of 'liberalization' of economic life in both countries—something like the New Economic Policy which Lenin and the Bolsheviks were forced to adopt in the Soviet Union in 1921, with a greater emphasis on the market and a redevelopment of artisan and small-scale enterprise in manufacturing, retail trade, and so on. The evocation of such 'liberalization' in economic activity tends to generate the cry of 'restoration of capitalism' among many purists. But this is a misconception. For the 'commanding heights' of the economy would have remained in the public sector, and the public sector would have remained massively predominant. It would surely have been exceedingly difficult to unscramble long-nationalized property and to restore factories, mines or land to their former owners. And there is one measure of 'liberalization' which would have been of enormous socialist significance, namely the restoration of the right to strike. Purists make much too little of the grievous dereliction, in socialist terms, which the suppression of that right in Communist regimes represents. Not only would the reaffirmation of the right to strike have been proper in itself: it would also have strengthened the credentials of the regime in the eyes of the working class, and made all the less likely the 'restoration of capitalism'. Moreover, this reaffirmation would have been one element among many to mark the loosening of the grip of the monopolistic state over civil society; other such elements would have included the reaffirmation of a whole range of civil rights suppressed earlier. And there would also have occurred a substantial and possibly a major reorientation of the foreign relations of both countries; and this raises the question of Soviet 'security', which will be discussed presently. Tito's foreign policy, it may be said here, may well afford an example of what might have been the most likely course of events in this realm.

The fundamental question that socialists have to confront is not whether the kind of regime that would have emerged from the convulsions of 1956 and 1968 would have been absolutely the most desirable; but whether it would have been a worse alternative than the imposition by Russian arms of a regime altogether lacking in popular support and whose most distinctive characteristic is the tight monopoly of power exercised by a Communist leadership acceptable to Moscow. I suggest that the answer—again leaving out for the moment the question of Soviet 'security'—is that, in socialist terms, it would not have been a worse alternative. The reason for saying so is simply that there can be no good socialist warrant for the imposition by foreign arms of a 'socialist' regime which the overwhelming majority of people resent and reject.

This is no more than the affirmation of a principle akin to that of national self-determination. 'Self-determination' means the right to national independence, expressed by independent statehood. It is a very old principle to which most if not all strands of the socialist movement have always declared allegiance. Admittedly, there was a current of thought in the international socialist movement most notably represented by Rosa Luxemburg, which rejected the 'slogan' of self-determination on the ground that it diverted the proletariat from its real revolutionary tasks; and Luxemburg continued to hold this view after 1917. But even she said in 1915 that 'socialism gives to every people the right of independence and the freedom of independent control of its own destinies'.[2] In effect, she believed that self-determination could not be achieved under capitalism, and that to seek it was a diversion from the main task; but she also believed that socialism would make self-determination possible and that it was indeed a fundamental right. So did the Bolshevik leaders, although with some qualifications other than those advanced by Luxemburg. They very reasonably held that, while self-determination could not be denied to a people who wanted it, and could particularly not be denied by the revolutionaries of an 'oppressor' nation like Tsarist Russia, it was not incumbent upon them to press it upon people who were content with regional autonomy or federal arrangements. The Bolsheviks' own most important saving clause, however, was that the demand for self-determination must not run counter to the larger requirements of the class struggle, nationally and internationally. Even though they had recognized Georgia's more or less independent status in May 1920, they cast aside its Menshevik Government by military action in February 1921 and brought Georgia back into the

Soviet fold. In due course, what had been a saving clause became a convenient excuse. From the early years of the Bolshevik Revolution until 1956, there was one centre—Moscow—to decide for the world Communist movement what was in the best interests of the class struggle on a global scale; and this made it possible for the Soviet leaders to interpret the principle of self-determination—and any other principle—as they willed.

Military intervention need not formally deny national self-determination expressed as statehood. The Soviet Union did not incorporate Hungary in 1956 or Czechoslovakia in 1968, and thereby bring to an end their independent existence as states. But military intervention, under the 'doctrine' of 'limited national sovereignty', does turn this statehood into a largely formal thing, by ensuring that a government wholly subservient to the intervening power is installed in the given country. Even this is much better than incorporation and the end of statehood: but it does deprive statehood of a substantial part of its meaning. The principle of self-determination is not unduly stretched by the inclusion within it of the right of the people or of a majority of the people not to have a regime imposed upon them by a foreign power. Such imposition does constitute a drastic infringement of the principle of self-determination, which may be taken here to mean popular self-determination. It would be unrealistic to stipulate that under no circumstances of any kind must that principle ever be infringed. But the onus is on those who defend the infringement to show on what other principle the infringement was justified in any particular case; and the point does hold that it is only in the direst and most extreme circumstances that it could ever be justified.

There are many different ways—and not only by military intervention—in which the imposition of unpopular rule can occur. One such way is by the extension of help to reactionary and repressive regimes in order to enable them to defeat popular pressure and resistance; and the United States and its allies have engaged in such imposition on numerous occasions since the end of the Second World War.[3] It is only in Cold War propaganda and apologies for Western imperialism that the Soviet Union and other Communist powers are the only ones to have imposed unwanted regimes upon other countries. But this does not negate the fact that Communist powers *have* engaged in such enterprises.

I have argued that the threat of counter-revolution was not a proper justification for military intervention in the cases of Hungary and Czechoslovakia. But what of Afghanistan? Here is a country where a revolutionary coup brought to power in April 1978 a left-wing government with strong Russian connections and sympathies. The leader of the new regime, Nur Mohammad Taraki, was himself overthrown and killed when he tried, in September 1979, to get rid of his Prime Minister, Hafizullah Amin. Amin took over but was in turn removed and executed at the end of December 1979, and replaced by Babrak Karmal. The removal of Amin and his replacement by Karmal was obviously instigated by the Soviet Union, which also marched into Afghanistan to provide Karmal with military backing.

In Afghanistan as in Hungary and Czechoslovakia, the notion that the Russians were 'invited' by any kind of legitimate authority is so absurd as not to require discussion. On the other hand, the question of counter-revolution in Afghanistan does require it. The regime that came into being in April 1978 had declared itself to be a revolutionary one, intent upon the thorough transformation of the country in socialist directions. In immediate terms, this meant setting in motion a number of greatly needed reforms—some measures of land reform, improvements in the position of women, some attempts at alleviating an illiteracy rate of more than ninety per cent, the granting of cultural rights to national minorities, and the cancellation of debts owed by peasants to richer farmers and landlords.

From the first, the government confronted stubborn resistance and was itself undermined by acute internal dissension and factional struggles of a long-standing nature. It never had more than a very slender basis of support, concentrated in Kabul, and probably numbering no more than a few thousand people in a country of nearly seventeen million, comprising some two and a half million town dwellers, the rest being country dwellers, with a substantial number of nomads. By all accounts, the Taraki regime was fiercely repressive and thousands of people were imprisoned and many executed. This further reduced the government's base of support and fed the strength of its opponents, some of whom were supported by Iran, Pakistan, the United States and China. From the beginning of 1979 if not earlier, the Russians played an important role in the country's government and administration, and also in the military struggle against opposition forces. At the end of 1979, this turned into full-scale military suppression, or attempted suppression, and this has since then assumed larger proportions.

In the case of the military interventions in Hungary and Czechoslovakia, it could be argued that Russian arms were safeguarding the economic, social and political transformations which had been brought about by the regimes which had come into being some ten years earlier in the Hungarian case and twenty years earlier in the Czech one. As I have said earlier, this argument, based on the threat of counter-revolution, is unconvincing. But even this justification is lacking in the case of Afghanistan. For the regime was new, had achieved very little, was exceedingly weak (except in the repression of those of its opponents it could reach) and did not appear to have any serious measure of popular support. There was no revolution to save in Afghanistan, only a government that proclaimed its revolutionary intentions but had extremely poor revolutionary prospects. The chances are that no government in Afghanistan resting on so slender a base as the Taraki and Amin regime could hope to achieve much; and that it would only be able to maintain itself—if at all—by continued repression and the help of foreign arms.

Here too, the question of alternatives has to be posed. It is of course convenient to argue that *no* alternative to Babrak Karmal existed save the blackest kind of reactionary regime, allied to the United States, Pakistan and China. This seems very unlikely. No doubt there would have been much turmoil if the Russians had not intervened. Probably, the People's Democratic Party of Afghanistan (PDPA), or rather its leaders, would have lost the monopoly of power which they achieved with the coup of April 1978. The chances are that they would have had to share power with 'outside' elements by way of a coalition; and that there would have occurred a loosening of ties with the USSR.

No option of this sort appears to have been explored, either by the leaders of the PDPA or by the Russians. The reason for this is two-fold: first, because it would precisely have meant the relinquishing of monopolistic power by the PDPA leaders, which was a difficult and risky enterprise that they were naturally loath to consider; and secondly because the Soviet Union feared that a loosening of power by the PDPA leadership would indeed have meant the erosion and possibly the end of their preponderant influence in a country which had come to be in their 'sphere of influence' and control. This, incidentally, would have restored a situation which had prevailed in the years preceding the coup of 1978, when Afghanistan under the rule of Mohammed Daud was the terrain of intense competition between the United States (via Iran) and the USSR. The coup of 1978 was in this sense a major victory for the USSR, which it was not prepared to see jeopardized by an attempted widening of the base of the regime. The question of security, which will be taken up presently, was obviously an important consideration. But the larger question, encompassing that of security, is that the end of monopolistic power in Afghanistan would have appeared to be a retreat of Soviet power, for which the only parallel or precedent is Tito's 'rebellion' against Stalin in 1948. The Soviet leaders were not prepared to risk such a retreat. Instead, they opted for the installation of a puppet regime backed by military force. It is possible that such a regime can be maintained by military force. But it seems more likely that the Russians themselves will be compelled to engineer some kind of compromise solution, since the present situation involves them in a war of pacification which, in the nature of the terrain and the opposition (and the help that the opposition will be able to get from outside), they cannot conclusively win. But however this may turn out, the fact remains that the military intervention altogether lacks legitimacy and has strengthened rather than weakened the forces of counter-revolution in Afghanistan.

III

'Preventing counter-revolution' and 'saving the revolution' is one argument that leads many socialists to accept the legitimacy of military intervention in, say, Hungary or Czechoslovakia or Afghanistan. A second, closely related argument, is not usually stated explicitly but exercises a powerful attraction and goes as follows: the revolution may or may not have been supported by a majority of the people, or even by a substantial minority. But even if it was not, it did happen; and it must therefore be maintained at all costs and if necessary by force of foreign arms, not only because the alternative is counter-revolution, or because an alternative poses a threat to Soviet security, but also because *in due course* the people will come to see the advantages of the regime which the revolution installed. They will come to accept the regime and to support it. Early progress towards 'socialism' will thus have been made more or less against the will of the people. But given the advantages of the system and what it will do for the people, later progress will be made on the basis of popular support. In this sense, what military intervention is doing is to give the revolution a breathing space and to make possible its later consolidation and successes. Military intervention buys time for the revolution and could even be said to be an extreme form of 'substitutism', with foreign armies rather than the party 'substituting' themselves for the will of the proletariat and allied classes. Of course, 'substitutism' is a deformation. It runs counter to the Marxist 'scenario' for a socialist revolution, or at least to Marx's view of it; and it also runs counter to Lenin's view of the party as being closely linked to, even though separate from, the working class, and as requiring a large measure of popular support to make a revolution. But, the argument goes on, circumstances impose hard choices, particularly in an international context of implacable hostility to the revolutionary cause; and theory has to be adapted to the requirements of real life, without self-defeating and dogmatic adherence to frozen formulas.

The trouble with the argument is not that its contradicts Marx's 'scenario' for a socialist revolution, or Lenin's: this is hardly a conclusive objection. The trouble is rather that the projection on which the argument is based is exceedingly dubious, and has, in fact, been shown by experience to date to be wrong.

The crucial factor here is popular support, or rather lack of popular support. The revolution which is being saved by foreign arms is one which the large—usually the overwhelming—majority of the people, including, of course, the working class and peasants, oppose: it is precisely because of this opposition that foreign military intervention occurs. But the intervention itself constitutes a further condemnation of the regime which depends upon it, and further adds to its already great unpopularity; and it also further alienates the mass of the people from the 'socialism' which the regime and its foreign backers claim to represent and uphold. Military intervention also fuels a powerful nationalist sentiment, itself fostered by antagonism to the regime, and nationalist sentiment is further exacerbated when intervention is carried out by the armies of a country which is viewed by the mass of the people as a secular enemy and predator, whose government is believed to be furthering traditional aims of national aggrandizement and domination. An obvious case in point is Poland; and it probably applies also to Vietnam and Kampuchea. Whether the belief is justified or not is not very material: it is deeply held.

These are very heavy burdens for a regime to bear, in terms of its minimal legitimation. Some regimes in Eastern Europe have borne the burdens more easily than others. But nowhere has a Communist regime imposed by foreign arms upon a hostile population been able to acquire massive popular legitimation. The reasons for this include foreign intervention but go well beyond it.

Almost by definition, a regime imposed upon a hostile population by foreign arms (or for that matter without the help of foreign arms) will be strongly repressive: opposition must be put down, civil rights must be denied, and civic life must be severely controlled, and thereby impoverished. This also deeply affects economic life and activity. The regime requires the cooperation of the working class, the peasantry, and the producers in general. But the working class, officially prevented from freely expressing its demands and grievances, and from using the one weapon which is most readily and immediately available to it, namely the right to strike, fights back by non-cooperation at work and elsewhere. Other classes and strata, also alienated and unable to express themselves, act similarly. The result is resistance or at best indifference, inefficiency and corruption. Poor performance and non-cooperation aggravate economic difficulties; and these in turn enhance popular dissatisfaction.

In this perspective, the notion that these regimes can eventually come to enjoy a large and growing measure of popular support must appear illusory. For not only are they deeply marked by their dependence on foreign intervention for survival (and for the most part by their origin in foreign intervention); but also by the essential nature of the regimes which military intervention (or the threat of foreign intervention) serves to maintain. The point is that the regimes in question are not monopolistic and repressive simply from temporary necessity and transient adverse circumstances, but by their very structure. I mean by this that they are based on a view of 'socialism' as *requiring* the existence of one 'leading' party whose leaders do exercise monopolistic power; and monopolistic power by definition means the exclusion from power of everyone else, and also the deprivation of rights—speech, association, publication—which are essential for the exercise of power or at least pressure, and which are, so to speak, the oxygen of civil society. To speak of this as a 'Soviet-type' regime is at one level inaccurate, since the rule of the soviets was intended to establish the opposite of concentrated and monopolistic power. But history has associated this monopolistic form of regime with the Soviet Union; and it is therefore convenient to refer to it as a 'Soviet-type' regime. Its early form was the largely unintended product of the circumstances of the Bolshevik Revolution; but it was perfected with every deliberate intention by Stalin. All Communist regimes that have come into being since the Second World War bear this stamp. Some of them are less repressive than others, with the extent of the repressiveness varying not only from country to country but also over time within countries. But they are all monopolistic regimes, not excluding Yugoslavia.

Much confusion is engendered by the discussion of these regimes as 'transitional', meaning in effect 'transitional' from capitalism to socialism. Most notably, Trotskyist discussion, which ever since Trotsky's *The Revolution Betrayed* of 1936, has most probingly sought to advance the Marxist analysis of Soviet-type regimes, has also fostered much confusion about them by insisting that they were 'workers states'; albeit 'bureaucratically deformed'. and that they were 'transitional' between capitalism and socialism. The main reason why this thesis is maintained is, of course, that in these regimes the private ownership of the means of production has been replaced by state ownership and control. Given this, it is argued, to my mind rightly, that the societies in question are no longer 'capitalist'; and that the description of them as 'state capitalist' does not fit any better. However, they are not 'socialist' either—hence the label 'deformed' or 'degenerate workers states'. But this label is also defective, not only because 'workers state', however qualified, is not an applicable description of these societies, but also because the label is intended to suggest or imply that, for all their bureaucratic deformations, they are *on the way* to being socialist, in a process which, though not painless, has been rendered inevitable by the abolition of the private ownership and control of the main means of production. This needs to be questioned.

The abolition of the private ownership and control of the main means of production is indeed a gigantic step; and it may be said to constitute an essential feature of a socialist society. But it is now very generally agreed that it is not a sufficient condition for the establishment of such a society. Even when this is readily acknowledged, however, it is also often believed that, given the 'base' which is provided by a predominant public economic sector, all other major features of a socialist society—notably democratic and egalitarian forms in economic, social and political life—must sooner or later follow. But this is much too simple and 'economistic' a reading of the 'base-superstructure' model; and an experience which is now sufficiently ample to be convincing shows that a predominantly (or for that matter an exclusively) public economic 'base' does not necessarily produce anything like democratic or egalitarian forms in economic, social and political life, or anything like a 'socialist consciousness' which would prepare the ground for them. On the contrary, such a 'base' may well produce markedly undemocratic and inegalitarian 'superstructures', with a strongly repressive state, a relatedly impoverished civic life, and general indifference and cynicism concerning the 'social good'. To be credible, the notion of 'transitionality' would need to point towards some degree of progress towards socialism in terms of socialist consciousness; for it is a mistake to speak of any kind of socialism which does not involve at least popular support for it. But it would surely be rash to claim that the *idea* of socialism (never mind the actual regime) is more securely legitimated in Poland in 1980 than it was in 1970 or 1960 or 1950.

It may be that the picture is more favourable in other countries in Central and Eastern Europe, or in the USSR; but nowhere in Soviet-type societies does there appear to have occurred the growth of socialist consciousness which an 'economistic' reading of the 'base-superstructure' model as applied to these societies would suggest or imply. In other words, there is no good reason to think that the regimes in question, because of their public sector 'base', are bound to flower into legitimated socialist democracies, enjoying a large and growing measure of popular support, with a base of genuine popular power, and therefore able to dispense with their vast apparatus of repression and their abrogation of civic rights. For they are all imprisoned in a very hard mould: not surprisingly, the people in charge, who exercise monopolistic power, have no wish to change in any fundamental way the system which gives them that power, and which they believe to be the only one capable of defending 'socialism'; and the forces making for *socialist* change are generally speaking weak.

On this view, the notion of Soviet-type societies as 'transitional' is not helpful. It is much more helpful to a proper assessment of these societies and their regimes to see them as specific systems, with their own particular mode of production and their own social and political structures. They lack an agreed label: but that does not detract from their reality or from their specificity. They are not capitalist systems. But they are also very far distant from anything that could be called socialism. The term is largely meaningless if it does not include a fundamental recasting of the 'relations of production' and the 'relations of life' in general in democratic and egalitarian directions: and this clearly requires the institutionalization of the means whereby this can be achieved, or at least striven for. Merely to say this, in relation to Soviet-type societies, is to indicate how great the distance is that separates them from socialism, and how inappropriate it is to apply the notion of 'transition' to them.

This is in no way to suggest that these regimes do not have some very considerable achievements to their credit in the economic, social, and cultural-scientific spheres, or that they are not capable of further achievements. Nor is it to underestimate the enormous obstacles placed in their path by economic backwardness and imperialist hostility. Again, it is hardly necessary to say that there are any number of regimes in the world, strongly supported and greatly lauded by the Western powers, that are infinitely worse for their own people than Soviet-type regimes. But none of this turns the latter into socialist ones.

The relevance of these considerations to the question of military intervention as a form of 'substitutism' is obvious. The 'substitutist' argument is that these socialist regimes need time to establish themselves, and must be defended against 'counter-revolutionary' pressure against them. But if these are *not* socialist regimes, what they need to become socialist is not simply time but a fundamental transformation in their whole mode of being. In some of the most dramatic cases of military intervention in the post-war decades— Hungary, Czechoslovakia—this is precisely what a large part of what was called 'counter-revolutionary' pressure was intended to achieve; and it is precisely what military intervention was intended to prevent. In other words, military intervention occurred not to save 'socialism', but to save monopolistic regimes.

IV

A subsidiary argument, which has sometimes been used to justify some military interventions, notably the Vietnamese intervention in Kampuchea, may be considered at this point. This is the argument that, whatever may be said against military intervention in most cases, it is defensible in some exceptional cases, namely in the case of particularly tyrannical and murderous regimes, for instance the regimes of Idi Amin in Uganda, and Pol Pot in Kampuchea. Idi Amin, it will be recalled, sent Ugandan troops into Tanzania and occupied a substantial area of border territory; and Tanzanian troops did not merely push Ugandan troops back into Uganda but went on to occupy the country and overthrow Amin. Similarly, in regard to Vietnam's overthrow of Pol Pot, the Vietnamese claimed that they were faced with repeated and large-scale incursions by Kampuchean troops into Vietnam; and the horrifying nature of the Pol Pot regime, it has been claimed on behalf of Vietnam, as well as imperative security considerations (of which more presently), justi- fied Vietnam's decision to march to Phnom Penh and to make an end of the Pol Pot regime.

The argument is obviously attractive: one cannot but breath a sigh of relief when an exceptionally vicious tyranny is overthrown. But attractive though the argument is, it is also dangerous. For who is to decide, and on what criteria, that a regime has become suffici- ently tyrannical to justify overthrow by military intervention? There is no good answer to this sort of question; and acceptance of the legit- imacy of military intervention on the grounds of the exceptionally tyrannical nature of a regime opens the way to even more military adventurism, predatoriness, conquest and subjugation than is already rife in the world today.

The rejection of military intervention on this score is not meant to claim immunity and protection for tyrannical regimes. Nor does it. For there are other forms of intervention than military ones: for instance, economic pressure by way of sanctions, boycott and even blockade. Tyrannical regimes make opposition extremely difficult: but they do not make it impossible. And the point is to help internal opposition rather than engage in military 'substitutism'. As noted earlier, there are rare and extreme circumstances where nothing else may be possible—for example, the war against Nazism. Hitler's Third Reich was not only a tyranny; nor was it merely guilty of border incursions against other states. It was quite clearly bent on war and the subjugation of Europe. But neither Uganda nor Kampuchea are of this order. In socialist terms, the overthrow of a regime from outside by military intervention, and without any measure of popular involvement, must always be an exceedingly doubtful enterprise, of the very last resort.

V

'Security' is perhaps the reason most commonly invoked to justify military intervention. In the case of Afghanistan, for instance, it has been said that the country has a 1,000 mile border with the USSR, that it is in its 'sphere of influence', and that the USSR could not therefore accept a regime in Kabul that was hostile to it, and liable to come under American influence. The same argument was used, *inter alia*, to defend military intervention in Hungary in 1956 and in Czechoslovakia in 1968; and it has been used to justify Vietnam's overthrow of the Pol Pot regime in Kampuchea.

In considering this argument, much confusion may be avoided if a clear distinction is made between two essentially different propositions. The first of these is that it is useful and desirable for any given country to have uncontentious, cooperative and friendly neighbours. This is indisputable. The second proposition is that the requirements of security make it not only useful and desirable for this or that country to have such neighbours, but essential, to the point, where necessary, of justifying military intervention when the requirements threaten to be no longer met. I think that this second proposition is dangerous and unacceptable from a socialist standpoint, and that it rests on shortsighted and mistaken calculations.

In the case of Afghanistan, it is worth repeating that the USSR found no difficulty in accommodating itself, before the coup of April 1978, to not having a preponderant influence there, and that the alleged security problem did not then appear in the least critical. It has been said that the USSR intervened at the end of 1979 because it feared a Khomeini-style revolution (or counter-revolution), which would have had a subversive effect on the Muslim populations of the USSR living in proximity to Afghanistan. But there is no evidence that such a revolution or counter-revolution was brewing in Afghanistan, or that the Russians were concerned with possible contagion. In short, security may well have been a consideration in the decision to intervene: but it is unlikely to have been decisive and compelling. As I have suggested earlier, there is a better explanation, namely the Soviet leadership's determination not to accept a loosening of the control it had been able to acquire since the coup of April 1978. Such a loosening of control would have represented a definite setback for them, and was unacceptable for a mixture of reasons—prestige, security, fear of repercussions, and so on.

In any case, security by virtue of occupation, and the maintenance of power of a puppet regime must be set against a number of contrary considerations. One of these is the fierce hostility that military intervention generates and the nationalist upsurge it produces. 'Security' is here turned into a mockery by the massive unpopularity of the occupier and his puppet government; and it is further degraded by the war of pacification that has been forced upon the Soviet Union, with all its attendant horrors. What kind of security is this?

The same question may be asked in regard to other countries upon which an unwanted regime has been imposed, for instance Poland. The Soviet Union believed at the end of the Second World War that a subservient regime in Warsaw was essential to its security. But here, too, 'security' is turned into its opposite by the implacable hostility which a Soviet-imposed regime engendered and by the consequent

inability of that regime to achieve a genuine measure of legitimation.

As against this, the argument is counterposed that the international context and the hostility of the United States and other
Western powers at the end of the Second World War forced the
USSR into the policies it pursued in Eastern Europe: faced with this
hostility, it had no option but to create a *cordon sanitaire* for itself,
and to prevent its erstwhile allies from using Eastern Europe as a
potential advanced base against the USSR. This required the establishment of friendly regimes; and the only regimes that could be
trusted to be truly 'friendly' were regimes firmly under Communist
control. Soviet security required no less, particularly after the Cold
War had got properly under way.

The argument not only leaves out of account the hostility
engendered by the external imposition of a Communist regime, particularly one of a Stalinist kind: it also ignores other possibilities,
such as are suggested by the case of Finland. 'Finlandization' is
often used by Cold War propagandists to suggest a state of virtual
subjection to the USSR. But this is inaccurate. It means in fact what
the Finns describe as 'active neutrality'; and it involves the acceptance of powerful constraints upon the country's external policies.
But Finland has remained internally independent. No country could
be geographically more important to Soviet 'security'. But Stalin,
no doubt influenced by the experience of the Soviet-Finnish war of
1939-40, decided in 1945 not to try to foist a Communist-controlled
regime upon Finland, which had fought on the German side and had
a long record of bitter enmity to the USSR and Communism. It does
not seem unreasonable to suggest that Soviet security would have
been at least as well served—to put it no higher—if the same kind of
arrangements that were made in regard to Finland had been made in
regard to Eastern Europe. Nor is it immediately obvious, on the
grounds advanced earlier, that the cause of *socialism* has been better
served and is further advanced in Eastern Europe than it is in Finland.

The major dimension which the argument from 'security' tends to
ignore is that of popular support; and the question of popular support relates not only to the countries concerned, but more widely.
'Revisionist' historians in the United States have been perfectly
right to claim that there were very powerful forces in the United

States and in Western Europe at the end of the Second World War which were determined to replace a shaky and conflict-ridden war-time alliance with the Russians by outright antagonism. But there were also masses of people in the United States, not least in the ranks of American labour, who appreciated the immense contribution that the Soviet armies had made to the defeat of Germany, and who wanted friendship with the USSR; and there were even more such people in West European labour movements, and beyond the labour movements. It is possible that these sentiments would not have prevailed against the barrage of anti-Soviet and anti-Communist propaganda that was launched after 1945 by reactionary forces backed by vast resources and influence. But the least that can be said about this is that these forces would not have had such an easy time of it, and would not have been able to mount such a powerful crusade, had the Russians not given that crusade valuable ammunition by the manner of the settlement that they imposed in Eastern Europe in the post-war years. That settlement was totally Stalinist in inspiration and character; and it was a typical Stalinist perspective which interpreted 'security' in the narrowest and most constricted terms, and which recklessly underestimated the impact of Stalinist infamies on working class and other opinion in Western countries. The search for 'security', interpreted as the establishment of 'reliable' governments and regimes in what Stalin regarded as strategic areas, produced the strengthening of the very forces whose policies posed the major external threat to Soviet security; and the weakening of those forces in capitalist countries, notably their labour movements, which were most likely to oppose anti-Soviet and 'hardline' policies. The same is true of Soviet military intervention in Afghanistan: this has obviously provided a very powerful reinforcement to the worst reactionaries in the Western camp.

Security considerations have also been invoked to justify the Vietnamese intervention in Kampuchea and its overthrow of the Pol Pot regime. Thus, it has been said that, with Chinese encouragement, the Kampucheans mounted massive incursions into Vietnamese territory, which were intended to 'destabilize' Vietnam. Nothing less than the overthrow of the Pol Pot regime would therefore do.

This is a weak case. Border incidents opposing Kampuchea to

Vietnam had occurred long before the Pol Pot regime came to power; and the later incursions were part of a pattern of deteriorating relations for which the Pol Pot regime cannot be held to be the sole culprit. The two regimes had maintained more or less 'normal' relations for some two and a half years after their victory in April 1975—it was only later that Vietnam discovered that the Kampuchean leadership was made up of 'fascists', and vice-versa. Not only is it inherently implausible to suggest that the overthrow of the Pol Pot regime was the only possible course open to the Vietnamese: it is also by no means certain that their security was thereby much enhanced. No doubt, a pliant regime now exists in Phnom Penh. But it lacks legitimacy and requires the support of a Vietnamese army of occupation. The enterprise has reinforced secular suspicions of Vietnamese designs upon Kampuchea. Like the Russians in Afghanistan, the Vietnamese have been drawn into a permanent struggle with Kampuchean guerrillas, with the usual accompaniment of repression and the killing of innocent civilians. The invasion has also weakened Vietnam's international position, and strengthened reactionary forces in the region and beyond. Here too, it does not seem unreasonable to ask 'What kind of security is this?'.

It has also been said that the conflict between Vietnam and Kampuchea is only an expression of the wider Sino-Soviet conflict. If so, it is difficult to see how the invasion of Kampuchea and its occupation helps the Vietnamese to cope with the dangers the Chinese pose to them. A hostile Kampuchean regime, allied to China, has been eliminated, but at very considerable cost. And this elimination leaves the main threat precisely where it was. The Chinese launched a major attack upon Vietnam after the latter invaded Kampuchea, in order to 'teach Vietnam a lesson', to quote the infamous justification invoked for the action by Deng Xiaoping and others. Thousands upon thousands of soldiers, Chinese and Vietnamese, as well as civilians—men, women and children—have died to satisfy the Chinese leaders' pedagogic ambitions. The Chinese armies were repelled. But Chinese hostility endures, and has hardly been diminished by the Vietnamese enterprises in Kampuchea.

It was in relation to American military strategists that C. Wright Mills coined the phrase 'crackpot realism'. But it applies as well to the leadership of Soviet-type regimes, so the record amply suggests.

'Crackpot realism' is here sustained by a narrow, Stalinist, interpretation of 'security' according to which what matters is territory
not people. But the strategies that proceed from this not only tend to
defeat their own purposes; they also have much larger implications
for war and peace.

VI

The USSR is not subject to the logic of imperialism; and the charge
that it is bent on territorial conquest to the point of 'world conquest'
is no more than reactionary ideological warfare. But the USSR does
seek 'security', and its interpretation of the concept has led it, and
continues to lead it, to seek the defence, consolidation, and, wherever
possible, the extension of its 'sphere of influence', particularly but
not exclusively in areas which it regards as being of strategic importance. This search for security has one specific feature which is of
extreme importance, namely that it is best served when traditional
structures in the countries concerned are revolutionized. This is why
Soviet help is readily extended to revolutionary movements in the
Third World: revolutionary strivings there and the Soviet search for
security are roughly congruent. On the other hand, such movements
and strivings are opposed by the United States and other Western
powers. This is the fundamental source of tension and conflict in the
world today: it is somewhere here that 'Sarajevo' is located.

It is obvious that an immense 'mutation', of global dimensions, is
now proceeding. The Brandt Commission Report is quite right to
stress the terrible poverty in which most countries of the Third
World are plunged. However, it is not the poverty that is new, but
the revolutionary stirrings in these countries. This is surely one of
the most remarkable and inspiring features of the present epoch.
For everywhere in the world, and in areas where passivity and resignation in the face of poverty and oppression have tended to be the
rule, with only episodic outbursts of rebellion, there is now sustained resistance and struggle, both against local oppressors and
their foreign backers and paymasters.

Quite certainly, this will continue to develop in the eighties and
beyond. The movements concerned are ideologically very varied; but

they are all nationalist and, to a greater or lesser extent, on the left. It must be taken for granted that the United States and other Western powers will seek to counter these movements and to prevent revolutionary upheavals (at least outside Soviet-type and Soviet-oriented regimes); or, if such upheavals do occur, that they will try to ensure that the new regimes, whatever they call themselves, do remain firmly in the 'Western' orbit. The means to be used for the purpose will differ greatly, according to circumstances, and range from economic pressure to military intervention. Conversely, it may also be taken for granted that many movements struggling for their country's independence from imperialist oppression and for social renovation, and that many regimes born of these movements' successes, will seek help from the Soviet Union, in the form of economic assistance, military material, or technical and military advisers; and that the Soviet Union will answer such calls for help, as a means of weakening Western influence and extending its own, in the hope of thereby strengthening its security.

Whatever the Soviet Union's motives may be, the help it accords to revolutionary movements and regimes is something that socialists cannot but welcome and support. The Cuban regime is now a repressive dictatorship of the Soviet-type model. But in comparison with other regimes in the Third World—many of them murderous dictatorships of a qualitatively worse kind, yet completely supported by the United States and other capitalist powers—it is also a progressive regime. The point about it, and about other such regimes, is precisely that they have these two sides—a progressive side as well as a repressive one. Apologists only highlight the first, detractors the second, but both are part of one and the same reality. It is wrong, in a socialist perspective, to ignore the dark side of the Cuban regime; but it would be equally wrong, from the same perspective, not to acknowledge and welcome the help from the USSR which has kept Cuba afloat. Soviet help is by no means given everywhere in a good cause; and there can be no socialist justification whatever for an unqualified endorsement of its policies in this or any other area. But where it does help serve progressive purposes, it has to be supported.

In terms of impact on the international scene, however, and quite apart from the question of socialist principle which has been discussed here, there is an enormous difference between help solicited by and given to revolutionary movements and regimes, and military intervention designed to maintain or install a deeply unpopular, unwanted and repressive regime. Even 'ordinary' help to revolutionary movements and regimes produces Western accusations of interference, subversion and expansionism; and it naturally comes up against American and other endeavours in 'counter-insurgency'. Even here, there are many possibilities for escalation of international tension and for the occurrence of explosive 'incidents'. But this is nevertheless very different from the impact produced by actual military intervention, even when that intervention occurs in a country such as Afghanistan, which had already come into the Soviet 'sphere of influence'. If it should occur outside that 'sphere of influence', in any circumstances, it must push the world to the brink of war, and quite conceivably over the brink.

The world of the eighties is in any case bound to be uniquely dangerous, not because of Soviet 'expansionism', but because there are certain to be many terrains on which the 'super-powers' will find themselves directly or indirectly engaged in competition and conflict. Independently of the Soviet Union or anybody else, revolutionary movements in the Third World and elsewhere will continue their efforts to destroy the local and international web of backwardness and oppression in which their countries are enmeshed; and some of these upheavals at least will occur in countries of high 'strategic' importance—for instance Pakistan, Thailand, the Philippines, countries in Latin America, Saudi Arabia, the Gulf States, South Africa and other countries in Africa. The gigantic paradox of the epoch is that these upheavals, which spell hope for oppressed peoples, are also fraught with great perils of clash and confrontation between one 'super-power' bent on 'counter-insurgency' and the other bent on 'security'.

Nor will the process of radical change, or at least the attempt to effect radical change, be confined to the Third World. It would be extremely suprising if one country or other of the 'Soviet-bloc' did not experience the kind of upheaval that has episodically been known there. Hungary 1956 and Czechoslovakia 1968 are much more likely to be repeated than not. And it is also likely that the pressure, now so greatly slackened, for radical change in Western

258

capitalist countries, will grow again, in the shadow of economic crisis. But this means that there will be innumerable opportunities in the coming years for clash and confrontation between the United States and the USSR. Revolutionary stirrings and 'super-power' strivings here come together in a dangerously explosive package.

Military intervention, as in Afghanistan, adds to the danger; and opposing such intervention is therefore all the more necessary. Socialists have in the past been, and often are still now, inhibited in voicing opposition to unacceptable actions by the Soviet Union and other Soviet-type regimes by the very legitimate fear of finding their voice merged in that of a loud reactionary chorus. But it should be possible for socialist opposition to be voiced in its own terms, on its own premises, and with its own concerns: what this requires, among other things, is that it should be coupled with the insistence, which opposition to Soviet actions should never be allowed to dim, that the fundamental source of tension and danger lies in the determination of the United States and other capitalist powers to stem and reverse the tide of revolutionary change in the world.

1. On the other hand, the Cubans had no business helping Ethiopia against Somalia, and their intervention in the conflict between the two countries is a very different matter from that in Angola. The point gains particular force by reference to the fact that Ethiopia is seeking to crush a legitimate movement of independence, namely the Eritrean one. Eritrea was annexed to Ethiopia by a purely arbitrary act of defiance of the United Nations. The country does not 'belong' to Ethiopia and is entitled to independence.
2. R. Luxemburg, 'The Junius Pamphlet: The Crisis in the German Social Democracy', in M.A. Waters, ed., *Rosa Luxemburg Speaks*, New York 1970, p.304.
3. For some recent documentation, see N. Chomsky and E.S. Herman, *The Washington Connection and Third World Fascism* and *After the Cataclysm: Post-War Indochina and the Reconstruction of Imperial Ideology*, these being Vols. I and II of *The Political Economy of Human Rights*, Nottingham 1979.

14
The Politics of Peace and War
1983

I am concerned here with the 'causes of World War III', to use the arresting (and, one hopes, over-pessimistic) title of a book which C. Wright Mills published in 1959.[1] More precisely, I am concerned with the reasons which render possible (some would say probable) a major confrontation between the United States and the Soviet Union, escalating into a full-scale 'nuclear exchange' between them, and leading to a nuclear holocaust of hundreds of millions of men, women and children, and to the lasting devastation of a large part of the planet. The gravity of the threat is sufficiently indicated by the fact that no one, whatever his or her opinion of its causes or remedies, can deny that its realization is, at the least, within the realm of the possible.

Threats of lesser wars also abound. 'The smell of blood rises from the pages of history', Joseph de Maistre said in the aftermath of the French Revolution. But it is in the twentieth century that the stench of death in war has become overpowering. Some two hundred 'small' wars of a 'conventional' kind have been fought in many parts of the world since the end of World War II, at a cost, it has been estimated, of some 25,000,000 lives. Such 'small' wars must be expected to go on as long as nation-states, or rather their governments, believe it to be in their interest to wage them, and are able to do so; and the ever-greater efficiency of the 'conventional' weapons with which such wars are fought guarantees that they will become steadily more murderous and destructive.

It must also be supposed that, as more and more countries acquire nuclear weapons, one or other of them, engaged in a 'small' war and facing defeat and disaster, may seek to retrieve the situation by using such weapons. The use of even low-capacity nuclear weapons would cause vast casualties and great destruction: all the same, this would be much more modest (if one can use such a term in this context) than the death and devastation that would be produced by a 'nuclear exchange' between the United States and the Soviet Union. The effects of even a limited exchange between them would be tremend-ous—many times greater than what occurred at Hiroshima and Nagasaki;[2] and even those people who do believe that a limited exchange might not lead to an unlimited one cannot deny that it might. The very fact that so much death and destruction would be produced by a limited 'nuclear exchange' would itself create condi-tions in which escalation, far from being inhibited by the impact of such an exchange, would be made more probable as a result of it. The question is why the prospect of such a catastrophe should now threaten the human race; and what hope is there of preventing it.

Two related reasons have frequently been advanced in recent years for thinking that a 'nuclear exchange' between the super-powers is possible or probable.

The first is that an accident is quite capable of occurring which would lead to nuclear war. On this 'scenario', military computers in the United States or the Soviet Union would indicate, mistakenly, that the one country had launched a nuclear attack upon the other. Further mistaken signals would appear to confirm that an attack was on the way. The time available to decide whether to launch a counter-strike would be measured in minutes, or it might even be eliminated altogether by an automatic 'launch-on-warning' res-ponse. A nuclear war would then be on.

A number of computer misreadings have occurred in the United States, and led to alerts which were called off when the errors were discovered, well before (so it is said) matters were in any danger of getting out of hand. It may be assumed that computer misreadings have also occurred in the Soviet Union and produced more or less advanced stages of alert.

It clearly cannot be taken for granted that any such errors, which are bound to occur, will always and inevitably be rectified in good time. However improbable, a chain of errors, misreadings, mishaps and accidents is possible. Moreover, accidents and their consequences are not purely 'accidental'. What is made of accidents is not only a matter of objective and technical appraisal: much also depends on the international conjuncture in which accidents occur. In a period of relative quiescence, when relations between the superpowers are not particularly bad and there is no major international crisis, there would be a very strong urge to treat alarming signals with great caution and scepticism, to check again, and to delay to the utmost an irremediable nuclear response. This is what makes the notion of an automatic 'launch-on-warning' response so sinister. In a period of intense and prolonged international crisis, on the other hand, possibly with some limited military incident having already occurred (a ship sunk, planes shot down, some soldiers killed), there would exist a strong predisposition to find in erroneous signals a confirmation of expectations and fears that the other side had decided to strike, and there would be a greater willingness to initiate what would be believed to be a counter-strike. We are therefore driven back to ask what are the forces which shape the international conjuncture and which produce crises in which accidents are likely to turn into catastrophes.

The second reason often advanced for thinking nuclear war possible or probable is the arms race itself. 'The immediate cause of World War III,' Mills wrote in the book referred to earlier, 'is the military preparation for it.'[3] On this view, the people in charge of affairs in the United States and the Soviet Union are governed by pressures and constraints which are driving their countries and the rest of the world towards nuclear war. Much the same view has been expressed more recently by E.P. Thompson, for instance in his article 'The Logic of Exterminism'.[4]

'To structure an analysis in a consecutive rational manner,' he writes, 'may be, at the same time, to impose a consequential rationality upon the object of analysis.' But, he goes on to ask, 'What if the object is *ir*rational? What if events are being willed by no single causative historical logic . . . but are simply the product of a messy inertia? . . . Detonation might be triggered by accident, miscalculation, by the implacable upwards creep of weapons technology, or by a sudden hot flush of ideological passion.'[5] To the left's 'anthropomorphic interpretation of political, economic and military formations, to which are attributed intentions and goals', Thompson therefore counterposes 'the irrational outcome of colliding formations and wills'.[6]

It is easy to see why the view that the superpowers are caught up in an irrational process should have gained so much currency. For it *is* irrational to prepare so feverishly for death and destruction on such an immense scale, and to devote enormous efforts and resources to the production and improvement of weapons of war; and it is all the more irrational when so much needs to be done to make life more tolerable for hundreds of millions of people who chronically suffer hunger and want, not to speak of all that needs to be done even in countries whose inhabitants are not on the edge of starvation and death.

But to say that the arms race is irrational is not at all the same as saying that it is itself a prime cause of war. It may well be argued that the arms race creates conditions in which any attempt to achieve a significant measure of disarmament is made more difficult and problematic; that the ever greater sophistication of weapons technology constantly reduces and may annul the time available to decide on response to alerts, and therefore make more 'accidents' potentially lethal; that the arms race poisons further the climate of relations between the superpowers; and that it strengthens all the forces—and there are many—which have an interest in opposing *détente* and disarmament. On any such count, the arms race must be reckoned to be an important contributory cause of World War III.

Even so, there are dangers in placing the prime emphasis on the arms race itself: for to do so obscures other and different factors which are at the core of the antagonism between the superpowers and which serve as fuel to the arms race. The chances are that, if nuclear war does occur, it will be as a result of an escalation of a crisis originating in these factors. If *they* could be made less explosive, the danger of a nuclear confrontation between the United States and the Soviet Union would be greatly reduced; and *détente* and disarmament would have a better chance. This is why it is important to locate accurately the reasons for the antagonism between the superpowers.

In essence, the danger of armed conflict between the United States and the Soviet Union stems from the proliferation of revolutionary movements which has occurred since the late fifties. By then, an exceedingly difficult and partial process of accommodation between the superpowers had been achieved, with the more or less reluctant acceptance by the United States of the Communist bloc that had come into being following the Second World War, and which included Eastern Europe and East Germany, North Korea, China and North Vietnam. If all revolutionary strivings in the world had then been frozen, and stayed frozen, the Cold War might have been replaced by 'peaceful co-existence'; and even if the arms race had continued, it is quite likely that it would have continued with much less intensity, and there would have been less danger than there is now of accidents escalating into nuclear war.

But revolutionary strivings were not frozen, and could not be. The Cuban Revolution and Fidel Castro's entry into Havana in 1959 mark the beginning of a new historical phase, which amounts to permanent revolution, though not of the kind and in the style which Marx and Trotsky envisaged. Some revolutionary movements since then have been able to achieve power, for instance in Algeria, Angola, Mozambique, Ethiopia, South Yemen, Nicaragua and Iran. Others have been able to pose a major challenge to their regimes, for instance in El Salvador and Guatemala. Yet others are at an earlier stage of development and can still be contained, usually with American help. In some cases, revolutionary movements have been temporarily crushed, as in Indonesia.

These movements differ very greatly in their specific ideological and political orientations. Unlike earlier movements, they are not Communist-led, though Communists often do play a part in them. But however much they may differ in other respects, they do have in common a very strong *nationalist* consciousness. Whatever the extent to which they are social-revolutionary, they are certainly national-revolutionary; and this is as true for those movements which proclaim themselves to be Marxist-Leninist as for any other. They may seek Soviet support: but they do not want subordination. Earlier (Communist) movements equated allegiance to the Soviet Union with allegiance to the cause of the revolution in general, and to the cause of revolution in their own countries in particular. These more recent movements do not.

Revolutionary movements challenge the *status quo* not only in their own countries, but internationally as well. The regimes which they replace are usually closely allied to the United States. The victory of revolutionary movements, whatever their specific ideological orientation may be, signifies a rupturing of military, economic and political bonds with the United States and other Western powers. and it requires the forging of a new relationship with them, which is marked by suspicion and hostility on both sides, with the constant and well-grounded fear by the new regime that it stands in danger of 'de-stabilization' by the United States and its allies. The revolution which overthrew the Shah in Iran shows well enough that the depth of suspicion and hostility on the revolutionary side is not simply a matter of how 'left-wing' and 'Communist' the new regime may be: what is at issue is the determination of the revolutionaries to establish a new set of conditions one of whose main features is independence from the United States and the West in general.

The international status quo which revolutionary movements challenge and disturb was established in the Second World War and after; and it was marked, most notably, by the predominant position which the United States was then able to assume in the world. That predominant position was sanctioned by the treaties, alliances, understandings and concessions which linked most countries outside the Communist bloc to the United States. It found expression, in practical terms, in the economic access which the United States had to these countries, and in the military bases, facilities and arrangements which it was able to obtain from them. It is to all this that revolutionary movements, to a greater or lesser degree, pose a real threat.

Revolutionary or dissident movements of a different kind also pose a threat to the predominance which the Soviet Union was able to achieve in a number of countries in the post-war period: Hungary in 1956; Czechoslovakia in 1968, Afghanistan in 1979 and after, Poland in 1956, 1970 and 1981 provide the most visible and dramatic signs of this challenge. Yugoslavia provided another as early as 1948. But the area of Soviet predominance is very much smaller than that of the United States: in global terms, it is the United States and not the Soviet Union which is the 'conservative' power in the world. For it is the United States which is mainly concerned to maintain the status quo, and which therefore opposes all the forces which seek to upset it—except of course in the area of Soviet predominance, where it is the Soviet Union which plays the 'conservative' role.

There is nothing particularly complicated about the reasons why the United States seeks to maintain the status quo in its area of predominance. One such reason is economic. The American government seeks to defend American business interests anywhere in the world, and wants to keep the largest possible part of the world open to capitalist enterprise, notably to American capitalist enterprise. The coming to power of revolutionary movements poses a clear threat to such purposes: revolutionary governments have a bias towards nationalization, often with the threat of actual expropriation of nationalized assets, or with offers of compensation to foreign interests which are not satisfactory. Moreover, such governments make more cumbersome and expensive the operation of foreign enterprises, where they allow them to operate at all. In any case, existing regimes are much more favourable to American and other capitalist interests than any revolutionary government is likely to be, and are much easier to deal with. The fact that they may also be vicious tyrannies, which keep the vast majority of their people in conditions of extreme exploitation and poverty, is a matter of secondary importance. After all, such regimes can be relied on to be ruthless with the left; and they also ensure that labour relations present no problem to the foreign interests in their country.

There are also important strategic considerations which affect American policy. As noted earlier, the coming to power of a revolutionary government brings into question existing military arrangements and threatens future ones. Moreover, it may open the way to a Soviet presence in the country, even possibly a Soviet base. To these strategic considerations may also be related the danger, from the American point of view, and from that of the West in general, that strategic mineral and oil supplies might come under the control of revolutionary governments, and be denied to the United States and its allies while being made available to the Soviet Union.

These would be grounds enough to explain American global interventionism against revolutionary movements. But how is this linked to the arms race and the conflict between the superpowers? The answer is quite straightforward: in seeking to oppose and defeat the challenge posed by revolutionary movements, it is not only these movements which the United States encounters, but also the Soviet Union. Fred Halliday makes the point as follows:

> '...the new wave of Third World revolutions occasioned a substantial and visible exercise of Soviet military power in support of them. The USSR supplied the heavy military armour needed for victory in Vietnam; it provided the airlift and strategic equipment for Cuban forces in Angola and Ethiopia; and it directly deployed Soviet forces themselves in Afghanistan. Even where there was no Soviet military involvement as such, states allied to the USSR or revolutionary movements in conflict with the West were in some measure protected by the fact that the new strategic potential of the USSR stayed the hands of US officials who might otherwise have envisaged direct intervention, as in Iran.'[7]

The Soviet presence in the world may, in many instances, be quite undramatic. But it *is* a presence, and it does make the maintenance of American predominance in the world more difficult. For some policy-makers in Washington, Soviet help to revolutionary movements or states, whether it takes the form of economic or military aid, is proof enough of Soviet 'expansionism'. But even those policy-makers who take a more moderate view of Soviet purposes cannot but be aware of the Soviet Union as a hindrance to their own purposes—not necessarily insurmountable, but real. They may know that revolutionary movements would exist, even if the Soviet Union did not. But it is a reasonable presumption that these movements would be easier to deal with if the Soviet Union did not exist. Cuba is the most obvious case in point. The Cuban Revolution owed nothing to the Soviet Union: but the survival of the Cuban regime would have been impossible without Soviet help, or at least exceedingly doubtful. The overwhelming chances are that it would have been strangled by blockade, even if it had not been destroyed by military means.

The reasons which impel the Soviet leaders to engage in their own global interventionism have nothing to do with a supposed irresistible craving for world domination. By far the most rational view of this Soviet interventionism is that it is produced by a primarily defensive concern for Soviet security. It is this above all which led Stalin to impose Communist regimes in Eastern Europe and East

Germany, since Communist regimes seemed to him to be the only real guarantee that these contiguous territories would not turn into bases for the Soviet Union's enemies. It was the same concern which led to the invasion of Hungary in 1956, of Czechoslovakia in 1968 and of Afghanistan in 1979. The point is not that the calculation was correct: there is much to be said for the view that it is very short-sighted, in that it fails to take into account the fact that an imposed and illegitimate regime is not reliable in an emergency, and that there is a very large price to be paid, in international terms, for 'security' bought in this way. However this may be, it is security for the Soviet Union, as the Soviet leaders understand it, which best explains their international strategy.

It is this, rather than 'expansionism' or ideological proselytism, that determines the degree and kind of support which the Soviet Union extends to revolutionary movements and states across the world. Such movements offer the hope of greater influence in the world for the Soviet Union; and they are also likely to be an embarrassment, great or small, to the United States. Here too, Cuba provides a good example of both points. It is similarly of some advantage to the Soviet Union that Nicaragua should be ruled by a left-wing regime rather than a reactionary one, closely allied to the United States. Even revolutionary regimes which are opposed to the Soviet Union, like Iran's Islamic revolutionary regime, are better than reactionary ones, since they are also strongly opposed to the United States.

Such perspectives do not make for 'ideological' politics; and Soviet foreign policy has in fact been extremely 'pragmatic', its one consistent thread being precisely the pursuit of security. This search, however, produces many Soviet actions and policies which help to confirm American policy-makers in the view that they are confronted by a country bent on aggrandizement and aggression. The search of Soviet leaders for security does lead to global interventionism in one form or another; and its motives matter less than its consequences. Not only does it confirm American policy-makers in their view of the Soviet Union: even more important, it helps them to convince the American people that they face immense dangers from the Soviet Union. The latter's 'image' is in any case greatly damaged by the repressive nature of the regime: its interventionism abroad completes the picture of a country which only armed might can contain. The propaganda value of drawing an analogy, however false, between this situation and that of the thirties, is obvious: 'Appeasement' of the Nazis then meant war, not peace: we must therefore not make the same mistake again. Much of the arms race is based on such *non sequiturs*. The emphasis on Soviet 'expansionism', and on the need to contain and fight it has many advantages; one of them is to obscure the fact that the containment which the United States is seeking to achieve is that of revolutionary movements throughout the world.

Even among those who most ardently believe in Soviet 'expansionism', there cannot be very many who hold the view that the Soviet leaders are only waiting for an opportunity to launch a nuclear war against the United States. In fact, there is probably a very general measure of agreement, even among people who otherwise differ fundamentally, that, accidents aside, a nuclear war would most probably be the result of an escalation of a local crisis that had got out of hand. Neither the United States nor the Soviet Union wants anything from the other: there are no territorial, or other, such bones of contention between them, as there are, for instance, between the Soviet Union and China. Their only real point of contact, in terms of conflict, is where revolutionary movements do threaten the status quo, either against the United States, as is usually the case, or against the Soviet Union. It is at these points of contact and conflict that lie buried the seeds of World War III.

For it is not difficult to imagine a set of circumstances in which a revolutionary movement is taken by the United States to threaten its vital interests, and in which it would therefore decide to intervene militarily, by sending units of its rapid-deployment forces to help a threatened regime. In doing so, it might well encounter the Soviet Union, or Cuba, or other forces allied to the Soviet Union. The chances of incidents of varying gravity would then be considerable; and so, in such circumstances, would be the chances of 'accidents' turning into catastrophes. How things would develop would depend in large part on the coolness and caution of the participants, and on their willingness or ability to compromise and even retreat, as happened in the Cuban missile crisis of 1962, when Nikita Khruschev did retreat. It is an indication of the immense dangers that now confront the human race that the possibility of escalation from crisis to full-scale nuclear war should depend on the response of a few people on either side, who may or may not be cautious and cool under stress, and who may in any case be overwhelmed by events.

These dangers are all the greater in that revolutionary movements are not only likely but certain to develop further in many parts of the world, including highly 'strategic' and 'sensitive' areas. It is not very rash to suggest, for instance, that revolutionary upheavals will occur in Saudi Arabia, or the Gulf states, or the Caribbean, or Guatemala, or Haiti, or the Philippines, or South Korea, and so on. The rise of such movements in the Third World has only just begun; and there would have to be very good prospects of a spectacular improvement in the conditions of poor countries, under their existing regimes, for revolutionary movements to subside, or to be permanently and effectively contained. There are no such prospects: the trend, for most such countries, is the other way.

Nor is it only in the area of American predominance that there exist potential points of conflict and crisis between the United States and the Soviet Union: they also exist in the area of Soviet predominance. In one or other country of this area, movements of contestation will seek to undo the status quo; and the United States may be tempted to help in one way or another.

Most parts of the world, in fact, provide dangerous points of contact between the superpowers. Unfortunately, 'crisis management' is not a sufficiently precise and assured craft to provide any sort of guarantee that it would necessarily be effective in all circumtances: the more reasonable assumption is that it could easily fail.

The conclusion is inescapable that, as revolutionary movements grow in the coming years, so too will the dangers of nuclear war. This is one of the great 'ironies of history', to use Isaac Deutscher's phrase. The rise of the 'wretched of the earth' against exploitation and subordination is the most remarkable and inspiring social phenomenon of the twentieth century; and its grandeur is not dimmed by the fact that it cannot achieve more, at best, than a small part of its aims. The irony consists in the fact that the endeavours of revolutionary movements also provide the occasions for crisis and escalation into nuclear war. The question is how such a consequence can be averted, and how the dangers of nuclear war, from whatever source, can at least be reduced.

To begin with, the fact has to be faced that no great reliance can be placed upon disarmament negotiations between the superpowers. Given the view of Soviet purposes which has held the field among American policy-makers since the Second World War, there is no reason why the arms race should not go on for ever, or until nuclear war brings it to an ultimate conclusion. The American assumption of Soviet 'expansionism' robs disarmament negotiations of any real meaning. For if Soviet leaders are believed to be moved by an inflexible will to expansion, it follows that they can only be deterred—if they can be deterred at all—by an American nuclear force so great as to turn Soviet nuclear blackmail in support of aggressive policies into an empty threat, since Soviet nuclear aggression would amount to certain national obliteration. This also assumes, of course, that Soviet rulers, irrational enough to seek world domination, and to threaten the use of nuclear weapons in pursuit of their aims, would be sufficiently rational to be deterred by any threat: it is a very large assumption.

As for Soviet policy-makers, they too clearly believe that they must have the capacity to threaten the United States with assured nuclear devastation, if they are not to be vulnerable to pre-emptive attack or to nuclear blackmail; and they too therefore strive to possess the strongest possible nuclear arsenal, which also means the least vulnerable one.

Given this belief in 'deterrence', it is not surprising that the arms race has if anything accelerated while negotiations over disarmament have been proceeding. But even if progress were made, and a substantial reduction in the capacity for 'overkill' which both superpowers now possess were to be achieved, this would still leave them with enough such capacity to make nuclear war between them possible, on a scale perfectly adequate for total devastation. Whether both superpowers have the capacity to destroy each other, and much of the rest of the world, a hundred times over, or fifty times over, is not a matter of huge significance. Richard Barnet has noted that 'even if the worst assumptions of American military planners prove correct and the Russians develop the capability in the nineteen eighties to destroy ninety per cent of American land-based missiles, the submarines, cruise missiles, and bombers would still be able to deliver far more than five hundred nuclear warheads to the Soviet Union'.[8]

The point also applies to disarmament. The only sound principle in this field is 'no nuclear weapons, no nuclear war'. Anything else is a potentially lethal second-best. This is not to say that partial disarmament should not be pressed as hard as possible: any such pressure, and any real gain, must be welcome in so far as it may help create a climate in which further gains can be made. But the prospects for really significant advances towards disarmament must be reckoned to be poor: not sufficient, at least, to offer real prospects that nuclear war between the superpowers might actually become *impossible*. Yet, nothing less than this will do.

It is the acceleration of the arms race, and the proposals to introduce new 'theatre' weapons in Western Europe in 1983 which have led to the resurgence in recent years of disarmament movements in a number of West European countries, notably Germany, Britain and Holland, with proposals for a nuclear-free zone in Europe 'from Poland to Portugal' (and from Iceland to Italy), with the elimination from European soil of all nuclear weapons, and of all bases for the launching of such weapons.[9]

This amounts in effect to *nuclear pacifism*, and it is the only reasonable response to the danger of nuclear war. There is *nothing* for which it is worth fighting a nuclear war. The slogan 'better dead than red' (or black or blue) still made sense, whether one agreed with it or not, *before* the advent of nuclear weapons. Any war that was then fought, however devastating, still left the survivors with a life to live; and however great the destruction, there was no doubt that the grass would grow again and that new generations would be able to treat what had happened as no more than history. Nuclear weapons have changed all that: it is now scarcely in dispute that nuclear war on any major scale must bring civilized life to an end over a large part of the planet if not over the whole of it. This is the new dimension of war; and it is this which makes any strategy based on the *possibility* of nuclear war the ultimate example of what Mills aptly called 'crackpot realism'.

As in the case of all proposals relating to disarmament, whatever specific and concrete gain can be made by European movements is

272

useful; and stopping the installation of Cruise and Pershing II missiles in Western Europe would be an important gain and a great encouragement to further endeavours.

Here too, however, it must be said that there are severe limitations on what the European peace movement can be expected to achieve, at least in the near future. For the purpose of achieving concrete results, 'Europe' means separate states and governments, all of which are opposed to the policies and purposes of the peace movement. The initiative would have to come from one country or perhaps two where a breakthrough has been achieved, and where a government had come to office determined to implement nuclear disarmament. No united European initiative, *at government level*, can be expected for a very long time to come, not least because the French left is not much less opposed than the French right to any policy that would appear to threaten France's *force de frappe*.

Moreover, the kind of disarmament proposals which the European peace movement quite rightly puts forward constitute a revolutionary project, which must be attended by the same difficulties as any other revolutionary project. The traditional Marxist view has always been that a government of the left, seriously seeking to implement fundamental measures of social and economic change, must expect great and implacable opposition from many different sources, at home and abroad. But the same kind of opposition must also be expected if the attempt is made to effect a fundamental change in the strategic orientations and policies of countries like Britain and Germany. The minimum condition of success for such purposes is mass support, and the bringing to office of a government pledged to implement peace policies. None of this can be achieved quickly.

A further point needs to be made about the contribution which Europe can make to the diminution and elimination of the chances of nuclear war. This is that Europe cannot itself be the decisive voice in regard to peace and war: it is not there that the crucial decisions will be made. This is why the real value of the European peace campaigns does not lie primarily in what they can actually accomplish, but in encouraging resistance to the nuclear arms race beyond Europe, and above all in the United States.

For it is above all in the United States that a major, fundamental change in policy is required, if nuclear war is to be averted. It is the determination of the United States to maintain the status quo in the world which mainly threatens to furnish the occasions out of which nuclear war may derive. What the Soviet Union does, or does not do, is also of the utmost importance: the two superpowers clearly react upon each other, and it is in this sense on both of them that the prevention of nuclear war depends. But it is in the United States that the major shift must occur, simply because it is mainly the United States which will, in the years to come, be confronted by major challenges and choices, produced by the occurrence of revolutionary upheavals in many different parts of the world.

It is not required that the United States should actually welcome such upheavals—though this might have unexpectedly favourable results for it. It is only necessary that the United States should not seek to defeat revolutionary movements by military means and in ways which create occasions for heightened tension and conflict.

Quite obviously, there are very powerful forces in the United States which will always press for the deployment of military power, intervention, the need for more and better weapons: economic interests bound up with the armaments industry, military interests seeking their own aggrandizement, ideological interests pursuing their particular crusades, political interests seeking political advantage through chauvinist overbidding. This is a formidable combination of forces, with vast resources and great influence in government, the media, the press, the universities, and throughout the country. Yet, the hope of averting nuclear war must to a large extent depend on the defeat of these forces.

This could only occur by way of an immense strengthening of counter-forces in the United States, which would have to be drawn from the ranks of labour, professional and academic strata, ethnic minorities, the women's movement, religious groups, ecology groups, the existing peace movement itself; and these counter-forces would need to acquire sufficient political weight and influence to be heard with political effect, and to be able to bring to power people who reject interventionist perspectives and who can stand up to great interventionist pressures.

To speak in this vein is to invite disbelief and derision, given the enormous disparity of power, influence and resources that exists between interventionist forces and their opponents. But much here depends on what is being sought. The point is not to bring to Washington a socialist President or Congress who would proceed to the creation of a socialist society in the United States. It may be assumed that this will not happen for some time to come. Similarly, it is obvious that all the difficulties which are present in the achievement of European nuclear disarmament are also present—and a hundred times greater—in the United States. But even limited measures by the United States in the halting of the arms race, provided they were not only cosmetic and public relations exercises, would be progress. Nor in any case is disarmament the only issue on which progress needs to be made. For it is American global interventionism that makes it possible or likely that nuclear weapons will be used in confrontation with the Soviet Union; and it is in a shift away from global interventionism that is required. Furthermore, disarmament itself is more likely to follow such a shift than to precede it. Far from being a condition of *détente*, disarmament of a significant kind may well be a consequence of it.

It would be foolish to deny that to achieve a shift of this nature in American foreign policy is itself a very large enterprise. But it is reasonable to hope that more and more Americans will come to see the direct linkage that exists between inflation, recession, unemployment and cuts in expenditure on health and other welfare services on the one hand, and the foreign and defence policies their country pursues on the other; and that, in seeking to find alternatives to reactionary policies at home, they may also come to reject global interventionism abroad. A modern version of the New Deal is one of the alternatives that may be produced by the economic and social pressures at work in the United States: such a New Deal would now be very likely to include a major reappraisal, not only of policies on arms, but also of the relations of the United States to the Third World and to the Soviet Union.

Of course, nothing of this may come to pass, in which case the danger of nuclear war will continue to grow. But the defeat of interventionist forces does not only depend on what happens in the United States; it also depends on what the Soviet Union does abroad and on what happens inside it as well. Any major Soviet intervention, anywhere in the world, even within its own area of predominance, inevitably brings about a heightening of tension, increases the chances of confrontation, and both strengthens interventionist forces in the United States and weakens the peace forces everywhere. It was not the Soviet invasion of Afghanistan that caused the failure of SALT II and produced a further escalation in the arms race: but it nevertheless gave a vast amount of excellent ammunition to all those in the United States—and beyond—who have an economic, military, ideological or political stake in the perpetuation and exacerbation of the Cold War. The rulers of the Soviet Union can do a great deal to strengthen the peace forces in the United States. But they can do so only by showing convincingly—by what they do and do not do, and not merely by proclamations of good intentions—that they are seriously seeking *détente*.

This is not only a matter of what they do abroad or of their policies on disarmament: what happens in the Soviet Union itself is also a matter of the greatest importance. The repression of dissent and the denial of civic freedoms are not only internal Soviet issues: they also have a direct bearing on the question of war and peace. The more repressive the regime is, the easier it is also for all the interventionist forces in the United States and elsewhere to proclaim that 'Communism' must be opposed in the name of freedom and democracy, and that this requires more and better weapons, and the deployment of military strength everywhere in the world. 'Liberalization', on this score, is not only desirable in itself and for the peoples of the Soviet Union: it is also necessary to reduce the danger of nuclear war.

1. C. Wright Mills, The Causes of World War III, London 1959.
2. See, for example, John Cox, 'A "Limited" Nuclear War', in E.P. Thompson *et al. Exterminism and Cold War*, Verso Editions, London 1982. The author discusses the consequences of a 400-megaton attack on Europe which would, he writes, be 'quite a "small" limited nuclear war': apart from the extreme material devastation this would produce, 'the death toll is likely to exceed 150 million . . .' (pp.175, 179).
3. Mills, p.85.
4. Thompson *et al., Exterminism*.
5. *Ibid.*, p.1.
6. *Ibid.*, p.2.
7. F. Halliday, 'The Sources of the New Cold War', in Thompson *et. al.*, p.299.
8. Richard J. Barnet, 'The Search for National Security', *The New Yorker*, 27 April 1981, p.61.
9. See K. Coates, 'For a Nuclear-free Europe', in E.P. Thompson and D. Smith, eds., *Protest and Survive*, London 1980.

III
Britain

15

Class War Conservatism

1980

Note: This article was written to mark the completion of the first year in office of the Thatcher Government elected in May 1979. The reference at the beginning of the article to inflation being 'sharply up' is no longer valid; and the reference at the end of the article to the use by the Government of a 'strident nationalist rhetoric' could be greatly strengthened in the light of the Falklands war. Otherwise, the article seems to have projected accurately the broad lines of the 'counter-revolution' on which the Government was then setting out.

On some familiar indices, the Thatcher government's record to date has been an unrelieved disaster: inflation is sharply up, recession deepens, de-industrialization proceeds, decline continues, unemployment rises, and ministers warn that there is worse to come for years ahead. Only the balance of payments is not now a problem: but this has nothing to do with the government and everything with North Sea oil.

However, the familiar indices are not the ones by which the Prime Minister and her most trusted colleagues measure the progress they are making. For they are engaged in a long-term enterprise whose success, they believe, is the essential condition for the achievement of economic recovery, and much else as well. The enterprise consists in the radical reduction of the organized working-class pressure to which governments have been subjected since 1945. Mrs Thatcher and her cabinet (some members of it with more enthusiasm than others) are quite consciously bent on something like a counter-revolution in British life and politics.

It is not at all their views on inequality, competition, free enterprise, state intervention, public expenditure, or even monetarism, which distinguish the Thatcherite reactionaries in the cabinet from their 'wet' colleagues. There may be differences between ministers on all these and other issues; but the differences are matters of emphasis and specific policy, not of fundamental principle. It is not true that if you scratch a 'wet', you find a social democrat. What you find is a Conservative, who is at one with his/her colleagues in wanting to preserve and defend a social order in which there prevail gross—and, at the opposite ends, fantastic—differences between classes in every conceivable aspect of life. The real differences between Thatcherites and other Tories who belong to a different strain of conservatism lies elsewhere—namely, in a sharply divergent appreciation of how class conflict ought to be managed, 'class conflict' is not what most of them would call it; but that is what it is, and what is at issue.

For a hundred years and more, Tory leaders (with rare and partial exceptions) have realized full well that the preservation of a system of great inequality and privilege, in conditions of extended and then universal suffrage, imperatively required that concessions be made to the working class; that 'ransom', as Joseph Chamberlain called it at the end of the last century, be paid; that conciliation be sought, and confrontation wherever possible be avoided.

The realization did not prevent the same Tory leaders from waging the class struggle with the utmost determination whenever they thought it necessary to do so. Stanley Baldwin in the General Strike of 1926 is the classic example, but there are many others. Toryism has been not one thing but two: a struggle against concessions, and a willingness ultimately to concede. There are certainly limits to this willingness, but the matter has never been put to the test—a tribute to the success of the strategy.

An important role in the containment of working class demands is allotted to the trade unions, or rather to trade union leaders. Tory policy-makers have long been aware—and never more so than since 1945—that trade union leaders could for the most part be relied on to be 'moderate', 'responsible', 'sensible', and so on. But they have also known that, for these virtues to be displayed, life must not be made intolerably difficult for the unions by ministerial obduracy, inflexibility and bloody-mindedness.

The strategy obviously works best under relatively favourable business conditions when economic growth renders concessions fairly painless. Unfavourable economic conditions, on the other hand, bring forth very familiar demands for retrenchment in social expenditure, for curbs on wage increases, and for stronger resistance by government and employers (and by the government as an employer) to pressure from below. This is the time when governments (Labour as well as Conservative) need trade union cooperation most. But it is also the time when that cooperation is most difficult to obtain, since retrenchment and resistance to wage and other demands generate rank-and-file discontent, which in turn makes more problematic the fulfilment of the trade unions' role as agencies of social control.

It is these difficulties which the Thatcher counter-revolution is intended to resolve, through a drastic weakening of such power and influence as organized labour and 'lower income groups' in general are able to exercise; and this of course also goes for all the pressure groups and lobbies which speak for them. This is what constitutes the fundamental theme of the government, and much of it is strongly marked by the Prime Minister's personal stamp. Mrs Thatcher's conduct and pronouncements in office, as in opposition, strongly suggest she has an almost irresistible wish to 'confront' trade union power and militancy, and to lead a crusade against this particular incarnation of un-British evil.

It does not stretch imagination very far to see her handing out white feathers to the faint-hearts in her administration who want to avoid confrontation. The Thatcherites have found it easy to persuade themselves that one of the government's most important tasks —if not the most important of all its tasks—is to shift the balance as far as it will go in favour of managerial power. Militants, strikers, pickets, subversives (all the same, really) must be subdued: for it is they who make greater productivity impossible, whose wage demands fuel inflation, who stand in the way of recovery, who ruin sound (toothless) trade unionism. This is the wisdom of outer suburbia; and it is in a commanding position at the centre of government.

The government's economic strategy is a rag-bag of hopes, hunches, prejudices and dogmas. But it does have a coherent *social* strategy, which is designed to produce a 'social climate' favourable to capitalist enterprise. This requires, in the name of 'incentives', that life should be made even more agreeable than it has been so far for people who are already in the higher income brackets; and that it should be made harder, also in the name of 'incentives', for those who are not. This is clearly the philosophy which has inspired the Chancellor of the Exchequer's two budgetary exercises in regressive taxation.

It is also the philosophy which inspires the cuts in social provision. The notion that they are simply designed to reduce public expenditure which 'we cannot afford' is spurious. In those areas which it deems desirable—for instance, defence—there is no limit to what the government is able to afford and is willing to spend.

The cuts are not ineluctably imposed upon the government by circumstances over which it has no control. They are a matter of deliberate and selective policy, part of the creation of the new 'social climate'. One of their major purposes is to reduce what wage earners may expect by way of social provision. The partial 'decommodification' of some aspects of life—which was one of the gains of the war and post-war years—reduces the dependence of workers and their families on the wage earned; it obviously saps their moral fibre, kills off their incentive to work, and enhances already far too well-developed tendencies to sloth and disobedience. The spirit which moves the government is well illustrated by the reduction by £12 a week of the supplementary benefit which families of strikers may claim. Another illustration is the deployment of an army of snoopers on social security 'scroungers'.

In short, the market must rule, and the lesson must be taught to those who need it that money is all. Private health services, private education, private transport, or whatever, are all readily available. If you cannot afford them, you must do with what is left. Don't blame us, blame yourself. Under the Thatcher dispensation, not to be rich indicates a rather serious deficiency of character; and to be poor is not much short of criminal.

An important element in the government's social strategy is the erosion by legislative means (and in due course by judicial and coercive means) of the right to strike. Shorn of verbiage, this is what the Employment Bill seeks to do. It is only because some ministers, including the Prime Minister, wanted (and still want) more drastic measures that it has been possible to present James Prior's bill as an innocuous little measure. It does, in fact, introduce substantial curbs on effective industrial action, and notably on the right to picket. Much, of course, always depends on how strictly—or on how arbitrarily—the police enforce what they take to be the law. The way the wind is blowing is indicated by the admonitions of the Attorney General and the Home Secretary to chief constables during the steel strike to act more energetically against stroppy pickets.

Another weapon in the government's arsenal is the threat—and the fact—of unemployment. Full employment strengthens the bargaining power of labour: mass unemployment, it may be hoped, will inject an element of fear and anti-militancy in the ranks of the labour force, and thus bring more improvement to industrial relations. This has happened to a limited extent; but the level of wage settlements shows that it will take a great deal more to achieve the deferential relations in industry which the government wants.

Taken together, the government's policies constitute the most formidable assault that has been mounted on organized labour, and the working class in general since 1931; and there is a long way to go yet. This assault is often presented as a liberty-loving attempt to 'roll back the state'. But this, too, is spurious. Certainly, the government does want to surrender to private capital such bits and pieces of national property as may yield an attractive return; and it does want to reduce some of the collective services financed and run by the state. But there are realms where the liberty-loving neo-anarchists are perfectly willing to accept and indeed encourage a vast increase in state power—namely, in the realm of police powers and prerogatives, law and order, and anything else that will ensure the more effective containment of the subordinated classes. The national slum which is being created must be well policed, and the government will be glad to provide the necessary resources, notwithstanding the protestations of libertarian bleeding hearts—probably all Marxists anyway. For the purpose of containment, Thatcherite reactionaries do want a strong state, and will seek to protect it from criticism by a strident nationalist rhetoric of 'the SAS make us proud to be British' variety.

For the time being at least the government does not have to worry unduly about opposition to its long-range plans—and Mrs Thatcher does have long-range plans. No doubt, as the local government elections indicated, it now commands a great deal less electoral support than the 43.9 per cent of votes which it obtained at the general election, but this is no great matter at this point. Nor are the occasional rumblings in the Conservative ranks.

The Labour Party is deeply embroiled in its own troubles. Its leaders are greatly handicapped in attacking the government by their own record in office, and by the fact that Conservative ministers, when challenged over their policies, are able to say 'You did it first', to which it is not much of a rejoinder to say 'Yes, but not so hard.' Nor in any case can effective opposition be expected from leaders of a party who are at least as much concerned to fight off their own militants as they are to fight the government.

As for the trade unions, the government may well have expected more trouble from them than it has so far, and is emboldened by their uncertainty of response. Three months ago, Mrs Thatcher was saying on television that she did not think it was possible to legislate for a reduction in the social security benefits to be paid to strikers' families. Two months later, the government was confident enough to introduce the measure, at a higher figure than it had dared to contemplate a little while back. It is a small point but a significant one: where the opposition is weak, the government is encouraged to press on.

The unions are still very reluctant to accept the idea—and to base their response on the idea—that Mrs Thatcher does not actually want cooperation with them but submission.

The reluctance is not surprising since the trade unions are beset with many grave problems. In a climate of deepening recession, mass unemployment, short time and redundancies, divisions appear, sectionalism grows, solidarity weakens. This is precisely what the government wants; and it is helped by a national and local press which is all but unanimous in its dislike of trade unionism, or at least of any trade unionism which is not tame and deferential. In this area, the only difference between newspapers lies in the degree of shrillness and malevolence with which they condemn trade union activism. And it is clear that the sentiments they express reflect as well as shape the opinion of large parts of middle-class and lower-middle-class Britain, and of parts of working-class Britain as well.

Even so, there is resistance and there will be more. But the forces of labour do not yet seem to have the full measure of the challenge which the Thatcher government is presenting to them. The Prime Minister and her colleagues are seeking a drastic weakening of the labour movement because their view of the good society requires it; and the good society in which they believe is a class society in which the subordination of the many to the few, on the basis of property and privilege, is the dominant principle.

Labour has long lacked the capacity to project a radically different view, and therefore to turn it into a major theme in political life. Until it regains that capacity, it will be fighting on Mrs Thatcher's ground rather than its own.

16
Socialist Advance in Britain*
1983

To speak of socialist advance in Britain a short time after the General Election of June 1983 may seem rather strange. For the election was a major defeat not only for the Labour Party but for all socialist forces; and while that defeat may eventually turn out to have had beneficial political effects, in that it may help to break the mould in which the labour movement has long been imprisoned, such a blessing is hypothetical whereas the immediate effects of Labour's defeat are very tangible. The election results have conferred a new legitimacy upon an exceptionally reactionary Conservative government; and they have also served to demoralize further a movement that was already in bad shape well before the election. It may be said—and indeed should be said— that only 30.8 per cent of the electorate voted for the Conservatives—42.2 per cent of votes cast—and that its vote was less than in 1979. But the system is designed to put the main emphasis on the number of seats won rather than on votes cast; and the fact that the Government obtained a majority of 144 seats in the House of Commons makes it possible for it to claim, however spuriously, that it has a 'mandate' for the policies it chooses to put forward.

The extent of Labour's defeat has another long term consequence which is clearly important: namely, that both a net gain of well over 100 seats for Labour and a swing from Conservative to Labour of over twelve per cent would be required to bring about a majority

* This is a much-revised version of the Second Fred Tonge Memorial Lecture given under the auspices of the Holborn and St. Pancras Constituency Labour Party on 29 June 1983. I am grateful to Monty Johnstone and John Saville for their comments on an early version of the text.

Labour Government. This kind of swing (to the Conservatives) has only occurred once in this century, in the exceptional circumstances of 1931, when a former Labour Prime Minister, Ramsay MacDonald, was leading what was in effect a Conservative coalition against the Labour Party. It is useless to speculate on how things will turn out in a General Election which is some years off: but it is nevertheless reasonable to believe that the extent of Labour's defeat, leaving aside all other detrimental factors, greatly reduces Labour's chances of being able to form a majority government for many years to come.

What adds further to the demoralization of defeat is that the election results—as is agreed by everybody in the labour movement, right, left and centre—are not the product of some extraordinary set of events whose impact will soon be dissipated, at which point the Labour Party will be restored to its former vigour, but rather the most dramatic manifestation of a deep-seated, long-term crisis, for which no immediate remedy is at hand. My purpose here is to discuss the nature of this crisis, in the light of Labour's election defeat; and to link this with the problem of socialist advance in Britain.

Of all the reasons advanced for Labour's defeat, two have obtained the most currency. One is that changes in the composition and character of the working class have been such as to erode drastically the support that the Labour Party might expect from its 'natural' constituency; the other is that the Labour Party presented the image of a party so deeply divided as to inspire no confidence in its capacity to govern. Other reasons that have found favour include the lack of credibility of much of Labour's electoral programme; the dangerously 'extreme' nature of some of its proposals, notably on defence; the mismanagement of the election campaign, to which may be linked the personality of Michael Foot; and the 'Falklands factor'. But it is upon the changes in the character and composition of the working class on the one hand, and the divisions in the Labour Party on the other, that most attention has come to be focused. I will argue that the first of these explanations is misconceived; and that the second is inadequate because it does not explain why divisions, which are nothing new in the Labour Party, have been so much more significant, intractable and damaging than in the past.

It is perfectly true that the Labour Party has suffered a steady loss of electoral support since its peak achievement of nearly fourteen million votes in the General Election of 1951, with 48.8 per cent of the votes cast. By 1983, this had fallen to 27.6 per cent, Labour's lowest percentage share of the vote since 1918, when the Labour Party did not contest over one third of the seats. In 1951, the Labour Party also had an individual membership of around a million: by the early eighties this had dropped to not much more than a quarter of that figure.

It should first be said about the explanations which have found most favour to account for this loss of support, that they have a strong ideological purpose: for thirty years now, a shoddy sociology has been invoked by anti-socialist politicians and commentators in the Labour Party and outside as part of an endeavour to rid the Labour Party of those of its commitments which ran counter to their own 'moderate' positions. A certain code language has grown up over the years to obscure the nature of these endeavours. After Labour had lost office in 1951, despite its remarkable electoral performance, it was widely said that the Labour Party must 'rethink' its policies—and who could be against 'rethinking'? After the electoral defeats of 1955 and 1959, it was widely said that the trouble with the Labour Party was that it was saddled with commitments that belonged to an earlier age, and that it must come to terms with a new 'age of affluence': Labour *must* lose, so long as it refused to renew its image and its message, meaning that it must shed what formal socialist commitments it had. After the defeat of 1983, it has been said that the Labour Party must 'learn to listen' to what 'ordinary' people were saying—and who could be so unreasonable as to refuse to listen? When all the verbiage and coded language is cast aside, however, what is left is the insistence that the Labour Party must dilute its policies and programmes, and adopt more 'moderate' positions. This was the whole burden of the battle that Hugh Gaitskell waged in the fifties to change the Labour Party, to 'adapt it to the modern age' and to 'bring it up to date'. The attempt focused on Clause Four of the Labour Party Constitution: unless there was a clear repudiation of this preposterous commitment to nationalize everything in sight, including street-corner shops and garages, it was said, the Labour Party was doomed to electoral disaster and annihilation. The attempt failed.

Clause Four remained in the Party Constitution (with as little effect as ever before); and notwithstanding the 'age of affluence' which was supposed to have anesthetized the working class, Labour won the election of 1964 on a platform not markedly less 'radical' than previous ones; and it went on to win the election of 1966 with a majority of ninety-seven seats. Nor did the 'radicalism' of Labour's electoral platform in February 1974, with its pledge to bring about a 'fundamental and irreversible shift in the balance of power and wealth in favour of working people and their families', prevent Labour from winning that election, or the one in October of that year, again with a much increased majority.

Nothing of this is to suggest that the fact of decline in popular support is not very real: it is simply to note that explanations for it usually advanced by anti-socialist commentators are highly suspect and an intrinsic part of the battle that has been waged against the left in the Labour Party and outside ever since the Second World War, (indeed ever since the Labour Party came into being) and particularly since Labour's electoral defeat of May 1979. Once again, it has been said from many quarters that the working class, in so far as it could still be thought of as a class at all, was no longer what it was, and could not be expected to support a Labour Party which obstinately refused to come to terms with these changes (read: 'refused to dilute its policies').

Here too, the point is not to deny that changes in the working class have occurred. 'Traditional' occupations and industrial production have declined, and their decline has been accelerated by the Conservative government's policies; white collar and public service employment has grown and those engaged in it form a larger proportion of the working class than heretofore.[2] It is also possible, but by no means certain that 'sectionalism' within the working class has grown; and it is unquestionably true that unemployment and the fear of unemployment have reduced the willingness of many workers to engage in strike action. The question, however, is what impact these and other changes in the working class may have on its political attitudes and allegiances; and it is here that instant sociology turns into special pleading and bad faith.

To begin with, a very large fact needs to be recalled about the political attitudes of the working class, namely that a very substantial part of it has never supported Labour at all, even in the inter-war years of depression, mass unemployment, the Means Test and Tory retrenchment. Instant sociology often seems to imply that there was a time of depression and poverty when the working class *of course* supported Labour: but that in the age of affluence, of home owner-ship (a new favourite in the explanation of working-class 'de-radicalization'), a car in every garage, consumerism, video cassettes and holidays in Spain, no such automatic support could be expected. This conveniently overlooks the fact that, even if one leaves out all General Elections from 1918 to 1935, when the Tory and Liberal Parties obtained a vast preponderance of working-class votes against the Labour Party, the General Election of 1935 returned the 'National' Government (in effect, a Tory Government) with a majority of well over 200 seats.

This betokens an enduring conservatism in large sections of the working class; and it was this conservatism (which does not neces-sarily betoken allegiance to the Conservative Party) that was greatly shaken—but not overcome—by the traumas of war. As a result, the Labour Party, after forty-five years of existence, two world wars and a Great Depression, was able at long last to win a majority of seats in the House of Commons—146—with 48.3 per cent of the votes cast. Even then, the Conservative Party was still supported by nearly ten million voters (39.8 per cent) and the Liberal Party by nearly two and a half million. Twelve million people had voted for the Labour Party.[1] In other words, the pro-Labour and the anti-Labour votes were more or less evenly divided. Nor can it be assumed that the majority of those who did vote Labour, then and later, were fired by particularly strong radical sentiments. Many perhaps were. But many Labour voters, in 1945, were probably doing no more than expressing a general sentiment that the time had come for a new deal for the working class in Britain, and that the Labour Party was the party to being it about. Nevertheless, and for all its limitations, the victory of 1945 was a great advance; but instead of being enlarged, that basis was steadily narrowed in subse-quent years. I will argue that the main responsibility for this shrink-age lies with Labour's leaders and the 'labourism' that provided their ideological and practical framework. But it is at any rate clear, on the historical evidence, that neither the deprivations and sufferings of the 'old' working class, nor the 'affluence' of the 'new' (in any case always grossly exaggerated) provides an adequate explanation for the support or lack of support that Labour has obtained: here is vulgar economic determinism indeed, whose inadequacy is further confirmed by the fact that Labour's loss of support has continued through the past ten years of economic crisis, retrenchment and retreat.

What has sometimes been called 'Labour Socialism' is a loose amalgam of many different strands of thought—Christian ethics, Fabian collectivism, a radical and democratic tradition of reform, based on age old notions of social justice, equality, cooperation and fellowship. Even so, 'labourism' seems a better label for the ideology that has moved Labour's leaders—and many others in the labour movement—for a hundred years past. Labourism has never been turned into a systematic body of thought; and its adherents and practitioners have frequently made a virtue of their 'practical' sense, their rejection of 'theory', and their freedom from all 'isms' (and they themselves have never adopted 'labourism' as a label for their views). But it is nevertheless strong ideological promptings, suitably called by that name, that have guided their practice.

Labourism is above all concerned with the advancement of concrete demands of immediate advantage to the working class and organized labour: wages and conditions of work; trade-union rights; the better provision of services and benefits in the fields of health, education, housing, transport, family allowances, unemployment benefits and pensions. These demands may be clad in the garb of 'socialism' but most leaders of the labour movement, however much they might believe in some vague and remote socialist alternative to the present social order, have in practice only had a very weak concern—in so far as they have had any concern at all—with large socialist objectives. The reforms they have sought have never been conceived as part of a strategy for the creation of a fundamentally different kind of society, but rather as specific responses to immediate ills and needs. Their horizons have been narrowly bound by the capitalist environment in which they found themselves, and whose framework they readily took as given; and it is within its framework and the 'rationality' it imposed that they sought reform.

This acceptance of capitalist 'rationality' helps to explain some notable features of their politics: for instance, why the reforms they sought were generally so modest in scope and substance, and so geared to what 'society' could afford; why Labour governments so quickly and so regularly moved from being agents of reform to being agents of conservative retrenchment, more concerned to contain pressure from below than to advance labour's demands; and also why these leaders were so ready to collaborate with Labour's class enemies. Trade-union leaders steeped in labourism might have had to fight the class struggle; occasionally, indeed, they fought it hard. But neither they nor certainly Labour's political leaders thought of society as a battlefield upon which the working class was engaged in a permanent and irrevocable struggle against the domination and exploitation to which it was subjected by a rapacious ruling class: or if they thought in those terms, they did not let it affect their political practice. But for the most part, they thought of 'society' as presented with 'problems' whose solution mainly required the kind of good will, intelligence, knowledge and compassion that their Conservative opponents somehow lacked.

Given these perspectives, labourism readily accepted the political system that was in existence when the labour movement assumed definite shape in the second half of the nineteenth century. Labour leaders might demand some reforms in this realm too—for instance, the extension of suffrage, or the reform of the House of Lords or of local government. But they took the system as a whole more or less for granted and capitalist democracy on the British model to be the most accomplished form of democratic government conceivable— hereditary monarchy and hereditary peers in the House of Lords included. They mainly thought of the political process in parliamentary terms, and of grassroots activism and extra-parliamentary activity as party work at local level for the purpose of supporting local and parliamentary representatives and helping to fight local and parliamentary elections. The notion that a local party might be a focus of struggle, agitation and education fell outside their ideological spectrum. Nor have Labour leaders ever shown much concern to bring about any large reform in the organization of the British state so as to change the closed, oligarchic and profoundly conservative character of its administrative, judicial, police and military branches.

Finally, Labourism has always had a strong national vocation. The Labour Party has regularly been accused by its Conservative opponents of being 'unpatriotic', heedless of British interests abroad and unconcerned with British 'greatness'. Nothing could be further from the truth. Labour Governments have always pursued foreign and defence policies (and in an earlier epoch colonial policies) that did not greatly differ from those of Conservative Governments —not, perhaps, very surprisingly since Labour Governments relied on the civil servants and military advisers they inherited from the Conservatives. Of course, there have been some differences: it may well be, for instance, that a Conservative Government, had one been elected in 1945, would not have accepted without much bitter struggle the inevitability of Indian independence; and divergences between Labour and Conservative defence policies have widened in recent years and were manifested in the General Election of 1983. It is permissible to doubt how far these divergencies would have been maintained, if a Labour Government had been elected, given the, at best, lukewarm support that senior Labour figures gave to major items of Labour's defence programme; but the divergences were nevertheless evident. On the other hand, it has to be remembered that, beyond these divergences, all senior Labour figures, without exception, continued to be committed to the American alliance and NATO, which have been the cornerstones of the defence and foreign policies of the Conservative *and* Labour Parties since the war years.

These being the main features of labourism, it is reasonable to see it as an ideology of social reform, within the framework of capitalism, with no serious ambition of transcending that framework, whatever ritual obeisances to 'socialism' might be performed by party leaders on suitable occasions, such as Labour Party or trade-union conferences, to appease or defeat their activist critics. Labourism, in other words, is not like Marxism, an ideology of rupture but an ideology of adaptation.

It is this ideology that has been overwhelmingly dominant in the labour movement for a hundred years and more, whatever 'socialist' label might be given to it. Marxism, as a main alternative to labourism, has not been a negligible strand of thought among activists and its influence has been greater than the proclaimed number of its adherents might suggest.[2] But it has nevertheless been marginal in comparison with labourism. For it is labourism which slowly made its way in the working class and became an acceptable perspective to a substantial part of it; and it is labourism which, from the peak that it reached in 1951, has been losing support in the working class. The question I now turn to is why.

An explanation of this growing alienation has to begin with the long-standing economic decline of the British economy, and with the aggravation and acceleration of this decline by virtue of the world capitalist economic crisis from the early seventies onwards; or rather, an explanation has to begin with the response of the Labour Governments of the sixties and seventies to decline and crisis. The chronic British economic malady and the recurring emergencies which it produced presented these governments with a challenge that they always promised to meet but which they always failed to meet. Instead, and well in line with their labourist ideology, they consistently pursued economic policies that were broadly acceptable to the capitalist forces at home and abroad on whose help and cooperation they relied. In so doing, they were also and naturally compelled to turn themselves, as I noted earlier, into agencies of retrenchment and containment.

The failures, derelictions and betrayals of the Wilson and Callaghan Governments of 1964-70 and 1974-79 have been amply documented and need no retelling here.[3] The point that does need to be made is that these governments did, to a quite remarkable degree, act in ways that were bound to alienate masses of actual or potential Labour supporters in the working class, and not only in the working class. It was the Labour Governments of those decades that inaugurated the 'monetarist' policies which the Conservatives pushed much further after 1979. It was those Labour Governments that launched repeated attacks on public expenditure by central and local governments for collective services whose level is of crucial importance to the large majority of people who cannot pay for private health, education, housing, transport and amenities; and it was also they whose budgets turned into tax exercises much more calculated to hit low incomes than higher ones. It was the Wilson and Callaghan Governments that made war on industrial activists; and that persistently sought to curb wages under the guise of incomes policies, wage norms, social contracts and national agreements. Nor could Labour's policies claim any measure of success: after a combined period of eleven years of Labour Governments from 1964 until 1979, with a Conservative interruption of only four years, there was no major improvement in the British condition to which Labour could point. Meanwhile, the rich prospered; and so did a Labour state bourgeoisie loud in its denunciation of militants and wreckers who were spoiling their enjoyment of the pleasures of office.

This record alone would be perfectly adequate to account for the progressive alienation of masses of potential Labour voters from the Labour Party. The argument is not, of course, that the working class wanted more socialism and turned away from Labour because Labour Governments did not give it to them. That is indeed nonsense. The point is that Labour supporters wanted, and voted for, programmes of economic and social betterment, but that the betterment they got from Labour Governments was easily overshadowed by the negative side of the record. As a result, many of them abandoned Labour in 1983, as more and more of them had been doing in previous elections, and did so all the more readily as there now appeared to be a plausible alternative to both Labour and Conservatives, namely the Social Democratic and Liberal Parties. Furthermore, many of them simply did not vote: one of the significant facts about the General Election of 1983 is that forty-seven per cent of unemployed young people between the ages of eighteen and twenty-two did not bother to cast a vote at all.

Even so, eight and a half million people did vote Labour. This is really very remarkable, when account is taken of the relentless and quite unscrupulous assault to which working-class—and other—voters were subjected during the election campaign, and for years before the campaign. The assault had two obvious objectives. One was to get voters to overlook the viciously regressive character of the policies of the Thatcher Government. The other was to persuade them that the Labour Party had been taken over, or was in imminent danger of being taken over, by political perverts and lunatics. Not the least persuasive element in that assault was the contribution made to it by senior and respected figures in the Labour Party through joining in the chorus of vilification which united all anti-socialist forces, including of course the ex-Labour renegade leaders and parliamentarians of the Social Democratic Party. In the circumstances, and given the intensity of the assault, the wonder is not that Labour lost, but that so many people resisted the propaganda, overlooked Labour's condition and record, and still voted for it. That so many did constitutes a precious asset, to whose significance I will return later.

The second main reason advanced to account for Labour's defeat, I noted earlier, is that the Labour Party was, and had been for a long time, so obviously and deeply divided. This makes good sense, but needs to be taken a good deal further. For there have always been deep divisions in the Labour Party and the labour movement, and they have not prevented the Labour Party from doing much better than it did in 1983. The difference is that the more recent divisions have run much deeper than before and that many more activists have opposed their leaders; and also, most significant of all in my view, that the Labour leaders, unlike their predecessors, have not been able to maintain their ideological and political hegemony over the labour movement. Here lies the root of Labour's troubles.

In this context too, account has to be taken of the economic decline of Britain and of the Wilson and Callaghan Governments' response to it. For just as the derelictions and betrayals and failures of these governments 'de-aligned' a mass of potential and actual Labour supporters, so did that record 'radicalize' a mass of left activists and given them a new determination to prevent a repetition of past performance. From the early seventies onwards, a new wave of activists emerged, not only more determined but better organized than the Labour Left had been earlier, and less susceptible to manipulation and seduction as well. Also, and not to be under-estimated, they found an articulate and resilient champion in Tony Benn, whose national position and place in the Labour Party gave them added strength. The Labour Left has always had problems with its parliamentary and ministerial standard bearers. Stafford Cripps was a weak and vacillating leader of the Socialist League in the thirties; and Aneurin Bevan in the post-war years was a very erractic and impulsive leader of the Bevanites, in so far as he could be said to have been their leader at all. Bevan soared above his followers, and did not really seek to mobilize support at the grassroots. Benn did.

No wonder that he was so bitterly hated and reviled, by his erstwhile ministerial colleagues and fellow parliamentarians no less than by all the forces of conservatism proper.

The new activism was not homogeneous in ideological and political terms. Some small part of it—on which its enemies naturally fastened—drew its inspiration from Trotskyism. Some of it proceeded from an unlabelled militant socialist iconoclasm, of which the most representative figure was Ken Livingstone; and most of it was probably the product of the deep but undoctrinal anger of rank-and-file activists who were utterly fed up with the retreat by their leaders into Labour versions of Conservative policies at home and abroad.

Furthermore, the new activists rejected the view traditionally held by Labour leaders (and by much of the traditional Labour Left as well) that the political process must have the House of Commons as its main and all but exclusive focus, with grassroots activism playing no more than a support role for parliamentarians. On the contrary, they were oriented towards work at the grassroots, and had a strong sense of the political process at local level—hence the importance they attached to what could be achieved in and through local government. Like the women's movement and the peace movement, the new generation of Labour activists (who were in any case often part of the other two movements as well) was strongly committed to extra-parliamentary pressure and did not believe that parliamentary work was so crucial as to dwarf all else: on the contrary, they saw parliamentary work as part of a larger and more important struggle in the country at large.

The new activists were, relatedly, intensely suspicious of all leaders, and notably of parliamentary leaders; and they tended to view most (but not all) left parliamentarians as being part of a 'soft left' that could not be trusted to offer sustained resistance to the retreats and compromises of the leaders of the Labour Party.

In so far as this response is unstructured, it may in time fail to protect Labour-left activists from appeals stemming from many diverse sources not to rock the boat or make a bad situation worse. From this point of view, the suspicion which many left activists themselves have of 'theory' is a source of real political weakness, which has very adversely affected many Labour activists in the past.

Nevertheless, the General Election defeat of 1979, coming on top of the record of the Wilson and Callaghan Governments, gave a powerful impulse to activist pressures which had been building up throughout the seventies. The left in the Labour Party was able in the following years to force through major innovations in the selection of MPs and in the election of the Leader and Deputy Leader of the Labour Party. Moreover, the left was also able to achieve temporary control of the National Executive Committee and of its important sub-committees; and it was thus well placed to make a marked impact on the programme which was eventually presented in the election of 1983.

The most remarkable feature of this pressure from the left is that, even though the Labour leadership bitterly opposed it, with the vociferous encouragement of a virtually united press, it was unable to subdue it. This had in part to do with the strength of the new activism in the Labour Party and in the unions; and also with the much less solid position of that leadership. For another consequence of the failure of the Wilson and Callaghan Governments was a drastic weakening of the moral and political authority of those people—drawn overwhelmingly from the Right and Centre—who had been in charge of those governments. In any case, when one recalls the relative ease with which an earlier Labour Left was brought to heel by expulsion or the threat of expulsion, or was manipulated into submission by the kind of rhetoric and deception of which Harold Wilson was the master, the inability of the Labour leaders to crush or curb their activist opponents stands out as the really new and significant fact in recent Labour history.

However, the new activists, notwithstanding their successes, were just as unable as their predecessors to dislodge the Right and the Centre from their commanding positions in the Labour Party and the trade unions. Even when they had a majority on the NEC, they were confronted by a powerful minority of senior figures (including the Leader and the Deputy Leader) who could marshal considerable resources to block the path of the left. Also, the majority of the Parliamentary Labour Party remained under the control of the Right and the Centre; and the parliamentary left itself was badly split between the 'soft left' and the Bennites. Nor did the left have many reliable allies in the upper echelons of the trade union hierarchy.

The high point in the activists' campaign after 1979 was the vote for the Deputy Leadership of the Labour Party by the new electoral college at the 1981 Party Conference, when Tony Benn obtained 49.5 per cent of the vote, against Denis Healey's 50.4 per cent. Had Benn won, it is conceivable that the balance of forces in the Labour Party would have shifted considerably to the left, with many more people in the Parliamentary Labour Party moving over to the Social Democratic Party, to which many Labour parliamentarians are in any case ideologically well attuned. But Benn did not win, and the Right and Centre remained in command, with a Leader, in the person of Michael Foot, who, for all his past Labour Left record and rhetoric, had long made his peace with the Right and the Centre. Foot had been a main pillar of the Wilson-Callaghan Government between 1974 and 1979, and a chief architect of that Government's alliance with the Liberals; and he was a determined enemy of the Bennite Left.

The successes of the new activists, coupled with their failure to win a commanding position in the Labour Party, thus produced the absurd and untenable situation which is at the core of Labour's troubles: the left was able to get major items of policy adopted by Labour Party and trade-union conferences; and these items subsequently found their way into Labour's electoral programme. But the task of defending these policies was left to leaders many of whom—indeed most of whom—did not believe in them, made no secret of the fact, and found many opportunities to denounce those who wanted these policies as wreckers or fools.

The full absurdity of this situation became disastrously evident in the General Election campaign. The Labour Manifesto was not the 'extreme' document that the enemies of the left, not least in the Labour Party, found it convenient to claim, then and later. It amounted for the most part to a reiteration of policies that had been put forward in the Labour Party's electoral manifestoes of the seventies and earlier. But, in addition to the pledge that a Labour Government would take Britain out of the European Economic Community, it did include some proposals in the field of defence that had far-reaching implications: thus, it pledged a Labour Government to reject the deployment of Cruise and Pershing missiles on British soil and to 'begin discussions' for the removal of nuclear bases in Britain, 'to be completed within the lifetime of the

Labour Government'. The document further proclaimed Labour's commitment 'to establish a non-nuclear defence policy': 'we will, after consultation, carry through in the lifetime of the next parliament our non-nuclear defence policy'. This appeared to commit a Labour Government to unilateral nuclear disarmament. But the document also said that, in addition to cancelling the Trident programme, it would propose that 'Britain's Polaris force be included in the nuclear disarmament negotiations in which Britain must take part'. The obvious question, on which the Conservatives and others naturally pounced, was what would happen if the negotiations failed. On this, the Labour Party spoke with uncertain and divided voices. In other words, the manifesto's attempt to square the circle had failed and the divisions in the Labour leadership on the issue of defence made it impossible for the Labour Party to proclaim what it was left to Enoch Powell to call the 'transparent absurdity' of the theory of nuclear deterrence, based as it was on the willingness to commit national suicide 'as a last resort'. Mrs Thatcher made the typically reckless and bombastic declaration during the election campaign that she would be perfectly ready to 'press the button'; Labour was in no condition to denounce this for the degraded nonsense that it was.

It is very unlikely that any major party in Britain has ever fought so inane a campaign as the Labour Party did in 1983. The basic reason for this was not incompetence and mismanagement, however much there may have been of both. These were only the manifestations of much deeper trouble, namely the division, essentially between social reformers whose perspectives do not for all practical purposes reach beyond labourism, and socialists whose perspectives do. This age-old division has now reached a point where any attempt at accommodation only produces fudging formulas which neither satisfy nor convince anyone.

Such a situation cannot permanently endure: or at least, no party or movement can be viable in which such a situation endures. Pious references to the Labour Party being a 'broad church' which has always incorporated many different strands of thought fail to take account of a crucial fact, namely that the 'broad church' of Labour only functioned effectively in the past because one side—the Right and Centre—determined the nature of the services that were to be held, and excluded or threatened with exclusion any clergy too deviant in its dissent. Now that this can no longer be done—the clumsy and largely ineffectual attempts to banish the Militant Tendency confirm rather than disprove the point—the 'broad church' is unable to do its job.

The question which therefore needs to be asked is: what should socialists, whether in the Labour Party or not, want to see by way of a resolution of this condition? The answer to that question is best considered by reference to two possible 'scenarios'.

The first of these involves the election of a new Leader of the Labour Party able to combine a vocabulary that would please the left on the one hand with a sufficient degree of flexibility over policy on the other to reassure the Right and the Centre. The task of such a Leader might be eased somewhat by the fact that no major policy decisions have to be incorporated in an election manifesto for some time to come; and a Leader who spoke an adequately left-sounding language might hope to confuse and divide the left sufficiently to isolate its more intractable elements, and thus reduce them to a marginal position.

The realization of such a 'scenario' would restore a certain degree of coherence to the Labour Party. It would not be quite the party of Clement Attlee and Hugh Gaitskell that Mrs Thatcher was calling for during the election campaign, but it would be a recognizable version of it. Labourism, suitably embellished with some socialist phraseology (but not too much of it) would again predominate. Persuasive appeals would be made to 'unite against the common enemy', and an enticing vision of electoral victory and a Labour Government would be held out as the reward for reasonableness and moderation.

There undoubtedly exists a considerable weight of support for such an outcome: a large majority of parliamentarians would be for it; so would a large number of trade-union leaders; so would the press and the media. It would widely be represented as a welcome sign that the Labour Party was returning to the sensible policies of old, and that it was abjuring the lunatic policies which had brought it to its present pass. Nor is there much doubt that it would meet with the approval of many Labour supporters and Labour party members.

It is, however, a very difficult 'scenario' to realize. For its realization would represent a massive defeat for the left in the Labour Party. There is no good reason to suppose that, having got so far, the left would accept such a defeat and desist from their endeavours. Inevitably, however, their endeavours maintain the Labour Party in a state of civil war.

This being the case, a realization of the 'scenario' in question requires nothing less than a thorough 'purge' of the left in the Labour Party, extending far beyond the Militant Tendency; and it would also need a redrawing of the constitutional rules so as to reduce drastically the increased influence that activists have been able to achieve since 1979 on such matters as the re-selection of MPs and the election of the Leader and Deputy Leader of the Labour Party. If this could be done, socialists in the Labour Party would be forced to decide whether the time had finally come to leave the Labour Party to labourism and its devotees, and to seek a realignment of the left by way of a new socialist party. However, this kind of action against the left seems well beyond the powers of any Labour leadership today.

The new activists, for their part, have proceeded from a very different 'scenario', which has not been clearly spelt out, but whose main lines are not difficult to draw. What is involved is a continuation of the struggles in which the left has been engaged, with the purpose of achieving predominance and turning the Labour Party into a socialist party free from the constrictions hitherto imposed upon it by its leaders. It must be presumed that many leading figures in the Labour Party would then want to leave it and seek new political homes elsewhere—in the Social Democratic Party, or the Liberal Party, or even the Conservative Party. In fact, it would be essential that such people *should* leave the Labour Party; for just as the left makes life difficult for a leadership which is opposed to it, so could determined Right and Centre parliamentarians make life difficult for a party in which the left had acquired predominance. No doubt a good many other Labour Party members, at constituency level, would also leave. But these defections would be compensated by the accretion of strength which would be provided by the many people who are not now minded to join the Labour Party but might then want to do so, and be actively involved in it. It is also very likely that some, perhaps many, trade-union leaders would wish to disaffiliate from a Labour Party that had gone beyond labourism. But any such attempt would meet with stiff resistance from the left in the unions; and though the attempt might succeed in some cases, it would probably be successfully fought in others.

I must enter a personal note at this point. I have for more than ten years written that this hope of the left to transform the Labour Party—which has always been nourished by the Labour Left—was illusory, and that, far from representing a short cut to the creation of a mass socialist party in Britain (which has never existed), it was a dead end in which British socialists had been trapped for many decades—in fact, since the Labour Party came into being. It was this view which led me to advocate the formation of a new socialist party able to do all the work of socialist advocacy and agitation that the Labour Party had been prevented by its leaders from doing.[4]

I am far from convinced that I was mistaken. For it is by no means evident that the new activists can realize the 'scenario' I have just outlined: on the most optimistic expectations, they have a long way to go, with many large obstacles on the way. But it is obvious that I underestimated how great was the challenge that the new activists would be able to pose to their leaders; and how limited would be the capacity of these leaders to surmount the challenge. I now take it that the question whether the activists can push matters further is more open than I had believed.

Rather than speculate further upon this, it may be more useful to ask what would be the prospects of a socialist Labour Party, such as the activists seek; and the same considerations would apply to a new socialist party, born from the disintegration of the Labour Party.

Such a party would seek to advance purposes and policies which have long formed part of the aspirations of the socialist left. One of its main concerns would be the democratization of the whole structure of government; the abolition of anti-trade union legislation and other repressive legislation, such as the Prevention of Terrorism Act, introduced in 1974 by Roy Jenkins, then Labour Home Secretary; the drastic curbing of police powers and the placing of the police under effective democratic control; and the end of the British military presence in Northern Ireland.

A socialist party would be pledged to return to public ownership the industries and services sold off by the Conservative Government; and it would take a major extension of public ownership under a variety of forms, and with the greatest possible measure of democratic control, to be one of the indispensable conditions for the transformation of British capitalism in socialist directions, and for the dissolution of the class structure which would be one of its central aims.

In the realm of defence and foreign policy, such a party would be committed to the nuclear disarmament of Britain, as part of a radical shift in the policies followed by Labour and Conservative Governments since the Second World War. A socialist party could not be true to itself if it did not include in its programme an end of British support for the world-wide counter-revolutionary crusade which the United States has been waging across the world ever since the forties, and if it did not support progressive movements throughout the world struggling for national and social liberation. Such defence and foreign policies are clearly incompatible with membership of NATO.

Conventional wisdom has it that such a programme can never be endorsed by a majority of people—indeed, that it dooms the party that propounds it to marginality and irrelevance.

Two points may be made about this. The first is that there is no point in pretending that there exists a ready-made majority in the country for a socialist programme. How could there be? One of the fruits of the long predominance of labourism is precisely that the party of the working class has never carried out any sustained campaign of education and propaganda on behalf of a socialist programme; and that Labour leaders have frequently turned themselves into fierce propagandists *against* the socialist proposals of their critics inside the Labour Party and out, and have bent their best efforts to the task of defeating all attempts to have the Labour Party adopt such proposals. Moreover, a vast array of conservative forces, of the most diverse kind, are always at hand to dissuade the working class from even thinking about the socialist ideas which evil or foolish people are forever trying to foist upon them. This simply means that a ceaseless battle for the 'hearts and minds' of the people is waged by the forces of conservatism, against which have only been mobilized immeasurably smaller socialist forces. A socialist party would seek to strengthen these forces and to defend socialist perspectives and a socialist programme over an extended period of time, and would accept that more than one election might have to be held before a majority of people came to support it. In any case, a socialist party would be concerned not only with office, but with the creation of the conditions under which office would be more than the management of affairs on capitalist lines. The first of these conditions is precisely a strong measure of popular support; and their support would be all the more essential, given the fierce resistance that a socialist government seeking to alter its programme would encounter from all the conservative forces in the land.

Ever since the Labour Party became a substantial electoral and political force, Labour leaders have taken the view—and have persuaded many of their followers to take the view—that government was all; and that politics is about elections: on one side, there is power, on the other, paralysis. This is a very narrow view of the political process. Elections are important, and no party functioning in a capitalist-democratic context can afford to neglect them, not least at local level. But this is a very different matter from the view that gaining office is the sole and exclusive purpose of politics. For office, however agreeable for those who hold it, has often meant not only impotence, but worse still than impotence, the power to carry out policies fundamentally at odds with the purposes for which office was obtained. Nor is it necessarily the case that opposition means paralysis. This has never been true of the Conservative Party and conservative forces; and it has only been true of the Labour Party because of the narrow ideological and political framework in which its leaders have dwelt, and because of their concentration on electoral and parliamentary politics. But it need not be true for a substantial working-class party. It is by no means obvious, for instance, that the Italian Communist Party, in opposition since it was expelled from office in 1947, has, *in socialist terms*, exercised much less influence on Italian life in this period than the Labour Party has exercised in government. The notion that the Labour Party is either a 'party of government', with all the opportunist compromises and retreats the formulation carries, or must resign itself to being no more than an 'ineffectual sect' may be useful propaganda for all the 'moderate' forces in the labour movement, but it does not correspond to the real alternatives.

This relates to the second point, namely that, while there is no popular majority for a socialist programme at present, it does not follow that there is no support for such a programme at all, and that more support for it could not be generated. This is where it is necessary to recall the fact that eight and a half million people did vote Labour in 1983. There is obviously no warrant for the view that all of them consciously and deliberately supported all the items in Labour's programme, or even that they supported many of them: many such Labour voters were no doubt simply registering a vote against the Thatcher Government. But among these eight and a half million voters, a large number may be taken to have voted as they did because they approved more or less strongly the general drift and many items of the Labour programme, and were not put off by the massive propaganda to which they were subjected, and which assured them that a vote for Labour was a vote for personal and national disaster. As I noted earlier, they resisted this assault, just as millions of Labour voters have resisted such assaults at every election since 1945, when the Labour Party put forward a programme which its leaders had striven very hard to dilute, in the belief that its more radical proposals must inevitably lose them the election. This stubborn popular resistance to the unrelenting campaign of indoctrination to which the working class is subjected at election time and in between elections provides a basis of support on which a socialist party serious about its business can build. Much of the propaganda conducted by anti-socialist forces—Conservative, Liberal, Social Democratic, and Labour—seeks to present a picture of the working class as irrevocably opposed to socialist proposals: but the propagandists would have to work much less hard if this was the case. They do have to work as hard as they do precisely because there is a vast degree of popular alienation from existing economic, social and political arrangements, which can be turned into support for radically different arrangements. I have called this alienation a 'state of de-subordination', as a result of which 'people who find themselves in subordinate positions, and notably the people who work in factories, mines, offices, shops, schools, hospitals and so on, do what they can to mitigate, resist and transform the conditions of their subordination'.[5] Unemployment and the fear of unemployment have undoubtedly had an effect, as was intended, in reducing 'desubordination' at 'the point of production'. But this hardly means that the experience of these years of Tory Government and mass unemployment and the attack on welfare and collective provisions have generated any more popular support for existing arrangements than was previously the case. On the contrary, economic decline and crisis, allied to the crying injustices generated by a grossly unequal class system, provide the ground on which socialist work can effectively proceed.

Socialist work means something different for a socialist party than the kind of political activity inscribed in the perspectives of labourism. I have noted earlier that political work, for labourism, essentially means short periods of great political activity for local and parliamentary elections, with long periods of more or less routine party activity in between. Socialist work, on the contrary, means intervention in all the many different areas of life in which class struggle occurs: for class struggle must be taken to mean not only the permanent struggle between capital and labour, crucial though that remains, but the struggle against racial and sex discrimination, the struggle against arbitrary state and police power, the struggle against the ideological hegemony of the conservative forces, and the struggle for new and radically different defence and foreign policies.

The slogan of the first Marxist organization in Britain, the Social Democratic Federation, founded in 1884, was 'Educate, Agitate, Organize'. It is also a valid slogan for the 1980s and beyond. A socialist party could, in the coming years, give it more effective meaning than it has ever had in the past.

---

1. The Communist Party, with twenty-one candidates in the field, polled just over 100,000 votes and had two seats, which they lost in the General Election of 1950. Over 100,000 votes were also cast for the Commonwealth Party and under 50,000 for the Independent Labour Party.

2. See, for example, Stuart MacIntyre, *A Proletarian Science: Marxism in Britain 1917-1933*, London 1980, ch. 2.

3. See, for example, L. Panitch, *Social Democracy and Industrial Militancy*, 1976; D. Coates, *Labour in Power?*, London 1980; and K. Coates, ed., *What Went Wrong?*, Nottingham 1979.

4. See 'Moving On', in *The Socialist Register 1976*, and 'The Future of Socialism in England', in *The Socialist Register 1977*.

5. R. Miliband, 'A State of Desubordination', *British Journal of Sociology*, Vol. XXIX, no. 4, December 1978, p.402.

Index

Allende, Salvador, 74, 79 ff.
Altamirano, Carlos, 102
Althusser, Louis, 29, 38
Amin, Hafizullah, 241-2
Amin, Idi, 249
Anderson, Perry, ii, 50 ff
Attlee, Clement, 86, 301

Bahro, Rudolf, 203 ff
Bakunin, Mikhail, 19, 20
Baldwin, Stanley, 280
Baran, Paul, 31
Barnet, Richard, 270
Bauer, Bruno, 7
Benn, Tony, 296, 299
Berlinguer, Enrico, 109
Bettelheim, Charles, 109 ff
Beven, Aneurin, 81, 296
Bismarck, Otto von, 12, 43
Bolsheviks, 143, 161-163, 170, 190,
    198, 208, 238, 239
Bolshevik Party, 142-143, 160, 175,
    190, 200
Bolshevik Revolution, 140-141, 149,
    161, 165, 195-196, 224, 240, 246
Bonaparte, Louis 10, 11
Bonapartism, 74, 75, 78
Brezhnev, Leonid, 225
Brezhnev, doctrine, 186
Bukharin, Nikolai, 140, 143, 145, 198
Bukharinism, 176
Bury, J.B., 133

Callaghan, James, 109, 294, 296, 298-
    299

Carillo, Santiago, 108 ff
Carr, E.H., 144-145, 160
Castro, Fidel, 263
Catherine II, 59
Chamberlain, Joseph, 280
Claudin, Fernando, 108, 112, 114, 116,
    119, 120
Cohen, Stephen, 143
Colletti, Lucio, 155
Corvalan, Luis, 80, 101
Cripps, Stafford, 296

Daud, Mohammed, 243
Debray, Regis, 102-103
Deng Xiaoping, 254
Deutscher, Isaac, 141-143, 176, 178,
    185, 203, 269
Draper, Hal, 17, 18, 63
Dubcek, Alexander, 235
Duverger, Maurice, 14, 87

Engels, Friedrich, 3, 8, 9, 12, 13, 15-
    17, 19, 21, 37, 43-45, 52, 56, 58, 63-
    64, 100, 110, 134, 138, 151, 155, 164
    165
Eriugena, 216

Foot, Michael, 287, 299
Frei, Eduardo, 90, 97

Garces, Juan, 83-84
Gaitskell, Hugh, 288, 301
General Strike, 280
Gierek, Edward, 207

de Goncourt, Edmond, 96
Gramsci, Antonio, 115, 174, 212

Halliday, Fred, 266
Healey, Denis, 299
Hegel, G.W.F., 4-6, 218
Hitler, Adolf, 139, 179, 250
Hobsbawm, Eric, 93, 96, 104, 106
Hook, Sidney, 137

International,
    First, 15, 16, 20
    Second, 190
    Third, 190, 191

Kamenev, Lev, 140
Kautsky, Karl, 12, 155, 156, 165
Karmal, Babrak, 241
Kolakowski, Leszek, 215 ff
Kosygin, Alexei, 183
Krushchev, Nikita, 184, 225, 268
Kugelmann, Ludwig, 100, 135

Jenkins, Roy, 303
Johnson, Lyndon, 69

Laclau, Ernesto, 26
Labour Party, 201, 284, 286 ff
Lenin, V.I., 3, 20, 37, 76, 100, 113,
    116-119, 123, 132, 140-145, 149, 154-
    166, 172, 175, 178, 182-183, 192,
    196-197, 198, 200, 208, 223-227, 238,
    244
Lichtheim, George, 14, 19
Livingstone, Ken, 297
Luxemburg, Rosa, 138, 175, 221, 239

Macdonald, Ramsay, 287
Mao Tse-tung, 132, 190, 196
McNamara, Robert, 88
Marchais, Georges, 109
Marx, Karl, 3 ff, 28-30, 33, 35, 37, 39,
    43-45, 52, 54-56, 58, 63-64, 76, 81,
    86, 94, 97, 99, 100, 110, 116, 119,
    120, 134-136, 142, 144-146, 148, 151,
    155, 159 ff, 192, 216 ff, 244, 263
Martov, Julius, 165
Medvedev, Roy, 167 ff, 175 ff
Medvedev, Zhores, 167

Mensheviks, 161, 230, 239
Michelet, Jules, 220
Mill, John Stuart, 81
Mills, C.W., 27, 254, 259, 261, 271
Molotov, Viacheslav, 173
Montesquieu, Charles, 220

Napolitano, Giorgio, 108 ff
Napoleon, 136-137, 139, 151
Novotny, Antonin, 186

Palme, Olaf, 109
Paris Commune, 15, 18-19, 94, 96, 99-
    100, 135, 160, 164-165, 182
Plekhanov, Georgii, 131, 136, 139, 142
Poulantzas, Nicos, 26 ff, 64
Proudhon, Joseph, 19
Preobrahensky, Evgenii, 141
Powell, Enoch, 300
Pol Pot, 231, 235, 249-250, 253-254
Prior, James, 282

Rakovsky, Christian, 178
Renan, Emile, 220

Saint Just, 106
Sartre, Jean Paul, 96
Schmidt, Helmut, 109
Skocpol, Theda, 65-66, 74
Stalin, Josef, 112, 132, 140-141, 161,
    168 ff, 184-185, 198 ff, 205, 225,
    233, 243, 246, 252-253
Sweezy, Paul, 31

Taine, Hyppolite, 220
Taraki, Nur Mohammed, 241-242
Tawney, R.H., 87
Thatcher, Margaret, 279, 281, 283-285,
    295, 300-301, 306
Therborn, Goran, 76
Thomas, Hugh, 81
Thompson, E.P., 261
Tito, Josip Broz, 236, 243
Trimberger, Ellen Kay, 65
Trotsky, Leon, 140-143, 145, 161, 168,
    175, 178, 198, 263

Vico, Giambattista, 220

Weber, Max, 42, 66
Weydemeyer, Joseph, 17
Wilson, Harold, 81, 294, 296, 298-299
Wittfogel, Karl, 14

Zinoviev, Grigori, 140, 145